PLAY WITH A PURPOSE

LEARNING GAMES FOR CHILDREN
SIX WEEKS TO TEN YEARS

PLAY WITH A PURPOSE

LEARNING GAMES FOR CHILDREN
SIX WEEKS TO TEN YEARS

DOROTHY EINON

PANTHEON BOOKS
NEW YORK

First American Edition

Conceived, edited and designed by
Duncan Petersen Publishing Ltd.,
5 Botts Mews, London, W2 5AG.
Text © 1985 by Dorothy Einon.
Artwork © 1985 by Duncan Petersen Publishing Ltd.

**Library of Congress Cataloging in
Publication Data**
Einon, Dorothy.
Play with a purpose.
1. Play. 2. Educational games.
3. Child rearing. I. Title.
HQ782.E36   1985   649'.5   85-6301
ISBN 0-394-54493-5

Manufactured in Yugoslavia

CONTENTS

Play with a Purpose
was written by **Dorothy Einon** with the help of
John Farndon
illustration features and games in margins
John and Elizabeth Newson
top twenty toys lists
Paul Parry
research
Joe Robinson
artwork

A list of photograph and other credits appears on
page 256

My first inclination in writing this book was not to include
any age ranges for the games. Children differ so much that
ages, however vague, are bound to be inaccurate. But on
second thoughts, I felt that approximate age ranges would be
better than none at all. The age ranges I give are only an
indication of when you might try to encourage your child to
play. If they err, it is on the early side: a time when you or an
older child might be able to lead a younger one into the game.
But if you can't, wait a bit – there's never any point in
pushing.

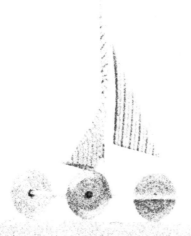

I N T R O D U C T I O N

It is a hot day, and you are sitting on the grass watching two children – for the sake of argument, your children – running in and out of the spray from a garden sprinkler. They scream with delight time and again as the cold water touches their skin. Their enjoyment shows no sign of palling; they have been at it for half an hour, and they will probably continue until stopped.

In the comfort of your deckchair, you could be excused for not thinking twice about your offspring's behavior. You probably register no more than the fact that they are having fun; if asked by some creature from another planet to define what they are doing, you would, without hesitation, use a single word: playing.

But is it so simple to define what your children are doing? And could you explain, convincingly, what keeps them at it for so long? You, after all, would probably give up the game after the first wetting.

I suspect that adults take juvenile play too much for granted. Because it is fun, and because it is usually harmless, we tend to see it as less serious than comparable adult activity. When children, or puppies, play-fight, they rarely hurt each other; in adult boxing or wrestling, the injuries are real.

Anyway, play is a feature of adult life as well as childhood. An old dog will chase and retrieve a stick, and grown-ups, like their children, enjoy a friendly game of softball after work. So what sets childish play – the subject of this book – apart from other sorts of recreation?

The learning game

Adults play when they have nothing better to do; in fact a philosopher once described adult play as "useless in the eyes of the beholder". But that is not to say it has no function at all; it is probably essential as a means of relaxation. The fact remains, though, that adult play is a means of *filling in time* between

Opposite: what keeps them playing for so long?

mainstream activities – like earning a living and rearing children. By contrast, practically everything a child does, when he has not been asked to do something else, is play. It can be joyful, it can be serious, it can be solitary, it can be social. It is frequently repetitive. And it is almost always creative.

When my children were growing up I made some video tapes of them playing. One episode was especially revealing.

The two youngest, aged ten months and three years, are in the bath, one at each end. My daughter sits with a small metal kettle and half a dozen cups. Solemnly, she pours water from kettle to cup and back again. Occasionally, she fills the kettle in the bath watching the bubbles as the water forces the air out through the spout. She is serious, intent in her activity, almost unaware of my presence.

My ten-month-old son is standing, holding the side of the bath because he is still unsteady on his feet. He stoops to pick up a toy duck; rising, he catches my eye as he holds it over the side of the bath for a moment before dropping it. I return it to him, and he drops it again. I smile at him, but leave it on the floor. He watches the duck on the floor, looks at me, then the duck. He waits for a moment before he stoops again to pick up a toy cup full of water. He holds it over the side of the bath, then looks at me in triumph before, encouraged by my shouts of "No", he drops it, laughing as it splashes to the floor.

His sister looks up from the other end of the bath and tells him he is a "naughty boy". Then, seeing me laughing, she slowly and deliberately pours the water from her kettle over the side of the bath. Watching me carefully to judge my reaction, she follows the kettle with a cup. Next, with mounting glee, they both empty the bath of all the bath toys, and much of the water. My cries of "you bad babies" only increase their excitement. Drying and powdering them is accompanied by squeals of delight, squirms of pleasure.

When people see this episode, few have any doubts that the children are playing. But the behaviors are not simple. If this is play, it has many different aspects. In my daughter's case, it was at first both serious and solitary. It was also repetitive: the pouring of the water over and over again. In my son's case, the play was always social, but at first it was quietly so, gentle enjoyment of a simple, repetitive action. Then, for both children, play became boisterous and joyful, a happy social occasion. But if it was also creative, what were the children achieving?

Consider my daughter. Simply by pouring water, she was learning many things, though primarily the physical action of pouring, the minute postural adjustments needed to hold the cup

Solitary, serious, repetitive or social, it is all play: but what does it achieve? What sets childish play apart from other sorts of recreation?

steady as it became heavier, and the kettle as it became lighter. She was also learning that it is necessary to tip the kettle only slightly when full, but that as it empties it needs to be tipped more steeply so that the water will reach the spout at a constant rate. She may have noticed, too, that containers are heavier when full of water, and that the kettle holds more water than the cup. She may also have seen that when filling the cup by submerging it in the bath, the water rushes in from the sides without forming bubbles, but that if she performs the same action with the kettle, bubbles are formed. Thus she was conducting her earliest scientific experiments.

Meanwhile, my son was learning to balance as he bent down in the bath. A few months earlier, he had learned to locate and grasp an object; now he was learning to let it go. But that was not all: in his play, he was constantly interacting, first with me, and later with his sister. He watched our faces, judged whether we were pleased or not. He took his turn in an unspoken conversation, one in which smiles, laughter and gestures played the major roles. In fact, the words used in the conversation, the "no's", the "stops" and the "naughty babies" were taken, quite correctly, as encouragement, for I could easily have stopped the game at its outset by speaking sharply. They were both learning not only to judge my mood, but the value of simple co-operation, the simple sharing of fun and enjoyment.

A child does most things out of curiosity. He wants to find out how to do things, or how objects behave – be they televisions, books or scraps of paper. Perhaps, then, this is what we call play: a way of learning.

I believe that for all practical purposes we can assume that it is. Play may be difficult to describe and to define, but it is easy to recognize. Few people have any doubts that my video sequence was play; so I shall use the word as it is most commonly used, to describe childish activity which is at once fun, and, although some may not realize it, a superb, natural way of learning.

But why learn through play?

The answer is not entirely obvious, especially if you consider how often play is fraught with danger. Young monkeys chase and wrestle in trees and may, and do, fall, breaking limbs. Young animals of many species are often eaten by predators while in the act of playing noisily and conspicuously. Playing animals, and playing children, are less watchful than at other times, yet the young of many species, including our own human species, play without parental protection. Moreover, children and animals often positively favor challenging and dangerous locations as

Playing children, and animals, are less watchful than at other times. If they learn through play, why do so in this apparently maladaptive fashion?

When children or puppies play-fight, they rarely hurt each other. But just because much childish play is harmless, it is not necessarily less serious than comparable adult behavior.

playgrounds. Young goats choose the rockiest parts of the hillside; children play in water, on frozen ponds, on railway sidings, roads and cliffs, in fact any place where they can come to harm.

So why put themselves at risk? Why learn in this apparently maladaptive way? The answer must be that it is in some sense the best or only way to learn what must be learned. But to fully understand this imperative, one has to consider the nature of learning.

We learn all through life, and in two distinct ways: directly or indirectly. By indirect learning I mean receiving knowledge through others as intermediaries; it encompasses everything picked up through reading, watching the television, witnessing cultural events or sitting in a classroom. Its essence is profiting from the knowledge of others, which in turn allows short cuts to be taken. One does not have to work out the principles of cake-making for oneself if one has learned them indirectly from a cook book. A sponge cake could win a prize at a show without the cook ever knowing that the reason for beating fat and sugar or eggs and sugar together is to incorporate air; and that it is added air which makes the cake rise.

Direct learning, on the other hand, comes without the benefit of other people's experience. One simply discovers for oneself.

Much of what one learns as a child, has, because of its nature, to be learned directly, often enough by trial and error.

The motor skills, those involving muscle movement, and ranging from writing to skating, are typical examples of skills that can be acquired only by direct learning. No one can explain exactly which muscles to use when riding a bicycle; you learn to master the machine just by riding it. The list of motor skills a baby, and a young child, must learn this way is practically endless; and it does not stop at motor skills. Vision, perception, language and social behavior all come largely by the same process, particularly in the first year of life. Indeed, they cannot be learned in any other way, for a child cannot go on to learn indirectly from parents or schoolteachers until he has these essential basic accomplishments.

This goes far to explain why young animals and children are capable of playing irresponsibly, wildly, and even dangerously. Play is the only way they have of learning in the early years, and learn they must in order to survive.

To be aware of this as a parent is a priceless asset. Encourage the right kind of play – be conscious of the enormous significance of playfulness – and you will greatly add to your stature as a parent and enjoyment of parenthood. Especially in the early years, it is easy to organize a child so that he has the maximum benefit from play – so that he learns directly in the way most suited to him. To assist in that process by providing a fund of ideas is the purpose of this book; but its emphasis is always on the side of encouraging, rather than directing, for given a choice, most children will prefer to play. You don't have to force down this particular medicine. How much a child plays will depend on when he last played. If you are stopped from eating for a day, you will eat rather more than usual at your next meal. In the same way, children prevented from playing will show an increased interest in play when it is allowed again. No special knowledge is needed to ensure that your child plays often enough. You need only be aware that if a child is totally deprived of play for a very long time – say months on end – there will come a point beyond which all desire to play is lost. Like the hunger striker who eventually loses any desire for food, the chronically deprived child does not seem to play.

From Birth to Two Years

VARIETY SHOW
First three months

Procedure You can fill a new baby's tiny world with interesting objects to look at simply by making a collection of everyday items from around the house and showing her two or three new ones every few days. Anything will do, from cereal boxes to colored yarn – but for preference, choose items which are colorful, boldly patterned and make a noise when moved. Hold them about a foot from her face, and for long enough to allow her to explore each object's appearance. Remember, too, that just now your face is the most interesting object of all to her.

Value
PERCEPTUAL New babies must learn about the world to a large extent through their eyes, and tests have shown that they love to look at noisy, colorful objects that have a well-defined, bold pattern. It takes time for their eyes to develop physically, and at first they only see objects which are nearby.

Variation Leave a display of two or three light objects hanging above her crib so that she can explore them in her own time, *and see page 19.*

SENSING A STRANGE WORLD

In the first six months of life your baby must make sense of the world. In doing so she will mobilize all her senses and start to work out where her body ends and the rest of the world begins. She will learn to control her hands, and to adjust her posture as she moves. For some time yet, she is dependent upon you, so she must learn to communicate with you. Most of all, she has to learn that the world is not random; that things happen for reasons, that there are causes and effects and that she is one of the causes.

Although there is a great deal to learn and she has, in the main, to learn it for herself, that does not mean you cannot help. If you provide the right environment in which to play with her, and tailor play to her abilities, she will learn more readily.

Seeing and perceiving

Your baby is not born with a fine understanding of what she sees around her. Indeed, people born blind and given their sight by an operation when adult do not immediately understand what they see; in some cases they never learn to interpret it.

A newborn baby's eyes are barely half the size of an adult's, and although they are structurally similar, they differ in two important respects. Their focus is fixed at eight to ten inches, which means that the baby has only a small 'bubble' of clear vision at this distance. Anything nearer or farther away appears blurred. She will be able to focus at about six weeks, but will remain short-sighted for some time after that.

The eye is often likened to a camera, but the pigments at the back of the eye which record the light falling upon them are much more complex than ordinary film. For a start, there is one system of pigments for dim lighting – the rods – and another system – the cones – which records color and fine details in brighter light.

In the adult the cones are particularly concentrated in a small sensitive area – the *fovea centralis* – at the center of the eye. This is why you see best if you look straight at an object. At birth the fovea is only partially developed; so her vision is less clear, and less detailed than yours. If you showed her a striped card, held at about eight inches from her eyes, she would only see the stripes if they were more than one-eighth of an inch thick. By six months, she will be able to tell them apart even if they are only one-sixty-fourth of an inch thick. By the time she is adult, she can distinguish stripes which are as narrow as one-three-hundred-and-twentieth of an inch. (The sensitive fovea is present in babies by four months but still not yet fully developed enough to give a significant appreciation of fine detail.)

Her eyes differ from yours in one other respect. The nerves which leave the back of the eye and carry information to the brain are, in the adult, covered with a fatty coat called the myelin sheath. Its effect is to speed up the transfer of the messages along the nerve, so that what the eye sees the brain can almost immediately receive. Many of the nerves of a newborn baby, including those at the back of the eye, do not have the myelin sheath, so that in comparison to an adult the baby responds slowly to a visual stimulus.

Does it matter that your baby cannot see as well as you? Probably not at all; in fact, it might even be an advantage. She needs to see you, to see your face as you feed and cuddle her, and she needs to see her hands and other objects in close proximity. Her eyes, with focus fixed at about eight inches, are efficient enough for present needs, and you must therefore match any visual stimuli offered her in play to their extremely basic abilities. By the time she needs detailed vision, to pick up small objects, to thread beads, to read and write, her eyes will have matured. Until then, too much detail probably confuses.

Between four and six months, she begins to reach for objects; to see farther afield becomes an advantage, and so by this time the eyes can focus on both near and distant objects. She will see you beside her, and also when you call from across the room.

Eye movement develops similarly. A newborn baby can follow an object with both eyes soon after birth (although probably not efficiently) and she can converge upon an object (that is, look at it with both eyes) from two days. As her need for following and convergence grows, so the ability improves. Quite soon she can follow her hands as they move in front of her face. Much of this improvement is brought about by practice – practice you can encourage by playing with her.

Research has shown that babies prefer looking at patterned areas rather than plain ones – worth bearing in mind if you intend to decorate a room for a newborn baby. Of all patterns that can be offered to a baby in the first months, one is greatly preferred: that of a human face. At first, such a face-pattern can be quite crude: at six weeks a baby will smile at two dots on a card – some indication of how much she has to learn. By eight weeks, she shows a definite preference for real faces, although still smiling at drawings, and by four months smiles only at real faces. Two months later she will probably smile only at faces she knows.

So, try livening up her carriage by lining the hood with boldly patterned material, or by providing a simple felt face. Equally,

MOVING STICK
Two to four months

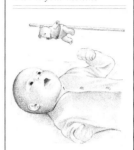

Procedure Once your baby begins to follow movement with her eyes, encourage this by fixing a little toy to a stick. Hold the toy on the stick about three feet in front of her in her line of vision. Then slowly move the toy from side to side so that she can follow it with her eyes. As she gets better at following the movement, swing the toy farther each way. Then try different directions, up and down, in and out. As she gets better still, speed up the movement and eventually try diagonal runs.

Value
VISUAL A new-born baby is able only poorly to fix her eyes upon objects and follow their movement. Head and eye movement is also poorly co-ordinated – in the first week or two, the eyes lag behind when the baby's head is turned to one side, a feature known by pediatricians as the "doll's eye phenomenon". This game helps to improve head-eye co-ordination and develop the baby's ability to visually fixate and follow objects.

WORLD IN MOTION
Up to six months

Procedure There are few things that babies like better than watching things move. So as she begins to gain a little control over her head movements, prop her up against some cushions on the floor – or in a baby chair – making sure her head is well supported. Then show her as many different types of movement as you can think of. Use your imagination to show her the infinite variety of ways things move. Blow bubbles to show the way they drift and float catching the light; play with balloons; roll balls across the floor; bounce them off the wall; use them to knock down blocks.

Value
VISUAL/PERCEPTUAL
Even when new babies begin to follow movement easily, they are still not fully aware that an object in motion is still just one object.
FUN Few babies will not giggle with delight when they see a wall of wooden bricks mowed down with a ball.

Later progress Soon she will begin to learn that objects continue to exist not only when they move but when they go out of sight (*see page 21*).

you could make a brightly colored bumper for her crib, adding a face or two for good measure. Don't forget the old favorites: hanging toys and large beads strung across the carriage are still useful, especially if they make a noise. Remember to place such objects at the right range.

Movement of shapes through the air also produces patterns – albeit moving ones – and this is why mobiles are so popular with babies. Remember to hang them where they can be seen, and remember that they will not move unless there are air currents. If you live in a house with high ceilings, or if your house is free from drafts, it is probably worth buying one of the mobiles that fix to the side of a crib, with a small motor to provide the motion. Some even have a musical box attached.

A mirror is an invaluable plaything at this stage, too, combining the fascination of a face-pattern with movement. Attach an unbreakable mirror to the wall near the changing table. Much later on, she will recognize herself in it.

Another high priority is the rod or frame, fixed above the cot, with objects dangled from it. The simpler alternative is to stretch a piece of elastic across the top of the crib or carriage. Bright objects can then be dangled from it: small stuffed animals or plastic toys being obvious examples. The advantage of home-made mobiles and hanging-frames is that you can change the shapes and objects hanging from them: large colored pegs, pieces of patterned material and yogurt cartons can all be pressed into service, and the bolder and brighter the shapes, the better.

Arranging objects close to your baby has a hidden bonus, too: it sets her up automatically for her next stage of development.

HOME-MADE MOBILES/*From birth on*

Taking the trouble to make mobiles really is worthwhile: you can match them to existing decorative scheme in your baby's room, and experiment to achieve best effects. If you put together a particularly fine mobile, the chances are you will leave it in place long after it ceases to be useful for stimulating her senses, and that is good, for it will contribute towards making her room a special place where she is happy to go to bed. *Basic requirements*: a hook set firmly in the ceiling; fine, but tough string or cord; a long string to allow extra movement; air currents to create the movement; light objects, so they move easily. Hang it where the baby can see it easily.

A strip of cardboard stapled into a shallow cylinder makes a useful mount for mobile objects: it has the advantage of being able to rotate. But a coat hanger is also perfectly serviceable. Keep the objects simple and brightly colored; shapes cut from felt look attractive: make templates by tracing images from a book designed for this age group. Change the objects as often as you like.

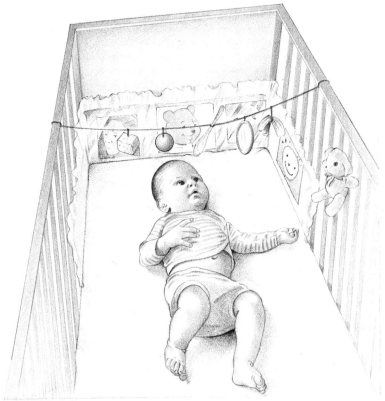

Elastic stretched across the crib makes a simple "cradle gym". Simply tie toys securely to it. Change the objects frequently: some suggestions for safe ones are given on page 18.

Value
VISUAL/PERCEPTUAL
Provided the objects are placed at the right range – *see page 17* – they can stimulate not only vision but a realization that the world out there is full of interest.

Procedure Of all moving objects, there is nothing more fascinating to a baby than you. So why not let him watch you when you cannot spare the time to play with him? Prop him up any way you like, but best of all in a bouncing cradle chair, so he can see you working about the house. Say "hello" now and then, and talk, sing, or whistle while you work – babies love voices, especially if high-pitched.

Value
VISUAL All the color and movement of housework is fascinating to a baby – however much of a chore for you. Think of how interesting the shiny iron looks as it is applied each time to colored clothes.
AUDITORY The noise and bustle of housework is equally attractive to a baby, and may help him take the first steps towards pinpointing the source of sounds.
SOCIAL He is deprived of your company for the minimum possible time.
PRACTICAL You can treat household chores as a game.

REACHING OUT

If one basic principle should govern early play, it is this: whenever possible, give your baby the opportunity to progress to the next stage of his own accord. Don't rush him; enjoy him just as he is, and let him play for as long as he wishes in his chosen way. At the same time, have a game at hand to which he can progress when the moment arrives. This is easy enough just now: simply tie a toy securely to the side of his crib. He can carry on watching the mobiles and, when he is ready, reach out for the toy.

Babies develop at different rates. It is never possible to say that at six weeks he will be ready for one game, and at twelve weeks for another. The best way to judge if your baby has reached a certain stage is to take a lesson from researchers: sit back and watch him. As he begins to reach out for toys you will notice, if you have been watching, that he also begins to realize he can do things himself. When he touches the toy it moves – a great moment for him, and for you. For the first time, he will have done something without your help. You will see him wave his arms – in the time-honored fashion of excited babies – and in doing so possibly knock the toy again, thereby increasing his excitement. Over the next weeks you can join in the game by dangling an object tied to a short piece of elastic in front of him; be patient; let him practice again and again until he can reliably reach out and touch it. He is learning a new skill, to him as difficult as anything yet achieved, or to come.

The reaching-out stage starts at around eight to ten weeks – but don't be disillusioned, or proud, if your baby begins it earlier or later. Early achievement is a very unreliable indication indeed of overall ability. Far better spend time observing his continued development so that you can anticipate his needs, rather than exult in hurdles crossed earlier than the baby next door; for a long time yet, he will be totally reliant on you to enable him to progress, undisturbed, one step at a time.

Things come and go
Sometimes a baby must lie alone: you cannot be in constant attendance. Obviously, you must fill his world with toys he can watch and reach out for in the waking moments. Not so obvious, perhaps, is the importance of one particular moving stimulus – your face – or rather, any face, for he cannot tell you apart for some time yet. So move in close to him as often as you can; even if it is only as you pass by, he will appreciate it. Just from this

simple movement of your face he can learn, in time, that objects get bigger as they come near, and smaller as they move away; that they remain the same object, only their size changes. Don't, however, move in too fast: babies do not like looming objects. From as early as they are able to avoid an object looming towards them, they will. It is good design that you naturally have to look at him as you feed him, for in time this look helps him see that a face viewed from different angles still remains a face. There is much he can learn from simply being close to you, and he will, of course, look at you from his earliest days. Study him carefully as he examines you and note how he looks at your hairline (particularly if your hair is dark), then moves slowly down your face to your chin, then back up to your eyes. There his gaze will rest for some time: note how slowly his gaze moves, and remember this when you show him things, or stimulate him with moving objects.

It is fascinating to realize that, at this early stage, he is quite unaware of where he ends and where the rest of the world begins, or that objects continue to exist after they move away.

Once he can focus, you can begin to show him toys moving in and out of his line of sight; but since your face is so favored, start by moving your head from left to right. Move slowly, so that he can always follow you. Then try it with a favored toy, again moving slowly, making sure he is following with his eyes. Trace the simplest patterns of movement – first left and right, then up and down. As he becomes more practiced, you can move the object farther and farther so that he has to move his head as well as his eyes. Then progress to different sorts of movement, the purpose of the game now being to show him not only that objects move in space but that they move in different ways. When you have tried jiggling movements, and slightly faster movement (but not too fast: if he cannot follow it he will get bored), try different objects. The ultimate game in this context is of course peek-a-boo, for it makes use of your face, the best stimulus of all. It is such a favorite with young children that psychologists even use it as a reward to make babies perform tasks. Take advantage of the fact that it has a number of forms (see margin) and can gradually be extended, as the baby grows older, into hiding games of many kinds.

PEEK-A-BOO
Two to 14 months

Procedure Simple peek-a-boo rarely fails to delight babies of all ages. All you need to do is sit close in front of him and cover your face with your hands, then open them and cry "boo!" But try varying the game by peeping around the side of your hands or moving to different parts of the room. Take the game a little further by turning your head away or hiding behind furniture.

Value
PERCEPTUAL It is a long time before a baby realizes that things continue to exist even when he cannot see them. This simple and natural activity is the perfect way to help him develop this concept at an early age.
SOCIAL As he begins to anticipate your reappearance and watch your face as you say "boo!", his squeals of delight are the first steps in social intercourse.

Procedure After a month or two a baby will turn her head to follow a sound. You can make this into a game if you prop her in a chair and try out various sounds from different positions. For instance, shake a box of matches a little to her left. Wait for her to look. Then shake it to her right. Wait for her to look. Finally, try moving the matchbox around slowly, shaking it all the time, so that she can follow the sound. Repeat the game with all kinds of different sounds – little bells, rustling paper, rattling cans and so on.

Value
AUDITORY Just as baby's visual fixation must be developed, so too must her ability to pinpoint sound. At first, she can only tell whether a sound is coming from one side or the other. After playing this game for four or five months, she will be able to locate sounds much more accurately.

Variations Try playing this game with your voice. Call to her from each side, from on tiptoe, from bended knee, always going to her to show that you are there. Then walk about the room talking or singing as you go, encouraging her to track your voice.

SOUNDS

Most of the sounds your baby hears are fleeting: a car passing, a door closing, the lid being put on a coffee jar. A few are more sustained: music playing, people talking, the vacuum as you clean. She must, in this first year, make sense of all these very different noises. Where do they come from? What do they mean?

The easiest way for her to learn is to keep her close to you while you work. Sit her near you as you chop vegetables, and she will hear the regular chopping sound of knife on board, and associate it with you and the kitchen. Carry her in a sling or on your back as you vacuum, prop her in a chair beside you as you type or play the piano.

Make a habit of creating familiar sounds in familiar places: a musical box in her crib at night, always the same lullaby to help her sleep. Most of all talk to her. Tell her what you are doing, ask her opinion – even tell her how you are going to vote in the coming election. It does not matter what you say at this stage, as long as you say it. She needs to know your voice, for she finds voices, particularly high-pitched ones, easier to locate than neutral sounds. Until she can locate a sound, she cannot begin to understand it. From an early age, your baby will begin to turn towards you when you speak, and when she gives you those first smiles, it is the sound of your voice, not the sight of your face, that she smiles at. In fact, so tuned is she to the sound of your voice that in the first weeks of life she will move to its rhythm, the segments of her movement matching the smallest segments of your speech. You, likewise, are tuned to her, for you raise your voice a tone or two to please her.

It follows that a noisy toy is easier for her to locate than a quiet one, and a talking face easier to find than a silent one. By adding sound to her early games you double their value: when she knocks her rattle by chance, its sound will draw her into a reaching game. Put a bell on a mobile and it is not just a visually exciting toy, it is a way of practicing sound localization.

Noisy games, played by you with your baby, are inevitably more fun, better value in terms of learning. Since your voice is a favorite sound, call to the baby often. At first, call when close to her, and when she is looking at you. Then progress, gradually, to calling to attract her attention, first from close by, later from across the room. Next, vary your position, in front, to left, to right. Stand on tip-toe, or stoop down low so that she looks up and down too. Always make sure she has seen you; if she cannot find you, move in towards her – remember it is a game, not a test. She will only play while she is having fun, and the point is to make learning fun, not to find out what she can do.

Once she can track the source of sound that is you, move about, talking as you go. Short distances are enough at first, but once she can follow you, make it more difficult. Go behind on her right-hand side, and then pop out on her left, talking as you go so that she turns one way and then the other. Or pop down behind the table and up again on the far side, so she has to follow your voice, even though she cannot see you.

Again, it must be stressed how important it is not to push a baby too hard. If you do, she will stop playing, and may even begin to cry. Watch her carefully: typical signals indicating that she wants to stop are looking away or avoiding your gaze. If this happens, give her a cuddle to let her know that all is well. Babies vary in their tolerance of sound: some like a wild rumpus, others are frightened by loud noises. Even a child who loves noise will sometimes prefer quieter sounds. The same sound may increase her excitement when she is happy, or frighten her if she is sad.

I have described these games in a rather formal way, but of course they do not have to be played like that. After all, they are the type of game most parents play without thinking. They can be – should be – played at any time. While you are cooking, sit her in her chair near you. Call to her as you move to the sink, when you go to the refrigerator, or as you bend down to take food from the oven. When you are getting dressed, call from beside the closet, or from the mirror as you brush your hair.

Understanding what you say

Although in the early weeks your baby obviously cannot understand what you say to her, she is amazingly clever at telling sounds apart, especially if they are the sounds made in speech. Tests have been performed in which babies are presented with a wide range of typical speech sounds originating in different parts of the mouth and throat – for example b's and g's. As early as the first days of life a baby can tell some of these sounds apart, and by the time she is three months, she can tell the difference between practically every speech sound given. By four months, she can even distinguish between the very subtle changes in the sound of letters in different words. The p in "sip", for instance, makes a different configuration of sound waves than the p in "split". Psychologists would like to be able to understand more of this amazingly early development; in any case, it leads them to the conclusion that of all the developing human skills, language is the most remarkable.

MUSICAL MAYHEM
Three months on

Procedure Babies love making noise, and as she grows older, she will do this more and more effectively. Encourage her, as long as your nerves can stand it, by providing her with "musical" instruments. Give her a rattle as soon as she can grasp one. The best on the market are brightly colored, and made of a plastic pleasant to chew. Once she gets the hang of rattles, introduce your own variations, such as a clean plastic medicine bottle with a screw-on safety top filled with a few dried beans. This is not so useful for visual stimulus, but it will make plenty of noise, of a different quality. In the second six months, or whenever her co-ordination has developed sufficiently, give her "drums" to hit – a saucepan and a wooden spoon for example. Play records to which she can bang and shout along.

Value
DISCOVERY Learning that it is she who is making the noise, and can start and stop it as she wishes, is an important addition to her understanding that by her actions she can control her environment.

LEG OVER, LEG OVER
Three months on

Procedure Sit on a chair with your legs crossed. Sit the baby astride your ankle and hold her hands firmly. *"leg over, leg over, the dog ran through clover. When he came to a fence . . ."* pause and uncross your legs to that the baby rides up . . . *"UP he went over."* Repeat at will.

Value
POSTURE CONTROL The change of position taxes the baby's sense of balance.
ANTICIPATION By nine months or so, the baby will start to wait excitedly for the leg to go over.
SOCIAL The face-to-face contact, turn-taking and shared enjoyment all foster the development of social skills.
LANGUAGE The rhythm and rhyme of the verses are invaluable aids to the development of language.

Variations Any popular riding rhyme.

We know that babies as young as six weeks prefer speech sounds to all others. They turn when you speak, and they turn to a loudspeaker that speaks rather than one that simply makes noises. It is as if babies are designed to tune into speech from the start, just as they seem instinctively to search for faces when starting to use their eyes.

So, talk to her as a matter of course, whenever you are with her; keep up a running commentary on everything that happens, and never lose heart, because it does make sense. She will learn to understand speech even if you don't do this, but she'll learn more readily if you do.

Rhythm
Listen closely to someone speaking, and it soon becomes clear that speech is more than enunciated words. Language has – or should have – rhythm. Listen to a baby before she has learned to talk and you will often hear the rhythm of speech in her babbling. Very young babies enjoy the physical sensation of rhythmical movement, rocking and joggling in your arms or in their cribs, but they like to hear it, too. The obvious conclusion is to give your baby music – as indeed parents have always done. The bolder and more simply rhythmical the music, the better – a characteristic of all the most popular old lullabies. Similarly, nursery rhymes often emphasize or mimic the rhythms or patterns of speech, and this probably explains their popularity too. Recent research suggests that some children who have problems reading have difficulties rhyming words. This does not, of course, prove that listening to nursery rhymes will help her reading – but it suggests that it might.

You will probably find that she enjoys rhymes long before she understands the words – if indeed she ever really understands the words. Later, rhymes can be a source of phrases and sentences, or experiments with sounds. When she is about six months, you can start to add actions to the words, and later you may find that she uses these actions like words. At about a year, she may clap her hands when you show her a cake, or go through the actions of "the wheels of the bus go round and round" each time she sees a bus.

Beneficial as it is, this type of sound-play should never be a burden to you, and you should never feel under pressure to provide this type of stimulus. There will be times when you are too busy or just not in the mood for spouting nursery rhymes, or singing silly songs. In which case, don't forget that you can buy from a wide selection of records or tapes of children's songs, or just sit her beside the radio.

MUSICAL MITTENS/*Six to ten weeks on*

The idea of musical mittens was originally
devised to promote hand and eye movement in
handicapped children, but even normal babies
may benefit enormously from this simple game.
It takes advantage of a baby's natural
attraction to sounds and bright colors to draw
her attention to her hands. You may find
suitable mittens in a shop, but if not, take two
different, brightly colored mittens – say one
red and one yellow – and sew a bell very firmly
to each. Start by putting on her right-hand
mitten. Her gaze will soon be drawn to the
tinkling bell. The next day, try the left-hand
mitten. Finally, after a few weeks' alternation,
try both mittens at once. Don't leave her alone
with the mittens on; she may try to chew off
the bells.

*Cotton "scratch" mittens (to stop babies scratching)
make ideal bases for musical mittens: it is easy to attach
things firmly enough not be pulled off and swallowed.*

Variation If it is too warm for the
baby to wear mittens, try tying a ribbon
with a bell around her wrist.

Later progress You can extend the
mitten game by sewing a face on to the
palm of each mitten to encourage her to
turn her hands. Include a hairline in each
face as well as eyes, nose and mouth –
this can be surprisingly important in face
recognition. Start with one mitten at a
time, as above.

Value
VISUAL
MOTOR SKILLS To see
the source of the noise
properly, the baby
moves her hand as well
as her head, promoting
eye-hand co-ordination.
CAUSE AND EFFECT She
begins to learn that
things happen when she
moves her hands.

25

A QUIET TIME
From birth

Procedure Leave a
baby to rest peacefully
every now and then. Or
sit quietly cuddling her.
Allow her to wind down
and *relax* occasionally.

Value
PSYCHOLOGICAL Babies
need to relax every now
and then just like adults.
Constant excitement and
stimulation can lead to
tension. They need time
to reflect on all their new
experiences.
PRACTICAL If you play
with her too much, you
may find that as she
grows older she can
never do without
constant amusement.

Smelling and tasting

Walk into the kitchen when you are hungry, and the cake in the oven smells good. Drive through the country after the fertilizer has been spread, and it smells bad. But between these two extremes, most of the smells of our daily life pass us by. The very young baby is, by contrast, surprisingly sensitive to smells. At a time when she happily smiles at the dots on a card, and cannot tell whether stripes one-eighth of an inch thick are really stripes or just plain grey, the breast-fed baby can distinguish her mother's breast pads from those of another woman. It is quite likely that she recognizes you by your smell long before she knows your face, or even your voice. It is not only babies that seem to be sensitive to smells. Young kittens are blind and deaf at birth, and they find the nipple by its smell: in fact each kitten has a "favorite nipple", which can be found by its smell alone.

Common sense indicates that this is an area of stimulation that can be left to look after itself. Taste is closely allied to the sense of smell, and likewise there is no need to encourage the ability to taste, or to enjoy tasting different flavors until after a baby has been weaned at five months or later. Weaning a baby too early is in any case counterproductive.

TOUCHING

One other sense remains: touch. As a matter of course, a baby discovers in her day-to-day activities how different things feel; but you can usefully extend this experience, for example by putting some talcum powder on her hands at bath time so that she can feel its smoothness, or by showing her the different textures of her clothes as you dress her.

Today's babies tend to be dressed in one-piece stretch suits by day, with overalls for outdoors. These may provide the most warmth, but the traditional baby wear – nightdresses and shawls – do give better opportunities to clutch the material. Babies often lie in the "fencer position": one arm by her head, the other down by her side. In this position it is easy to clutch the folds of a nightdress, and in the ensuing excitement to pull it up to her face. Alone in her crib she can develop not only a feeling game, but a game of control: of holding and lifting, of cause and effect.

I am the last to advocate returning to old-fashioned baby clothes that must be hand-washed and ironed, but nightdresses can be an interesting change for a baby from time to time. In any case, give her plenty of things to hold. Scraps of cloth, crumpled paper, wooden dolls and rattles, selected for their different textures, are all invaluable.

As she reaches three months, she will begin to uncurl, and from then until she becomes mobile, she will enjoy kicking. So let her feel with her feet and body, as well as with her hands, by giving her different objects with different degrees of solidity to kick against; or, lie her down on different surfaces. Play peek-a-boo with an old shawl or diaper by throwing it over her face: she will enjoy the sensation of being temporarily covered, then quickly uncovered to see your face smiling down at her. In fact some babies find this so funny that it becomes an essential part of the routine of going to bed.

I have discussed each of the senses separately, and suggested ways of encouraging looking and listening, smelling and touching, but a baby's world, like our own, is made up of all these sensations together. Play games with her that combine all or several of the senses and you can be sure that you are providing an exciting level of stimulus. Babies are more likely to look at noisy objects than quiet ones, they are more likely to look at you and smile if you talk to them. Encourage her to use all of her senses, but not in isolation. After all, she will not be using them in isolation as she grows up.

FEELERS
Birth to 6 months

Procedure Give a baby different objects to touch with her hands and feet from the very first moment. Dress her in loose clothes with interesting textures whenever possible – she will naturally fondle the material. But also put into her hand objects that feel different: hard, soft, firm, squashy, silky, coarse, cold, warm, wet, dry, furry, smooth – anything she can safely handle.

Value
TOUCH A baby lying in a crib or sitting in a chair may experience many different sights and sounds but receives only a limited range of tactile sensations. Giving her plenty of different objects to touch helps to develop her awareness of how objects can be distinguished by feel.

Variations Whenever it is warm enough, take off her clothes and lie her on different surfaces to let her feel different textures and surfaces with her whole body.

27

Procedure Provide a baby with evidence that her actions affect the world. Make sure that when she makes a positive movement something happens. Try tying toys to her cot so that when she hits them they move. If necessary, encourage her by sitting behind her and guiding her hand towards the toy. Help her to use both hands, not just one. If the toy makes a noise as well as moves, so much the better. Ideal toys are bells in plastic cages, plastic bottles filled with beans (*page 35*), balloons, squeaky toys and paper in a cloth bag.

Value
CONTROL At first, a baby's participation in the world is passive. Once she becomes aware that she can make things happen, however, her role will become more and more active. As she finds she can control her world, she will try all kinds of little experiments in cause and effect. The child who is only dimly aware that she can make things happen will have little natural curiosity and will learn slowly.
MOTOR SKILLS

Achieving control

At first, your baby receives information passively. Her contribution is to look, to listen, and to respond with the reflexes programmed into her by nature. If her hand is touched, she closes it: if her cheek is touched, she turns and opens her mouth. But by three months she is beginning to make an impression on her world; she is reaching out to touch with her hands, holding her head up, and beginning to kick and wave her arms with vigor. If she has a bouncing cradle chair, or a reclining chair, she will have a better view of the world about her. She is no longer restricted to her ten-inch vision bubble and can focus on more distant objects. Soon, she will sit in her chair and follow you with her eyes and head as you move about. When you come towards her, she will smile directly at you.

At around four months she will begin to explore for herself, a significant step because it means she has learned to control the movements of her arms. At first she learns to locate her hands and to reach out towards objects, but as yet makes contact only by chance. Gradually, the head movements become deliberate: an object is seen and a hand is guided towards it. She is achieving visual-motor co-ordination.

Now, when she sees you hold a rattle in front of her, she reaches for it directly, using her eyes to guide her hands. The next stage is reached when she can grasp an object, and soon she will move everything she holds to her mouth to suck it, to chew it, and otherwise explore it. The fourth stage in this progression is reached when the baby becomes mobile. This can be as early as five to six months, or as late as 18 months, but when it comes she will seek out objects on shelves, in corners, and inside cupboards until nothing is safe from her prying fingers unless it is too big, too heavy, or too high to reach.

Encouraging visual-motor co-ordination

A newborn baby keeps her hands in tight fists; they only open out gradually. Most babies do not begin to really "find" their hands until after they start opening out, although some learn to suck their hands and fingers almost from birth.

To begin with, the hands seem to come together by chance, and the baby grasps them, not because she intends to hold her hands together, but rather because she always grasps if the palm of her hand is stimulated. But once she is able to touch one hand with the other, she practices the movement. At first it is as if her other hand is just another object to touch and feel. But gradually she beings to reach with one hand for the other, and to watch her hands in front of her face, until by about three months she begins to connect what her eyes are seeing with what her hands are doing.

A baby is more likely to notice an object if it is brightly colored, if it moves, and if it makes a noise. So one way to help her notice her hands is to make them bright and noisy. Nothing is better suited to the purpose than the traditional rattle, only make sure it is brightly colored – much easier, and more interesting to follow with the eyes. At this stage, the best rattles are probably dumbbell-shaped, because this gives a narrow gripping area. Dropping rattles is an occupational hazard at this stage, and if you find this is a particular problem, it is worth trying musical mittens (*see page 25*) as an alternative.

The next step is to help her practice both controlling her hands and estimating how far her hands must reach in order to touch an object. Once again, the traditional toys, and methods of helping her play with them, provide stimulus second to none. Dangle objects in front of her whenever you can, and if you have not already rigged up a row of dangling objects across the crib, do so.

If you have a bouncing cradle chair, be sure to attach one of your baby's favorite rattles to the side. It not only encourages the baby to reach out, but, as a result of reaching out, to shift her height and so bounce the chair. When she discovers the one action causes the other, she is on the way to controlling the movement of the chair, and just now learning to control is vitally important.

From a baby's point of view, the world must be a disturbingly random place, even chaotic, with herself as the butt of much incomprehensible treatment. People visit her and clean her, pick her up and put her down, with no apparent reason. Playing games with you is a welcome relief from this chaos, because it enables her to see the results of her actions. Any games, or toys, which encourage a feeling of control or contributing are good. The bouncing cradle chair is probably the best of them, but there are many variations on the theme that you can set up with minimum effort (see margin).

BOUNCING CRADLE CHAIR
Six weeks on

Procedure A bouncing cradle chair is more or less standard baby equipment nowadays, but be sure to maximize its benefits. Whenever possible, place it at a high level rather than on the floor. Bouncers are generally equipped with four rubber donuts on the base to make them non-skid — but still never leave a baby like this unattended. A solid table top makes an ideal baby bouncer stage, from which she will get the best view of you going about your work. Never leave a baby unsupervised in this situation.

Value
SOCIAL You stop and talk as you go by.
CONTROL Babies left in the bouncer soon learn that as they move, the bouncer moves. Her awareness of the relationship between cause and effect will develop accordingly.

LEARNING TO HOLD

After learning to swipe and grab at objects, your baby progresses to the more refined art of deliberately holding them. Now mobiles should be moved up out of reach, and he should always have suitable toys close by to grab. Suspending them in front of him is still the best approach – he finds it hard to home in on things lying beside him. Your role now is not so much as provider of suitable objects but as patient attendant. Sit in front of him and offer toys. It will take him some time to organize his movements, but don't take pity on him and put the object into his hand. Let him do it himself – even if you find it frustrating to watch.

By now he is probably happiest to play in a sitting position. So prop him in his bouncing cradle chair or, if he has an adjustable chair, settle him in it with some toys on the tray. Remember when offering him objects that he is likely to put them in his mouth. Even if he cannot do so yet, never leave him with anything that could be swallowed or might be dangerous to chew. Be careful, too, with anything that he might poke into his eye. He does not yet have the control to avoid poking his eye when randomly raising an object to his mouth.

You do not have to go out and buy toys. The problem at this age is not stimulating him to reach, but stopping him: your hair, earrings or coffee cup will be grabbed as readily as a rattle or teething ring. So always have an eye open for appropriate makeshift toys.

Parents often worry that the toys going to a baby's mouth are not sterile. This is quite natural. Sickness and diarrhea are extremely serious for a young baby because they produce dehydration, which in turn can cause heart failure. As the baby grows, the amount of fluid in his body increases and this danger is reduced, but at five months it is worth taking precautions.

Since sickness is often caused by the bacteria in food, it is common advice to sterilize any plaything that you have used in cooking, such as a sieve or a plastic dish, or that has been used for eating or drinking, such as spoons and cups. It you live in an area with a high level of disease, such as in Africa or Asia, it would also be wise to sterilize all his toys. Elsewhere it is probably unnecessary. Make sure they are clean, and that you put him to play on a clean surface. I always used a play mat or the tray of a child's chair, but a freshly laundered sheet would serve the same purpose.

As he grows older, and more mobile, you will be forced to relax these rules.

Procedure There is practically nothing a baby likes better, once he begins to gain control of his hands, than to hit things. Objects to hit should be as varied as possible; hang them, within reach on his crib or carriage.

Value
CONTROL In hitting things, he is furthering his experience of the cause-and-effect relationship, learning that when he hits things, he can make a noise happen.
MOTOR SKILLS He will gradually appreciate that to take hitting one stage further – to grab hold of an object – he has to make more precise hand movements than when simply hitting.

TICKLE ME
Six weeks on

Procedure Of course, all children, especially when they are small, love to be tickled gently. But the anticipation of being tickled is almost as exciting as the tickle itself. So when you tickle a baby, try to build up his sense of anticipation by using rhymes and involving him as much as possible. Simple catchphrases like *"Stroke a bunny, stroke a bunny, tickle his little tummy"* then arm, leg, hand and so on, are ideal. He will soon be giggling with delight as he waits to be tickled again.

Value
ANTICIPATION Learning to predict what is about to happen and taking appropriate action are a vital part of growing up and surviving.
SOCIAL The constant to and fro and the shared enjoyment of tickling games help develop his ability to communicate with people.
FUN For parents and baby.

Later progress These early tickling games develop naturally into finger rhyme games – *see page 43*.

The security of movement

In Japan and China, and throughout most of Africa, mothers traditionally carry their babies at all times. Tradition has it, too, that their babies cry much less than Western babies – something no one will ever prove, but which makes sense – for there are respectable indications that carrying babies does in fact do more than just stop them crying. There are, for example, a few reports that premature babies may have less breathing problems if they are gently rocked from time to time. I am not certain how valid these findings are, but there are certainly many reports that rocking may be important for emotional development. When monkeys are raised on artificial mothers made of wire, they grow up to be emotionally disturbed, as one would expect. But if they have furry artificial mothers that rock, they fare very much better. If raised with siblings, they cling and rock with each other. Of course these are monkeys, not human babies, but it is perhaps worth noting that emotionally disturbed children (and adults) often rock themselves, as do deprived children.

Mothers who have used baby slings to carry babies, as African mothers do, report that their babies seem happy and content in the carriers. Not having to take a carriage or stroller makes shopping easier, and is essential if you enjoy walking. Carriers are useful, too, for those times when your baby seems to sense you are too busy to play. I have lost count of the meals I have prepared with a baby on my back.

All the time you carry a baby in this way, you can talk to him, and he can hear the sounds and smell the smells of you and your work. He can also practice changing his posture and balance as you move, for many subtle changes are required to remain comfortable while attached to you in this way. At one time, it was thought that babies who were carried at all times learned to sit and walk much earlier. However, this is probably not true: observations comparing European and African babies show that African babies are probably more advanced in this respect than European babies, even when they are not carried.

Perhaps we should all go back to carrying our babies everywhere, but however much one enjoys motherhood, there are times when one wants a break from the baby – and why not? You can give your baby this type of stimulation in other ways: a rocking cradle, a bouncing cradle chair, a carriage with springs, or any of the traditional games like riding on feet or trotting on knees. It is no coincidence that these are so popular with babies – and parents. Not only do they provide movement, but in most cases they are played face-to-face: he can observe your face, listen to you describing the game, and anticipate the next move.

EARLY SOCIAL SKILLS

Although a baby's first word may not be spoken before her first birthday, from the earliest weeks of life she is learning how to carry on a conversation. Look at her, and she looks at you, smile at her, and she smiles at you. There are no words yet, but already, in such simple games, there is the pattern of a conversation; and in a year's time she will add words to those looks and smiles.

For a conversation is more than the mere exchange of words, and in order to converse a baby has more to learn than simply speech. As we talk, we watch and listen for cues from our audience: we meet their eyes, and pause to offer them a turn at speaking. As we listen, we wait for breaks in the flow of speech and fill these with looks, nods or words of encouragement. Even when we are not taking turns at actually speaking, our behaviors alternate: your turn, my turn, your turn, my turn.

At first, babies are not directly involved in conversation, they merely provide the gaps for parents to fill. They give us cues to play with them, but as yet do not join the game. Gradually, however, they begin to take a more active role. Just when this happens varies from baby to baby, but some time in the first month or so you will become aware that she is interacting. She looks where you look, meets your eye and may even begin to imitate your facial expressions. You begin to respond to each other in a you-me, you-me sequence.

By six months, a baby is capable of most of the skills of adult conversation, except of course speech. She will take her turn, meet your eyes, return your smile, and look away to break an interaction. Much of this she will have learned from the simple games you play, and from the way in which you automatically fill any pauses in her behavior. As with everything she learns, she will need to practice and refine her skill: and her best – indeed her only – opportunity to do so is when you talk and play together.

So the simplest baby games, especially those involving turn-taking and exaggeration of facial expressions, are of great importance: creative in the fullest sense because they are forming the basic building blocks of behavior. Luckily, most of us play these games without having to think about them: try saying "coochy-coochy-coo" as if to a baby. It is almost impossible not to move your face forward (acknowledging that babies are short sighted), widening your eyes and raising your eyebrows. In doing so you adopt, without effort, the "correct" way to play with your baby. The more of it the better, and there is no need to worry about

Procedure Skills she cannot learn by herself may be acquired by imitation. Start with simple facial expressions and see if you can get her to mimic them. Try a big smile, or poking your tongue out. Or try puffing and blowing. Don't worry if she does not respond at first – some babies will not even give you a smile in return for the first six months. Once she is a little older, you can prompt her into copying you by copying her first. She can then lead the way to a to-and-fro copying game. You can introduce slight variations to her movements: if she shakes her hand, for instance, you could extend this to a full-scale wave.

Value
NEW SKILLS Imitation is a key method of learning a wide range of new skills.
SOCIAL Surprisingly, perhaps, full or mature facial expressions are not inborn and a new baby must learn much in order to use her face to suggest different moods.

MIRRORS
All first year

Procedure Many babies never even see a mirror – and thereby miss out on an attractive and valuable toy. Because they catch the light and reflect different colors, mirrors make marvelous mobiles for new babies. Hang a little unbreakable mirror, like those made for parakeet cages, above her crib. After a month, mount a bigger mirror on the side of her crib where she can see her face and catch herself moving. Then when she starts to sit up and take notice of the world, from six months onwards, sit her on your lap facing a mirror. Talk to her and point to both her and the reflection. Ask her who is it in the mirror. Show her that when she moves, the reflection moves too, but don't expect her to appreciate this fully in the first year.

Value
LEARNING BY EXAMPLE It is an enormous and important step for a baby to acquire the ability to imagine herself in someone else's place. Once a baby can do this, she can learn by example and follow instructions. If she can see herself "out there" and realize that it is her, she is half-way to acquiring this skill.
PLANNING Being able to "see" yourself doing something "out there" is essential for planning a course of action in advance.
SOCIAL A baby can see in a mirror whether her expressions are really matching yours.

whether your technique is correct. All you need to remember is that practice makes perfect and a baby cannot practice alone.

Saying "coochy-coochy-coo", waiting for her to respond with a smile then showing her how you appreciate her smile, may seem a silly little game, but you really should not underestimate its importance – and not just for learning to converse. To see a result – a response – is a revelation for a baby. It means that she has some control over her world, and that in turn is vital for her sense of security.

In these early games, children also learn adult facial expressions. Babies born blind never smile or look angry in the way that sighted children do; they may frown and look cross in the rather fleeting way that all babies do in the first weeks of life, but these early expressions never mature to the "whole face" expressions we see in sighted babies by six months. Researchers who have watched parents of blind babies say that the parents seem highly disconcerted by this lack of facial expression, and often play quite rough games in an attempt to make their offspring smile – an indication that parents somehow "know" the rules of these games, and how important they are to a baby's development.

The precise mechanism by which a baby learns to make facial expression is akin to learning a part in a play. Imagine you are acting a character who has to speak without facial expressions. In order to achieve this difficult feat, you would almost certainly practice in front of a mirror, and this, in essence, is what a baby does. The parent or other care giver acts – often unconsciously – as the mirror; even strangers are often more than willing to oblige with this useful service. A baby smiles at you, and naturally you smile back; a baby frowns, and you say "what's the matter?", frowning as you do so.

Try this game with your baby. First, catch her attention by making a mock surprise face, opening your eyes wide, raising the eyebrows and opening your mouth. She will probably look at you, and either smile or make a similar face to yours. Whatever she does, you will probably then find yourself copying her. In fact, mothers do this so unerringly that there is some dispute as to whether mother copies baby or baby copies mother. As babies develop they certainly begin to copy adults, but initially it is probably the parent who copies the baby.

The great virtue of these early games of interaction is that you can hardly get them wrong – unless of course you forget that her nervous system works comparatively slowly, and that her reaction time will seem to be delayed. In fact, most parents seem to know instinctively that they should allow for this. Researchers who watch parents interacting with babies have found that they

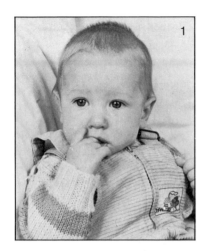

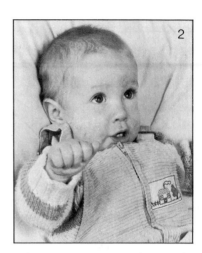

TURN-TAKING
Six weeks on

This routine is so natural that most parents go through it without even thinking. But it is not just a silly little game. Because you take turns reacting to each other, you rehearse, for the baby's benefit, the basic skills of adult conversation and it is well worth taking the time to make the most of this rehearsal.

1 A blank but attentive face is cue enough to start the game. You respond naturally, just as you would to fill in a gap in adult conversation, by looking at him, eyebrows raised.

2 The baby returns the gesture with a small but definite smile.

3 Then, of course, it is your turn to smile.

4 Give him time to make his next move – his nervous system works relatively slowly. It does not matter if his smile is still a little half-hearted, as long as he takes his turn in the "dialogue".

5 If you do get a full smile from him, you naturally return it, even more broadly, showing you have received the message.

6 He may respond with an even bigger full-face smile and may even laugh now. You can underline your response by lifting him into the air and making noises.

Value
SOCIAL;
LEARNING FACIAL
EXPRESSION

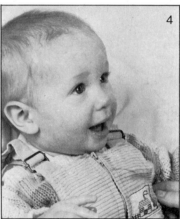

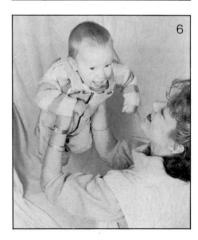

BLOW BY BLOW
Six to ten months

Procedure Puff your cheeks out and blow on a baby's face – she'll love it. With any luck, she'll try to blow back. If not, try again, only this time, waggle your head as you blow. If she has trouble blowing, show her how to blow with a short, sharp puff – she will find this much easier, and get the hang of blowing much quicker this way. When she can blow a little, try teaching her to blow a small feather from the palm of your hand.

Value
VOCAL Blowing is excellent for developing breath control and it improves the muscles used in speech.

Later progress At the age of about one year, you can try getting her to blow soap suds across a bowl or even blow out a candle. At 15 months, she should be able to blow bubbles in water through a straw – and will enjoy it immensely. She'll also love blowing through a straw on to flour in a dish – but be careful not to let her put the straw into the dish: she could inhale some flour.

not only move closer to the baby than they would to an adult, but also that they hold facial expressions for much longer. They also exaggerate the expression, which almost certainly helps the baby to see it.

There is more to making faces than just copying the expression; facial expression often needs to match mood, and this ability is part inborn, part learned. So remember, she will learn from watching your moods. She may feel upset when you are upset, and when you are excited, you may notice she senses something is about to happen.

Parenthood seems an awful responsibility when one stops to consider how much is learned straight from us; but you will be fulfilling your role very well indeed if you behave naturally with your child, if you remember that turn-taking is the essence of early social games, that you may have to wait for her response, and that there is maximum benefit if you can move in close. Take into account the fact that play is a means of practicing new skills. Of its nature, it is bound to be repetitive – sometimes, from the adult point of view, irritatingly so.

Play these social games as often as you feel inclined. Talk to her, smile at her, pull faces, tickle her or lift her up high – there are dozens of useful variations of this basic form of play and old favorites are as good as new inventions. Wait for her response before continuing – and be prepared at first for this to be no more than a squirm, a cry, or a slight movement.

Finally, remember that she will sometimes want to stop the interaction. Sometimes a game is too rough or too loud. If she looks away, it probably means she wants to escape. If she cries, the play was probably too intense. Respect her feelings.

OBSESSED WITH OBJECTS

In the first six months your baby began to make sense of the world. She turned to you when you spoke to her, smiled when you came near, and reached out to touch anything new. But it has been faces, particularly your face, and voices, particularly your voice, that have been her main interest. Through her overriding interest in people, she has come to learn where things are and what they mean. She has loved to look at the things you have shown her, to hear the sounds about her, but in many ways these have been a substitute for your face, your voice.

Sometime around five or six months, her preferences change. She still likes to see you, but in the next few months her overriding interest will be in things, not people. Offer her a rattle, and she will take it; offer her another, and she will take that too, and then she will drop both of them to take a third. For a baby of this age, it is strictly one thing at a time; if it catches her eye she cannot resist it and forgets about everything else.

Each toy will be taken to her mouth to chew, to explore with lips, tongue and gums. This is not because she is teething. At the moment her mouth is much more sensitive for exploring than her still-clumsy fingers. As soon as she can control her fingers well enough to prod, poke and feel, she will stop using her mouth so much.

Her waking day is now spent playing, and is probably the first time in her life that you can use the word unreservedly. It is not very elaborate play, focused almost exclusively on objects she encounters. There is little variety; she grasps, but at first cannot let go. She endlessly takes things to her mouth; she bangs the objects ceaselessly on any available surface.

As yet, only her interests have changed. It is true she is more skillful at reaching, but once she grabs the toy, the way she handles it has not altered. A baby at this age moves her arm, hand, and fingers as if they were one. She sees something, and her whole body responds. Later, she will begin to use her hand and arm in different ways: she will reach with her arm, and fold her hand around the object. In the second half of her first year, she begins to use her hand and fingers separately. Watch your baby's hands move as you offer her toys, and you can see this happening. When she grasped a toy at four months she used the same grip as in the first days of life: the fingers were spread over the toy and folded in towards her palm. This is quite an efficient way of dealing with rattles and other narrow objects, but in

COMING TO GRIPS
Six to ten months

Procedure After six months or so, many babies can grasp a wide variety of shapes, if only crudely, and you can try this game. Try handing her a rattle with the handle held vertically, but before she grips it, pause for an instant and look at her hand. Is the palm ready to grasp the vertical handle? Repeat this movement a number of times and help her to get her hand ready. Be careful not to let her become bored or frustrated. Try the same experiment with the rattle handle horizontal and then with a variety of orientations.

Value
MANIPULATIVE SKILL Learning to ready your hand and fingers to grasp an object is a crucial manipulative skill. This procedure will help your baby to develop this skill at an early age.

TOYS TO GRAB
After four months

Procedure When she starts to reach out and grab things, make sure there are plenty of interesting shapes for her to encounter. Provide her with small items to hold such as: a napkin ring, a plastic tea strainer, a soft, clean hairbrush, plastic cups, a straight clothes pin, and so on. But provide her also with things to chew, for at this stage she likes to feel things with her mouth. Soft teething rings, of course, are ideal but try to give her a variety of shapes and textures, e.g. little plastic jars, clean dish towels, an old sock – anything that she can chew safely. Be careful with paper, though, for she can easily get too much in her mouth, and avoid newsprint altogether (*see page 39*). Beware also of narrow objects which could be pushed into the throat. Finally, give her a selection of objects to grab that make noises – rattles, secure plastic bottles (*page 23*) containing small stones and an enclosed bell.

Value
VISUAL/MOTOR SKILL Providing her with a rich variety of objects encourages her to reach out and grab to satisfy her curiosity, improving her ability to guide her hand towards objects. Toys that make a noise provide further inducement.
TOUCH Providing her with a variety of shapes and textures develops her ability to distinguish by the way things feel.

essence it is no more than a means of gripping. She cannot deal with small or heavy objects in this manner, nor is it an efficient way of holding anything she wants to move. It is true she manages to transfer objects to her mouth using this grip, but often more by luck than judgment.

Matching grip to object

By nine months, she no longer uses her early grasp. Her hand movements are determined by the object she is grasping, and she will have started to use her thumb to push things into her hand. With practice, her hand movements slowly mature. She learns to cup her hand around an object and to use the base of her thumb to grip firmly. She begins to reach out for small objects using thumb and forefinger in a fine pincer movement. Her hands are no longer clumsy, and she can begin using them in more mature ways. As she plays with objects, she refines her skills, and learns to anticipate what kind of grip is required for a specific object. Pick up an imaginary pea from a table, and you will notice your finger and thumb move to the right position before making contact with the pea. In an adult this is a reflex action, but a baby must learn it. This early progress in manipulation is quite difficult to pinpoint because it is so gradual. For your part, it is enough simply to be aware of the complexity of the challenge facing her, and since it is through playing with objects that she learns this skill, start paying particular attention to what she plays with. Essentially, this means ensuring she has access to an interesting variety of objects – large and small, heavy and light, squashy and firm, balanced and unbalanced. Do not be tempted to shower her with toys; if you do, she will not know where to start, constantly dropping one to pick up another, with no chance to practice holding. Give her toys, one, two or three at a time, and change them frequently. You may find she has a favorite; if so, leave it with her, adding a single new toy at intervals.

Rattles should be carefully selected now, and there is no need to buy new ones. Improvise them from household items (see margin) and you could provide as great a range of interest as the manufacturer. She will need small objects too, and since these are likely to go into her mouth, it is safer if they are edible. Let her feed herself some of the small bits of food she is now being offered, such as peas and cooked carrot cubes – or indeed whatever types of food you are now introducing.

As she learns to use her hands and fingers separately, she will find anything which can be poked or prodded quite irresistible. She will be attracted by levers she can grip and will soon use her hand and wrist together to turn a small handle. She will need plenty of practice at these skills, and for this reason alone an activity center is an excellent buy.

Fixed to the side of her crib, it will enable her to try each movement at will. Later, you can place it a little higher so that she must pull herself up to play. An activity center is, however, much more than a manipulative toy. It is an outstanding teacher of "cause and effect": she will spend hours finding out how the components operate.

The telephone is the other irresistible toy at this stage. Toy ones – and there are some excellent versions on the market – never quite have the fascination of the real thing. A telephone can be prodded or poked, and will make a sound as she moves the dial. Later on she will lift it to her ear as she has seen you do, and later still she will pretend to ring her friends. Like many of the best toys, its play potential develops with her, stimulating first manipulation, later imitation and pretending.

Paper

Many babies develop a passion for chewing paper, often in preference to all else, and you may find this disconcerting. Newsprint, which is slightly toxic, is not a good idea, but unprinted paper will do a baby no bodily harm. Babies will not usually attempt to swallow the large objects they put into their mouths; danger arises only when objects accidentally slip into or roll down their throats. It is a wise precaution to rehearse exactly what to do if a baby chokes, doubly so if she is the sort of child who fills her mouth with paper or small objects. Obviously no child should be left alone with anything potentially dangerous, but if you are on hand, she can derive enormous pleasure from chewing and handling paper.

I grew up watching babies play with paper, and have always automatically given it to my own children. It is exceptionally versatile. She can take a crumpled sheet in her hand, and the harder she squeezes, the smaller it becomes. She can rip it, and put it into her mouth. As she chews, she can roll the shape around, and the large flat sheet becomes a small wet ball – the texture completely changed. Paper rustles as she crushes it, it changes color as she handles and chews it – in fact it stimulates all her senses. A flat sheet of paper held in front of her face will hide the room from view, but will soon flop forward to let her see you again. So don't be surprised if she finds paper more appealing than other toys – whatever their price.

Feeling for texture

Up to now, the sense of touch has been deployed in terms of "see-

---

SURPRISE PACKAGE
Ten months plus

Procedure To pique the insatiable curiosity of young children, wrap a little toy in three or four layers of paper – just fold the paper, don't tape it. Then get her to unwrap it. Repeat the game with different wrappings – or simply hide a toy under a cloth, letting her see you do it.

Value
PERCEPTUAL At first, a baby is very self-centered and is unaware that objects continue to exist even when she cannot see them. This game helps to make her aware of the permanence of objects.
MOTOR SKILLS The process of unwrapping improves hand and finger control.
PRACTICAL Giving her a number of parcels to unwrap will keep her happy in her crib for a long while.

Later progress As she grows older, you can play more and more difficult hiding games such as cloth and tumbler games (*page 49*).

SAND GAMES
From one year

Procedure A sandbox is not wasted, even if given as early as the first birthday. Keep it securely covered against rain, and against cats, who will use it as a litter box if given the chance – it is a shame if the sand becomes a source of infection. If you don't have the space outdoors, you can do just as well for your baby by setting up an indoor sandbox: a cardboard box, or even an old tire on an ample plastic sheet is perfectly practical. Use the finest quality white sand, *not* low-grade builder's sand, which stains everything yellow. Provide a choice of tools: spades or kitchen spoons, buckets or mops, a strainer or colander and jell-o molds with which to make shapes. Do keep an eye on her – she may want to eat the sand.

Value
DISCOVERY Sandbox play helps her learn about textures and about the behavior of fluid substances (pouring), weight and use of tools. EYE-HAND CO-ORDINATION

Variations A bowl of rice or cracked wheat is less messy but useful enough for a short session.

it-and-grab". Before, she reached out to try to pick the flowers off your floral dress; now, she wants to feel them. Acknowledge this by putting her to play on different surfaces – the carpet, the wooden floor or grass, so she can feel the textures at leisure. It follows that now is the time to start introducing her to specific items, naming them as you do so, and encouraging her to touch them. Learning the physical distinction between objects is a necessary prelude to learning to distinguish them with words.

Sand and water
She will not yet be able to use sand toys or to pour water, but she will enjoy the different textures they present. Let her sit in the sandbox and run her fingers through the soft sand, or bury her toes and watch her find them. Eating the sand can be a problem, especially if the sandbox is outside and normally uncovered. Cats also find sandboxes irresistible (see margin). So at this age, let her use a sandbox under supervision, or give her a bowl of sand, or some substitute (see margin) to play with in a corner, still under supervision.

By six months, most children start enjoying bathtime. As soon as she sits firmly, and can reach forward without losing her balance, you can begin to give her cups and other bath toys. Even at this age, she will benefit from a generous bathtime play period; if time is short for an evening bath, bathe her after she gets up from her morning nap. Use the kitchen sink – and prepare supper as she bathes.

Pets
Once she strokes, rather than pulls, your hair, you can let her stroke the dog, cat or rabbit. To my mind any animal who will not tolerate this sort of attention should not be in a house with a baby; but do ensure your baby is gentle – it will help the animal to be tolerant.

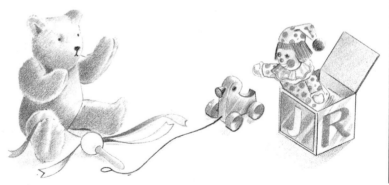

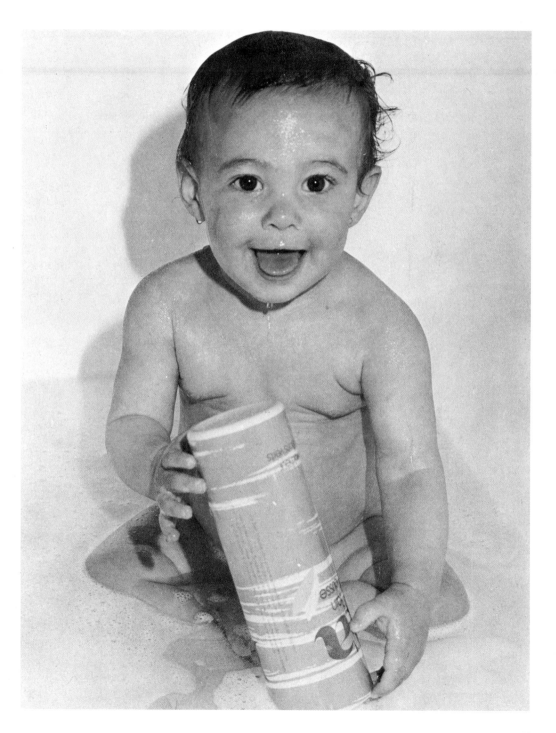

Procedure Babies love throwing things out of their carriages or cribs and are often happy just dropping a toy and waiting for you to pick it up. Although it may be frustrating for you, this game represents an important stage in a baby's development of manipulative skills. But you can take it a stage further and make it much more interesting by finding a large tin or box and a selection of toys that make a nice sound when dropped into the tin. Place the box where he can easily drop the toys in. Once he gets used to, and likes the idea of, making the noise by dropping the toys in the box, try placing the toy in his hand farthest from the box. This means he must either pass the toy to his other hand to drop it in the box, or swing his arm right across.

Value
MANIPULATIVE SKILL At first babies tend to use their hands completely independently. But to develop the ability to use tools, a baby must learn to use both hands together. Passing things from hand to hand is one of the first and most important manipulative skills.

Variations To get him to use both hands together, try giving him a toy so big and awkward that he has to use both hands to pick it up and drop it.

LEARNING TO LET GO

If there is a universal babyhood game, it is throwing things out of the carriage. The sequence is invariable: he drops the object and then watches you as if to say "come on, pick it up for me". As always in these situations, you take your turn, you smile and speak as you hand him the toy, which of course he immediately drops again. So you pick it up, he throws it down – and so on until you call a halt. There is clearly a strong, social, turn-taking element to this game, and he derives great benefit from the reciprocal contact with you. But why is it so especially popular? Why does he practice his social skills in this infuriating way?

The answer is that this is not only a social game, but a way of practicing the new-found ability to let go. The game may seem maddeningly simple to you, but it changes in quite interesting ways. If you watch, you will notice that at first he looks at his hand, not the toy falling. Also, he will let the toy go in different ways: he will uncurl his hand and drop it directly, or, keeping his palm upwards, uncurl his hand and then turn it over to empty the toy on to the floor, or simply let his hand flop so that the toy haphazardly rolls off.

While he may have a great deal to practice, you, like anyone else, have a threshold of boredom. If the game becomes a chore for you, he will probably sense your dissatisfaction, and that could be confusing. So instead, introduce variations: after a few bouts of "letting go", invite him to play a less tiring give-and-take game. Pass him a ball, then ask for it back. By nine months he will probably understand when you say "give it to me".

If you find he is readier to take than to give, try this game: first, let him drop objects directly into your hands; then, extend the game by hiding the toy behind your back, or under a cushion, after he has dropped it. Wait a few seconds, bring it out of hiding, and make it "creep up" on him. He may become readier to give once he realizes the fun which can follow. Sequences such as this practice more skills than simple letting go; there is an element of social turn-taking, and encouragement to anticipate the toy's return, to start realizing that objects still exist when they are out of sight.

When you can supervise, try tying some toys on to a length of elastic, the other end attached to the carriage or crib. Show him how, when he throws them out, they can be hauled back: this is the age at which he can start learning by watching you. Any object on the end of a piece of string is a fascinating cause-and-effect toy, and once he has mastered it he will have endless fun. When he is able to throw the toy down and pull it up again with ease, swap the tethered toy with another, leaving the original toy on hand. If he enjoys the surprise, try it again another day. If he does not like change, don't bother to persist.

Letting go for its own sake

Babies go through several phases of "letting go". At first he is most interested in the physical mechanism of releasing objects from his hand, but gradually he will pay more attention to the objects he drops, and to the game itself. As objects fall, he will notice how some roll and some stay where they fall. When you are playing with your child give him a range of items that behave in different ways: heavy things that fall quickly, light things such as balloons or sheets of tissue paper that fall slowly, bean bags that fall with a plop and stay put, balls that bounce, and plastic bottles that roll. Observing their different behaviors when dropped or thrown will be highly absorbing.

He may also come to see that throwing things out of his chair is a game that sometimes infuriates you. Possibly the more annoyed you become, the more he will feel that he is playing an interesting game. The only way out of this bind is to find ways of reducing the amount of bending and stretching you have to suffer when retrieving the toys. In the early stages of the game, when letting go is of prime importance, try sitting him in a chair at a low table. He will be able to pick things up and put them down without dropping many of them on the floor. Later you can give him a box or bag of objects to empty.

It makes sense, too, to place a sheet under his chair at meal times. I have found that tying some toys on short strings to a child's chair can distract him from emptying his food on to the floor; but he may find the string more interesting than his food. Finally, try putting a box under his chair and encouraging him to drop objects into it. Praise him when he succeeds in getting things in – and hope that it reduces the wear on your back.

Learning to store

Once he can let go, you will notice a difference in the way he plays. Before he could let go, he put things down by chance. Deliberate letting go is a new and important skill, because he can begin to place objects. He can put his peas back into his dish, and pile one block on top of another: there is so much more to be done with a toy once he can put it where he wants it. He used to take toys to his mouth, or bang one toy with another. Now he has many different ways of playing with them; he collects them in

---

MY DRAWER
Eight to 18 months

Procedure Many babies and toddlers can be kept happy for hours just emptying and filling containers. Set aside an old, solid wooden drawer, or a colorful box, that is his alone, and fill it with all kinds of interesting objects and toys. The contents need not be expensive, or elaborate. He will be absorbed by the simplest little things. If you want, you could just give him your sock drawer, or a kitchen drawer of his own. Bear in mind that he will find it easier to empty than to fill the drawer, and that at first he may need some help putting things back.

Value
SIMPLE TASKS He is learning to pick things up and put them down as well as to guide objects in and out of their container.

Later progress As he becomes more and more skilled at taking objects out and putting them back, you can lead him into more elaborate games with containers: containers with lids, containers with different compartments, and, of course, shape-sorters.

FIRST STEPS

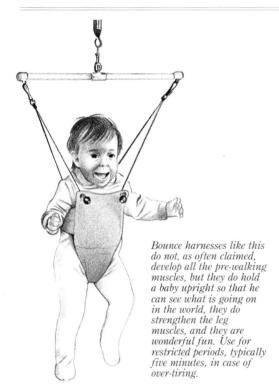

Parents are often perturbed if their child seems
late starting to walk, but there is rarely
anything to worry about. Babies are very
individual creatures and will learn to walk in
their own good time, whether it is after nine
months or 18 months. If a child takes a long
time to begin walking, it may simply be
because he can move around far more
efficiently by crawling. This variation is worth
remembering; you should never try to make a
baby stand if he does not want to: the activities
shown on these pages are playful ways to help
him once he has decided to stand himself. He
will only walk once his back, hip and leg
muscles are strong enough to support him (they
develop in that order). You can help strengthen
these muscles and improve balance in the pre-
walking stage by allowing him to "jump" on
your knee as you hold him and, after six
months, sitting him upright on the floor.

*Bounce harnesses like this
do not, as often claimed,
develop all the pre-walking
muscles, but they do hold
a baby upright so that he
can see what is going on
in the world, they do
strengthen the leg
muscles, and they are
wonderful fun. Use for
restricted periods, typically
five minutes, in case of
over-tiring.*

*You two are the best
supports for his first steps.
But let him make all the
moves – don't try to
"walk" him, holding his
hand: that is far too
insecure. With two of you,
though, you can encourage
him to cross gaps – and
catch him if he stumbles.*

When he first tries to stand, he will pull himself up in stages, pulling on anything available, and it is essential that this all-important support should not topple over. Low, solid furniture that will not move – for example, a soft, heavy settee – is ideal, and a chest of drawers can be useful, too.

His progression from standing to walking will be in stages. At first he clings to his support with both hands, only gradually learning to take all his weight on his feet, and using his hands for balance as he works his way along furniture or other upright objects. Soon, though, he will have the confidence to swing across gaps between furniture: so try arranging furniture so that he can work his way all around a room – and supervise his efforts.

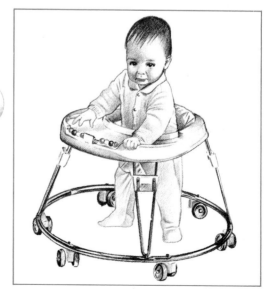

A baby push-cart (above) is a worthwhile investment, for it is not only a walking aid but, with a set of blocks, a toy that can be loaded and unloaded. A baby walking frame (right) is expensive but excellent: if tired, he can rest in the seat (whose height is adjustable); and placed centrally within the frame, he cannot reach far enough to grab breakable or harmful objects about the house.

FINGER RHYMES
One year on

Procedure Finger rhymes and clapping rhymes are ever popular. But to get the best out of them, you should start them at the right stage in the baby's development. Simple clapping games like "patty-cake" can be tried as soon as a baby shows signs of being able to use both hands together. This game involves clapping and patting the baby's palms alternately while you say *"Patty-cake, patty-cake, baker's man, bake me a cake as fast as you can"*. The more elaborate finger rhymes should be tried later when signs of independent finger movement emerge. One of the best of these games is: *"Put your finger in the foxy's hole"* (guide his finger in between the middle fingers of your clenched fist). *"Foxy's not at home! Foxy's out the back"* (keeping his finger trapped, turn and open your hand), *"chewing on a bone"* (chew baby's finger).

Value
SOCIAL Shared activities are always valuable aids to social awareness.
LANGUAGE The rhythmic repetition of words helps linguistic development.

piles, he puts them together, and he gradually begins to manipulate them in increasingly complex ways.

Between about six and eight months he will learn to transfer a toy from one hand to the other. At five months, if you give him one toy after another, he will probably drop the first to take the second. But by eight months he may pass the first toy to his other hand before he takes the second. A simple skill, but the first step in learning that he can put objects to work – that they can be tools. A hand was for grasping, for holding, for dropping; but now he can use it to keep things in. From this knowledge it is a small step to realizing that he can put objects into boxes and bags, cups and pans. Store a rattle in the hand while you pick up another, and inevitably the two rattles will bang together. Now he is but a step away from learning that two hands may be used together. Store a cup in one hand, and put a ball into it with the other. Hold a rod in one hand, and turn it with the other. This is the very basis of manipulative skill. It is because he is learning so many different skills that he is so obsessed with objects at the moment.

At this time, you can begin to play simple clapping and finger games. Try "patty-cake" to encourage him to put his hands together, "one, two, buckle my shoe" to encourage him to poke his finger, and "five currant buns in the baker's shop" to encourage him to copy your gestures. It is worth buying a book of these rhymes, or borrowing one from the library.

First birthday toys

His first birthday is not far off; perhaps it is imminent. With it comes the excuse – the opportunity – to buy some toys. He has come a long way in the past year, from helpless baby to young toddler, and already he has begun that spurt in mental and physical development which will take him out of babyhood. Now he looks for the play potential of each new situation and his behavior is guided by what he sees. Good toys can be of enormous value now, drawing him into varied modes of play.

Toys should provide him with interesting things to do: not so simple that he soon becomes bored, nor so difficult that he becomes frustrated. Look for versatility: if a toy can stimulate him in different ways so much the better, for it will hold his interest for longer. Before you buy large numbers of toys, remember that not all children like the same things. Just because your older child, or a friend's child, loved a certain toy, does not mean he will play with it. My daughter's favorite toy at this stage was later completely ignored by her younger brother. Whenever possible, let him play with a toy before you buy it. If you have a mother-and-baby group, or friends with children of a similar age, this should be possible. Otherwise, look out for second-hand toys at school and playgroup sales.

By now he will enjoy popping things into and out of all sorts of containers. Many of the most successful first birthday toys use the child's fascination with containers to teach him to manipulate and match objects. Shape-sorters are perennial favorites with babies, and many of the modern ones are very good. He may particularly enjoy the versions that reward his efforts with a noise or by delivering the shapes back to him. These are excellent "cause-and-effect toys" and will encourage him to peep inside to see "why".

"Peg people" can fascinate a baby for a long time. They have round bases which fit into a wide variety of containers – a pull-along car or fire engine complete with peg firemen would be a wise choice if he is mobile; a merry-go-round or musical ferris wheel encourages manipulatory skills, and later pretend play.

Now that he can use his fingers to poke, and his hands to turn or place objects, he will enjoy toys that he can manipulate: large popper beads which push together and pull apart again, or a jack-in-the-box or some other pop-up toy that he has to push down with his hand and release with his finger. If he is particularly clever with his hands, he can probably manage a set of blocks. A set of cups or beakers is ideal for the bath and sandbox as well as for stacking, or try some rings to thread on an upright post.

A large-scale push-along is an excellent investment – a real "must" for the toddler. If he is not yet walking, consider a specially designed baby walker. This is a small push-cart that should remain firmly in an upright position when the baby uses the handle to pull himself up. Once on his feet he will be able to toddle safely behind the truck at his own speed. The walker will not tip, nor will it run away from him as a doll's carriage or wheelbarrow would. It will increase his mobility now, and later he can use the truck to collect blocks and other treasures. He will also be able to use it as a wheelbarrow or even a doll's carriage. It will give him hours of enjoyment. Once he is walking, noisy push-along toys will be greatly enjoyed, but he will have to be quite steady on his feet before he can manage a pull-along. Don't be tempted by doll's carriages or other lightweight trucks or wagons until he can walk absolutely steadily: he will not be able to stop them tipping or running away until his own balance and control have matured – at least three or four months after his first steps.

All children love to ride on bikes and cars. You will probably find that the sit-and-ride vehicles and tricycles you buy over the next few years are among the best-loved toys of his childhood. Once he is able to walk steadily, he may be able to manage a "sit-

MAILBOX
One year on

Procedure You can buy a toy mailbox, perhaps as a first birthday present, but these are fairly expensive and they may well be too difficult for him to use just yet. The alternative is to make your own simple mailbox by piercing the lid of a shoe box. Start with a round hole and give him a ping-pong ball to "mail". Then progress to a box with a square hole, and a square, wooden toy brick to mail. Square items are harder to put in the hole than round ones because the corners have to be matched. Finally, try a mailbox with both round and square holes.

Value
HAND-EYE CO-ORDINATION To drop the object into the box, he must develop the ability to guide hand movements with the eye. SHAPE RECOGNITION Learning to classify and recognize different shapes.

Later progress When he becomes adept with the shoe box, buy him one of the more elaborate shape-sorters to encourage further exploration.

COPY-CAT
One year on

Procedure One of the best ways of learning is through imitation, and copy-cat games are useful and fun. For example, try putting a toy under a towel. Now give him the toy and towel and encourage him to do the same. Praise him when he does. Or make a telephone call with a toy telephone and get him to make one too. Gradually increase the complexity of the action. Next steps could be, for example, drilling a pretend hole with a toy drill, feeding a teddy bear or hammering a pretend nail.

Value
BASIC SKILLS You can teach a baby all kinds of basic skills by this method. Learning to imitate will also help him pick up new skills independently in the future.
SOCIAL The turn-taking nature of copying games is a valuable social stimulus.

Variations Saying what you are doing when you play copy-cat games will help to develop his linguistic abilities.

and-ride''. These are low, stable vehicles – plastic or wooden cars and animals – with castors or small wheels. The child sits and pushes himself along with his feet. Riding toys increase his confidence and give him enormous pleasure. They will help him balance, plan, and begin to solve simple problems. Later he will use his car in pretend play, and will ride socially with his friends. You might also consider a small wooden or plastic tricycle. These are pushed with the feet (he will not use pedals for another year or so), and are fast and easy to turn. They are not quite as stable as four-wheeled vehicles, but have one great advantage for those who live in a small house – they are less likely to become wedged between furniture. My children inherited both tricycles and sit-and-ride cars from older cousins and it is hard to say which were preferred. There is little doubt that together they have been played with more than any other toys.

Once again, don't forget the humble toys. A chunky crayon and a large piece of paper taped to the floor, some sand or water in a large bowl, your saucepans to stack, a little bag or bucket to carry things in: all will enchant him as much and as long as anything you can buy.

RULING THE
WORLD
Nine to 15 months

Procedure Babies are egocentric and think they are very clever once they believe they can make things happen. It is worth encouraging this belief for a while with this game: wait until she does something definite, such as bang her spoon, then say "Ooh!" or do something else she enjoys. If she bangs the spoon again, repeat your response. Try the game with a whole range of actions and responses – facial expression and spoken exchanges are both useful.

Value
LEARNING Games like this encourage a baby to experiment and explore – to find out what happens when she does certain things.
LANGUAGE AND SOCIAL A baby needs an incentive to start communicating properly and games like this provide that incentive. If she knows you will fetch teddy bear when she says "uh, uh", then it is worth her while learning to talk so that she can communicate ever more complex demands.

Later progress Later on she will begin to learn that things do not always happen as she wills.

THE GROWTH OF UNDERSTANDING

As she lies kicking in her bed, the toys you have placed around her begin to move. She kicks, they move; she stops, they stop, and she learns that she makes things happen. But although in these early months she may learn that whenever she kicks the toys move, she has no understanding that it was the bouncing of her bed, not the movement of her legs, that makes the toys dance. As she grows a little older, you might even find that she bounces in your arms as you pass a mobile, trying to simulate or create movement.

In the first months of life, babies behave as if they are very clever; as if everything that happens to them happens because they have made it happen. Of course, they are often right. A baby smiles, and you smile back, she smiles again, and you smile too. She bounces in her chair and you look at her, and say "Hello, little one"; she bounces again and you talk some more. She touches the toy and it moves, she touches it again and it moves again. Or perhaps you are feeding her stewed apricots, her favorite food. She opens her mouth, you pop in a spoonful. She opens again, you pop in another. Is it surprising she believes she makes things happen?

The disillusioning
We are all egocentric, of course, full of our own importance. The very young baby is completely so: she sees herself as the center of the world. Things exist when she looks at them, things happen when she makes them happen, and looking at the world from her point of view, she is right.

But now consider how a baby might act around the time of her first birthday. She wants her toy duck. She looks at the duck, then, turning, she looks directly at you and says "uh, uh". Or, she drops a cup from her high chair, and turning to you she holds up her hands and shouts. Now she has learned that, alone, she cannot always make things happen; sometimes she needs help.

Why should this be important? By itself, it is a small step, but it leads to a very much bigger one: she learns that if she cannot do something for herself, she can ask someone else: a crucial stage in the development of communication. Why should a child who thinks the world is under her control ever bother to learn to talk? It is only when she realizes it is not as simple as she first thought, that the world is not completely under her control, that the motivation to communicate her intentions will develop.

Language before words

At first, her communication is not through words. She uses noises, actions and looks. Words are difficult, actions are direct, and much easier for babies. Even when she begins to use words, her requests are still often given in sign language. Her earliest words are merely comments, something she adds to pointing when she wants to share her pleasure. She sees her car in the garage, thinks it is exciting, so points with an emphatic "car-car". She is happy, and happiness must be shared with you. But when she wants you to carry her, it is quite different. She puts up her hands and makes a pathetic sound. She could say "carry", or perhaps, "car" or "arry", but she does not. Instead, she will use a sign, the method she knows best. Many of the signs we use are universal, even transcending language barriers – a nod, a shake of the head, and so on. Most of us recognize "come here" or "go away". A smile shows happiness – but it can show reassurance too. Eyebrow raising can show surprise, but also greeting. Turning the head to one side, so it bends towards the shoulder, is a gesture which asks permission. So look out for her signs.

"Round and round the garden" is one of those baby games whose simplicity belies its value – especially for early communication. You take her hand and draw a circle round the palm, saying "Round and round the garden, like a teddy bear". You pause, then, walking up her arm with your fingers, saying "one step, two steps and *tickle her under there*", you then tickle her under her arm. Playing this game, you probably do not consciously think of the possibilities for her to communicate, yet, like most parents, you play the game quite naturally, in the most appropriate way. You wait for her anticipation, her looks, her laughter, before you set your fingers to march up her arm. In doing so you unconsciously encourage early language because it is so much more fun to play when she starts to squirm in anticipation. Those squirms are like words: they are saying "I know you are going to tickle me". And from knowing, it is but a small step to asking. She progresses from knowing what comes next to asking for more, from bouncing in anticipation to bouncing with a knowing look which clearly means "come on then, let's start the game".

Plenty of other games develop this early form of communication. Watch parents playing traditional games in which children ride on knees or feet, and you will see that pauses are quite naturally included. Sometimes parents wait for a signal to begin: the baby sits on a knee, and only when she looks at the parent in anticipation does the game start. Before starting a second turn you may even wait for her to rock herself. Playing face to face,

FINGER PUPPETS
12 to 18 months

Procedure One of the most enjoyable ways of playing together is opened up with finger puppets. Simple finger puppets can be made with paper – a little cap taped to fit over the end of your finger with a face and hair drawn on. More elaborate, and durable, puppets can be made from felt with face and hair sewn on. Make one puppet for her – slightly smaller – and two for you.

Value
SHARED ACTIVITY
Playing together as partners is not only fun, it also helps to develop social and communication skills.
MANIPULATIVE SKILL
Finger puppets improve finger control.

Language
IMAGINATION
Pretending that the puppets are really little people helps to develop her imagination.

FUN WITH PAINT/*About 12 months on*

Start a child off with short, fat, non-toxic crayons which are easy for tiny hands to grasp. Later on he can use a stubby paint brush and powder paints. Mix paints yourself at first, keeping them fairly thick – with thin paints a child will simply soak the paper. At first he will simply run the brush up and down or in zig-zags, never lifting it from the paper, and the result will be a shapeless scrawl. After a while, he will learn to move the brush round and round, but it still stays firmly on the paper. It is not until much later that he finds out how to draw a circle, joining the ends.

Stir paints are a wonderfully messy variation on standard art materials. Simply mix cornflour with food coloring and add water to make a stiff paste. He draws in the paste with a short, blunt stick.

Finger paints are just as much fun. To make them, mix $\frac{1}{2}$ cup of instant cold water starch with $\frac{1}{2}$ cup of soap flakes (not powder) and $\frac{5}{8}$ cup water and add food color. She can dip her fingers in this and paint on windows, tables, or any washable surface.

Value
FUN, PERCEPTUAL, MANUAL SKILL, "I DID THAT!"

you are naturally tuned into each other; even when there are no obvious pauses, she will communicate her enjoyment to you. Gradually, she will begin to ask for more. As she grows older and stronger, you can start playing rocking games, such as "See-saw Margery Daw". These are marvelous for communication and for strengthening your baby's back muscles.

Becoming play partners

By the end of her first 12 months, she is changing, and so are you. In the beginning, you did the playing, she did the watching. Then she became obsessed with objects and your role changed: you became the provider of playthings. Now your role changes yet again. At ten months, she starts to control your games, and to say how you two should play together.

You can see this in her favorite game – throwing things to the floor. Initially, she is very much in control: she does the throwing, and she starts the game. However, the control then switches: you finish the game, usually by refusing to pick up any more toys. This is an ideal situation, for she can progress to the next step, "asking" you to pick up for her. Once she realizes you can be used like an extra-long arm to pick things up, you will find that she begins to use you quite unashamedly.

I'll do it if you ask

Once she begins to "ask", many new games and variations on old ones start to open up. A simple example is the "give and take" sequence. In the basic game you sit opposite each other and pass a ball or toy, one to the other. Now, you can incorporate requests. You say "give me", using words and gestures: indicate with your hands, and turn your head to one side. When it is her turn, she must ask you. Start with some "free turns", but then wait for a sign before giving her the ball. There is no point in this game if she does not want to play, so don't wait too long for her request. If she does take to it, try some further variations. Move a toy car across the room, spin a top or wave a hand puppet at her. Show her once or twice, then wait for her to ask before you do it again. As you feed her, ask "Do you like it?" "Do you want more?" Look at her as you say it, and wait for a reply.

This early language without words takes widely different forms from child to child. Some children use looks, some noises, some may even wave their arms, or bounce up and down; most use a combination. How much they communicate varies, too. Some children "talk" in this way all the time, others seldom, just as later some children never stop chattering and others are relatively silent. There is no such thing as a standard child, or

THROUGH THE TUNNEL

From eight months

Procedure Once she starts to crawl confidently, make a small tunnel from an unwanted cardboard carton. Encourage her to crawl through, and stand at the far end. As she emerges, say "hurray!" and make a fuss over her.

Value
PERCEPTUAL It is important for a baby to learn that the world stays the same even when she cannot see it. It reinforces her sense of security.

Variations Make a tunnel from an old cereal box and push toy cars through, showing that they go in and come out again. See also page 54.

HUNT THE TOY
Nine months

Procedure Hide-and-seek games can start at an early age. One interesting game is to take three clear plastic glasses (or fine metal strainers) and, with the baby looking, "hide" a toy or snack under one glass. See if she can find it. If she does, make a fuss over her. Another hiding game is to cover the toy with one of three towels, again letting her watch while you hide it. If she finds this too difficult at first, help her by leaving the toy peeping out.

Value
PERCEPTUAL Children learn surprisingly late that objects have an independent existence – they tend to believe that objects disappear when they cannot be seen. Hiding games like this help take their growing awareness of the independence of objects one stage further than the tunnel game, *page 53*.

Later progress Once she can confidently find the toy under clear glasses, try the same game with unbreakable opaque cups. But always let her see where you put the toy.

even an average child, as anyone with more than one child quickly realizes. One asks for help at the slightest difficulty, another struggles with a problem until you can hardly bear not to interfere.

A child's early sign-language is not simply confined to requests for toys, food and help. Some are used more like conventional nouns. My daughter used to poke her tummy when she saw her penguin, and snap her fingers when she saw a picture of a crocodile. My youngest son used to make a sign with his hands every time he saw a bus. Before your baby talks, she will probably use at least a dozen different signs. If you record them in a diary, you will probably notice some you might otherwise miss – an interesting record for the future.

Games in which the baby has to anticipate our actions obviously encourage the development of communication, but so, too, will trust between mother and baby. A baby who has regularly been left to cry herself to sleep is unlikely to now feel that she can ask to come out of her crib. If you have always refused to pick up the objects she has thrown down, she is unlikely to feel that looking at you will change things. If her world has not included your smiling face when she smiles, or your voice when she makes a noise, she will not have developed that confidence in her ability to alter the world which will make her later learning so much easier. Nor, on the other hand, will she have any need to communicate with you if you always anticipate her every move. In between is the happy medium.

The independence of objects
One of the greatest spurs to communication in the second six months of life is her understanding that objects have an existence of their own. This happens surprisingly late, and until it happens there is not really much to talk about.

Suppose that your six-month-old baby is playing with your strainer while you make a sauce. Your sauce goes lumpy, as sauces do, and you need the strainer back. If you take it, she will cry, and, after the sauce, you still need the strainer for a salad. What to do? Offer her a nice, red slotted spoon, and she drops the strainer immediately to take the spoon. Out of sight is literally out of mind at this age: as soon as she sees the spoon, the strainer no longer exists for her.

Watch her with a rattle. She shakes it, and is fascinated by the sound, but when she drops the rattle, she does not look to see where it has gone. It is as if the rattle is an extension of herself: to her, the movement of her hand, not the beads in the rattle, makes the sound. When she drops the rattle, of course, the movement of her hand no longer produces sound. She may shake her hand to make it rattle, but when it is silent she soon forgets that hands make interesting noises. When she next sees the rattle, she will not remember the noise. Only when her hand starts to make the sound again will she remember and begin to shake her rattle with obvious delight.

When she is a little older, she will remember that rattles make sounds, and that mobiles move. She may even make the appropriate movements when she sees them. But still she does not realize that they exist without her. Only at about nine months does she begin to watch the rattle when she drops it. Only then does the rattle begin to have a life of its own. Because she plays her dropping game so often, she gradually becomes aware that the rattle on the floor was once in her hand. In other words, she starts to realize that the rattle has a separate existence, a permanence. Once there is a world of objects beyond her hands, there are reasons to make requests, things to comment upon, the motivation to communicate.

Remembering

When the supermarket checker packs your groceries as usual after a shopping session, you probably recognize her and pass the time of day. But if you meet her next day at the zoo, you might well walk right past her. It is seeing people or objects in context which makes remembering easy.

Your baby's first memories will be of events that happen in context: your face as she looks up from the breast; your milky smell; her daily routines; the sound of running water while you undress her for her bath. Gradually she will begin to anticipate these routine things. Going to the bathroom and hearing the water running will mean bath-time.

You can assist the development of memory by making sure that some features of her life are unchanging, always in context. Don't keep changing the toys around her bed; keep some old friends in the same place. Don't keep altering her room; give her a chance to learn where things are. Making games out of routines is also helpful. Improvise your own patter to accompany bathing, dressing and feeding – no matter how simple – and as long as you make the sequence invariable, she will benefit. "Arms up like a soldier" as you take off her sweater is not just silly talk: after a while she will raise her arms when you say it.

When you play together, some toys and games should be new and stimulating, others old favorites. Keep some games to play when you sit in a certain chair or to play in bed in the morning. End the day by sitting and reading a book together.

SURPRISE BAG
12 months on

Procedure Give her a little surprise to look forward to in the morning by putting a bag by her bed last thing at night. Fill it with things like: a soft toy; something to make a sound; a favorite toy; a little plastic jar with a screw-top lid; a little book with stiff covers and cardboard pages – by 18 months she will be able to turn the pages.

Value
MEMORY Familiar pleasures like this are comforting and can aid the development of a baby's memory.
PRACTICAL The bag may keep her occupied long enough to give you a little extra sleep.

Variations By day, a bag makes an excellent toy for a child of about 18 months for: collecting things; practice at putting in and taking out and pretending to go shopping like mommy and daddy.

Procedure To help create secure routines, you can make little games out of a few daily activities. A useful combination would be: a game for dressing; a game for washing; a game you play in bed in the morning; and a book in the same chair last thing at night. The best dressing and washing games involve pretending. For example, "Arms up like a soldier, leg up like a stork, stand stiff as a lamppost", and so on. A good game for playing in bed in the morning is "Foxes and rabbits" where the child plays the rabbit hiding under the covers in her warren, and you play the fox who has come to eat her.

Value
MEMORY Like adults, babies need cues to remember things by and familiar routines help the development of memory. PRACTICAL Making a game out of daily chores.

From these simple routines she will begin to recognize that the world is not new every morning. As her memory improves, you will find she is less dependent for her experiences on things she can see and feel. She will show you this by, for instance, becoming attached to certain toys and throwing others aside if they are offered. She will treat new people in the same way, no longer being open and friendly with strangers in the street. You may find too, that she is very upset by a change in routine. Take her on vacation, and she is miserable and fretful: before the change of environment she was beginning to realize that her world had a comforting degree of predictability. By plunging her into a new environment, you take away all her cues. Quite suddenly she finds she cannot remember: it is like meeting the grocery checker at the zoo, rather than where she "belongs", at the cash register. The more "context" you can maintain when you are away from home, the happier she is likely to be. Familiar toys, games, and little routines will help. So will having her own crib, chair or blankets around her.

Making plans
While she is still at the "out of sight, out of mind" stage, opportunities for improvising useful play are relatively limited. But as her memory improves, she will be capable of more complex, and, to you, more interesting games. She can attend to her hand and the toy, hit one toy with another, and fetch her car from across the room without forgetting why she wanted it. She can make plans. If she cannot reach the toy from this side of the table, she can crawl around to the other side. She begins to behave as if she is guided by "pictures in her mind".

Up until now, she has treated all objects similarly. She banged on the floor with the cup, the pan, and the blocks. Now, as she approaches her first birthday, toys do not inevitably go to her mouth. The doll is cuddled, and she may try to put the lid on the pan, or to stack the blocks. Offer her something new, and she no longer grabs; instead, she pauses, as if she is thinking what she might do with it, before she reaches out to take it from you.

Now, more than ever, is the time to lead her into play. Without your help, she may stick in the groove of repeating the same actions over and over again. Now is the time for toys and games which need a little planning. Chase her around the room or, better still, get her to chase you. Try a game of hide-and-seek, but not just the two of you: include her father, brothers and sisters, even friends. Make a large tunnel with a cardboard box for her to crawl through, or put two chairs together and drape a blanket over them. Give her a non-toxic crayon and a big piece of paper.

PULLING AND PUSHING/*A month after learning to walk, and on*

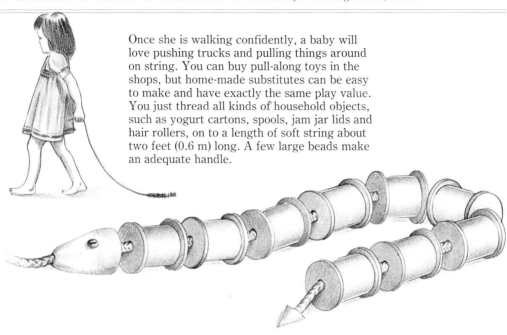

Once she is walking confidently, a baby will love pushing trucks and pulling things around on string. You can buy pull-along toys in the shops, but home-made substitutes can be easy to make and have exactly the same play value. You just thread all kinds of household objects, such as yogurt cartons, spools, jam jar lids and hair rollers, on to a length of soft string about two feet (0.6 m) long. A few large beads make an adequate handle.

Learning to push and release toy cars takes some time, but you can help her to learn by providing her with a ramp to roll them down. Show her how to let go once or twice, then let her find out for herself. See if she can transfer her new-found skill to flat surfaces.

If you make a snake of spools, set the spools about ¼ in apart, close enough to keep the shape but far enough apart to flex. Paint in bright colors with non-toxic paint.

Pull-along toys are most entertaining if noisy. If you make a friendly cart like this from a plastic bottle, fill it with macaroni – if the lid can be sealed firmly.

Value
CONTROL These toys reinforce awareness of her ability to control: "I can do it!"
MOTOR SKILLS Pulling and pushing improves balance and co-ordination.
PLANNING AND PUZZLING When a pull-along gets caught, she must work out how to free it; when pushing a toy car, she must discover how to make it roll independently.

THE MULBERRY BUSH
12 months on

Procedure You can make a language game from the song *"Here we go round the mulberry bush"*. Start by simply touching various body parts and singing, *"This is the way we touch our . . . head . . . nose . . . hand . . ."* and so on. Then try a new set of words, based on furniture, or toys.

Value
LANGUAGE This game helps to extend her vocabulary rapidly and painlessly.
SOCIAL She can copy you and join in with the song.

Variations Try introducing actions (and so verbs) as well as objects. For example, *"This is the way we lift our arms . . . up above our head."* Or *"This is the way we stretch our arms . . . right out in front."*

She will not do much with it before 18 months – but she will make marks, and gradually she will learn there is more than one game to play.

The threshold of speech

At first, she will not, of course, understand your words; but she will appreciate their context; babies are especially tuned to voices, and ready to form associations. By seven months, she will turn to anyone who calls. A little later, she will follow a conversation between two people, by turning from one to the other. She is ready and waiting to understand, finely tuned to what you have to say. So begin to talk about things that interest her: her food, her bath, her favorite toys.

Gradually she will realize that a certain sound is made at a certain time. She will notice that you make the sound "chair" as you sit her down for her meals, and she will associate "chair" with sitting down, just as she associated kicking with the movement of her mobile. At the playground you might say "swing, swing" as she swings to and fro; the association between the pleasant swinging feeling and the word is easily formed. When you sit and play together, look where she is looking. When she is happy she will be particularly keen to do as you do. Take the opportunity to name something for her. Gradually, this sharing will include words.

It is fortunate that when we talk to babies we naturally tend to include all the words necessary to make the sense apparent: "Mommy will slice the bananas now", not "I'll get you something . . ."

FIRST TALKING GAMES

Sit together in front of a mirror (babies love to look at themselves) and begin to show him things. Tom's hands, mommy's hands; Tom's nose, mommy's nose. Then clap his hands and yours, smile, frown, or put out your tongue. Once he gets the idea of following suit, you can play simple "you do what I do" games. Remember he is just beginning: the sequences must be simple. Once he can copy, it is a small step to following simple commands. From about nine or ten months, he may stretch up tall when you ask "how big is Tom?", or wave "bye-bye" at bedtime.

Walk around the house with him, telling him what things are. Sit him on your lap and show him a book. Simple pictures are best, especially pictures of familiar objects, like his cup, chair or shoes. See if he can point to his own shoes as well as the picture. Later he may fetch his shoes from across the room. My children love picture friezes made from cut-out pictures: put them where you can look at them together. Babies favor clear, simple pictures. Find one picture of a cow, and another of a sheep – easier to cope with than a large picture containing many different animals. If you have an older child, making a frieze for the baby can be a worthwhile activity for a wet afternoon.

Hiding

One reliable way to start a conversation is to sit on the floor with two or three toys. Tell him what the toys are, and what they do. "This little teddy bear can walk all the way to the chair." Then expand the game: hide the teddy bear under a cloth, making sure he sees where you are hiding it. Then say, "Where is the teddy bear?" Allow him time to look. From ten months, he will begin to search, with his eyes only, but when he knows the game, he will be delighted to lift the cloth to reveal the bear.

After you have played the game a few times using the cloth, let him watch you putting the bear under a blanket, but leave the cloth nearby. Although he sees what you are doing, you will probably find that he looks under the cloth for the bear. He has not yet understood what hiding means. Learning that things remain when you cannot see them, and that one object can be under or inside another is difficult for him, and it will be some time yet before he fully understands. So don't complicate the game by hiding the teddy bear in too many places.

Giving toys special roles is another conversation starter. His

Procedure This is a development of the hiding games played when he was younger (*see page 54*). Fill a small carton with crumpled up paper and hide a toy in it for him to find. When he is a little older, try the same game with wood chips or rice or lentils – sand is a little too difficult.

Value
PERCEPTUAL This game further develops a child's awareness of the independent existence of objects.
LANGUAGE Some research suggests that an appreciation of an object's permanence promotes language development.
MANIPULATIVE SKILL The desire to seek out, grasp and retrieve the toy improves a baby's skill with his hands.

FISHING
18 months and after

Procedure You need a cardboard box for the "sea" and some metal bottle tops for the "fish" – paint the bottle tops bright colors for the best effect. A stick about one foot long, some string and a magnet act as rod and tackle. Stand him in the box so he can see the fish clearly and play the game for him yourself, describing what you are doing. He won't be able to manage by himself, or to understand much of what you are saying, but this does not matter: the point of the game is that you do it together.

Value
SHARED ACTIVITY
Anything you achieve *together* contributes to the development of social and communication skills.

Later progress When he can start fishing for himself – considerably later on – the game will develop visual-motor skills and demonstrate the purpose of tools.

toy penguin can, if you choose, peck his tummy, or his bear can say something senseless but simple like "ah cuddle". Initially, pecking penguins and "ah cuddle" bears provide simple turn-taking games, but the constant repetition of "I'll peck your tummy" will be learned and later he will ask for the game by name. Incidentally, be careful when you use phrases like "I'll eat you up". My three-year-old was terribly worried when she heard a mother say this to her baby.

Possibly the most serviceable of all the speech games is down-to-earth pointing. Most first words are embellishments of pointing, copied from you. As he begins to point for himself, he begins to understand more and more of your pointing. At this time it is a good idea to draw his attention to your hands. He is beginning to learn by watching what you do and if hands do interesting things, he will watch and learn; here, in fact, is the value of finger rhymes – and there are a great many you can play together. You should soon find a favorite, or you could try some variations of your own. Make your hands into a snapping mouth, snap up a little toy, and take it to him. Improvise: the action itself is unimportant as long as you draw attention to your hands and fingers. He can, of course, watch you using your fingers at other times. Let him see you stacking blocks, peeling potatoes, rolling balls and shelling peas, and don't forget to tell him what you are doing. Gradually, he will begin to watch your hands and fingers as a matter of course.

Just how first words are used differs between children. Some children point and say "gi" for give, or "ps" for cat, others feel that it is not a word unless it is in a sentence, so that "is it bed-time?" comes out as "gangoo dang bed gage?" Many families have a favorite story about a baby asking a definite question like "ga do gaga goli?", to which the mother says "of course you can", and the baby promptly takes a cookie from the plate on the table. It is often hardest to pick out first words if a child uses bab-ble sentences. Many early words lack endings: "beh" for bed, "cu" for cup. Some will be repetitions, "chch" for chair, "car-car" for car, while others will be the child's special words: "nana" or "numnum" for food. Among these early words, which are understood clearly only by a baby's nearest and dearest, there is often a party piece: a single word which can be uttered with un-canny precision. My youngest child said a perfect "hedgehog" at a time when it was quite difficult to understand his other words. Little children are often great show-offs, and party pieces make them the center of attention, so the word is repeated often. Don't let this make you impatient for a richer vocabulary: the lesson – people like it when I talk – is well learned.

PLAY DOUGH
18 months to five years

Procedure You can buy play dough and similar substances in the stores, but it is much cheaper and much more fun to make your own. The recipe is: two cups of flour, one cup of salt, one cup of water and coloring, and two tablespoons of oil – you can manage without the oil, but dough feels much more attractive with it. Knead the ingredients together and warm gently in a pan until it forms a soft lump. Give it to the toddler or child to play with while still warm.

Value
DISCOVERY Playing with dough is a lesson in basic science, showing how things change weight and shape when pulled, pushed or torn apart, and how different shapes can be built up.
PRACTICAL Start a child with play dough young and she will soon get used to the idea of sitting down for a quiet constructive period each day.

Later progress As she grows older, you can give her all kinds of tools to work the play dough – blunt knives, cookie cutters, small pots, rolling pins, bottle tops, and more.

LEARNING AND EXPLORING

Sometimes you sit and pore over a problem for hours, and then suddenly the solution clicks into place. For your baby in her second year, learning is rather like this. Her skills develop in the first year, and in the second year everything suddenly comes together. She learns to reach, to hold and to let go, she becomes mobile. Her senses mature, she sees, hears and touches as an adult does, and she begins to understand. The understanding is limited of course: she still sees all sorts of magic in the telephone, the radio and the television.

In some senses, though, she really is becoming relatively sophisticated. She can remember things from day to day, and she knows that the table stays in the kitchen, and the tree in the yard, even when she is not around to see them. Now she can hold things in her mind, she can puzzle things out, try them this way, and that way, and remember what she has just done. Because she can plan, she no longer rushes into things. In fact, she is all set for a great explosion. For now she is hungry to learn, insatiably curious, and absolutely nothing is safe from her prying fingers. She does not just take everything from the cupboard, onto the floor; she looks at each object as she takes it, and if possible pulls it apart. She drops things to see how they fall, she sucks them to see how they taste, she bangs them to see how they sound, and when they break, she examines the pieces. All the time she learns. In her way, she is a scientist; she is never bored or at a loose end. While awake, her mind, and her hands, are constantly active, as you often learn to your cost.

You are about to do a little baking when the phone rings, so you leave her for a moment while you answer. Left alone to investigate, she takes the flour from the cupboard, and when it spills, she explores the movement of the white powder on the floor. If she scrapes with her fingers she can see the floor through the pile of white. If she kicks her legs up and down in the powder, it floats in the air. It is soft and silky on her hands, and easy to push across the floor; but then she sees a jar of strawberry jam. She can prise the lid off – she just needs to turn and lift. She puts her hand in the jam. It is nice and sticky, and she can squeeze it through her fingers. Then she finds she can make red hand prints on the wall. Next she turns her attention to the shortening. It squeezes in a very pleasing way and will slip if she rubs it on the floor.

It happens to us all. You are furious, but she has had great fun.

It was a good game, an interesting experiment; she has made a dreadful mess, but she has learned a great deal. She has to find out how substances feel and move, but must it be with the baking ingredients?

The lesson of such incidents is that clay, sand and water are essential playthings for toddlers. There is so much she can learn sitting in the bath with a few simple toys. Cups and kettles to pour with, strainers from which the water escapes, cups it stays inside; balls that shoot up in the air if you hold them under water; boats that first float, then sink as you fill them with water. Sometimes you can add bubbles, sometimes you can add a few drops of coloring to a bowl of water and let her stir it with a spoon. Bath-time is ideal for these experiments, but so is a bowl of water on the floor, or a chair at the kitchen sink.

And, of course, there is the sandbox, which does not have to be a summer-only activity. A modest pile of sand on a tray or other container is acceptable enough for wet days or the winter. A large groundsheet under the tray should contain any overspill. Clay is difficult to manipulate at this age, and messy, but dough is ideal. It can be squeezed and pulled, rolled out, cut up, and if you make up two mounds with two different colors, they can be mixed together with interesting effects. Pretend cakes, animal shapes, big piles for hitting, all will absorb her for at least half an hour. When she cuts out a shape, she creates a hole as well as the shape. She took the shape out, but she could put it back; she can begin to plan and puzzle.

Puzzling now covers a whole range of exploratory fiddling. She may well develop a passion for unscrewing any thread-mounted device with irritating, sometimes dangerous consequences. If you find this is a problem, try giving her small plastic bottles with screw tops: those with really large chunky caps are the most suitable.

The puzzling, not the solution, seems to be most fun. She will be engrossed while she tries, and lose interest when she succeeds. If she seems to be having difficulty with a shape-sorter, or erecting a pile of blocks, don't rush in to help – you may spoil the game. If she is obviously frustrated, help her; and if that does not work, wait a while before you introduce these toys again.

Collecting and classifying

In learning to name objects, the toddler is learning to classify, too: an essential part of speech. Don't be disconcerted if, during the latter part of the second year, as speech develops, some of the classifications are rather odd. My eldest son loved tractors. At 17 months he would point with great excitement, and say "tractor,

FIND ME A PIG
14 months on

Procedure You can encourage a child to classify with a small pile of plastic farm animals. Select a pig and ask her to "Find me a pig like this". Show her the pig and see if she can find one to match. If after a while she still cannot find a pig, give her some assistance. Repeat the game for all the different animals.

Value
LANGUAGE Classification is the basis of language and learning to sort things into different types is an important step on the road to speech. Saying the word also helps her to name each type of animal.

Later progress
Towards the end of her second year, you can ask her to sort out all the animals into their types.

Variations Try the same game with all kinds of things. Sorting vegetables can be fun, and it helps to give the child the sense that she is doing the same as mommy and daddy in the kitchen.

BLOCK PATTERNS
18 months on

Procedure An important extension of basic sorting games like "Find me a pig" (*see page 63*) is matching shapes. Take three identical blocks and make a pattern. Ask her to make the same pattern. Show her how if necessary, but if she has trouble, let the game wait. If she enjoys it, repeat with different patterns.

Value
CONCEPTUAL Learning to build up abstract shapes is a vital step in the development of conceptual thinking. The need to match the number of blocks introduces basic math; the need to position the blocks correctly in relation to each other promotes logic.
LANGUAGE Grouping objects together abstractly is as important to the acquisition of language as sorting objects.

tractor" whenever he saw one (and since we lived next to an agricultural auction lot, this was quite often). At first, only tractors produced this excitement. The large crane in the center of town was always called "cra, cra". He could say car too, and he used this word for small trucks and vans, but jeeps, pick-ups, and army trucks were very definitely tractors. There was a logic here, a similarity in shape, and we were fairly sure we understood his classification. When he called road rollers and earth movers tractors too, we were convinced. But then he saw a map of Paris, and on the cover a picture of the Eiffel Tower. Pointing with great delight he said "tractor, tractor", most emphatically. He was certain, and we are still puzzled.

Once the inclination to classify is apparent, foster it in every way possible. You can make it your cue to buy her a modest collection of farm animals (the farmyard, building and other accessories can then make a complementary second birthday present). Collect a simple range of animals and colors, so that she can pick out all the pink pigs and brown horses, without being perplexed. Naturally, you will encourage her to use blocks in the same way and if she is with you in the kitchen while you are busy at the stove, suggest she separate the potatoes from the carrots in the vegetable tray, or the large from the small cans in the cupboard.

MAKE-BELIEVE

When it is time to exercise the broomstick horses, hats and boots have to be found, and the horses brought to the door from their stable. Sometimes one of the horses becomes impatient, waiting at the door, sometimes he even stamps his foot, but it is worth it for the gallop to the park. Once there, the horses are happy to be tied to the fence while the riders – children once more – play in the sandbox or on the swings.

Watching children make-believe, and listening in to the accompanying conversations, are surely among the great delights of parenthood. Make-believe games like broomstick horses are of course a joy to come, probably reaching their peak of complexity around the fifth birthday. The ability to pretend develops gradually – but it does start earlier than many parents believe: during the second half of the second year, occasionally sooner. It has its roots in the toddler's imagination, and the first signs, if you notice them, will be fleeting. As she plays, she may lift a cup to her mouth, or a telephone to her ear: from these simple acts, she will progress to more sustained sequences such as feeding her teddy bear with a spoon, or vacuuming the carpet with a stick.

It would be reasonable to ask yourself at this stage whether, delightful as make-believe may be, you should encourage it. Who, you may say, needs fantasy? She may not be cut out to be a poet or an actor, so why waste time on such childish pursuits? Would it be more productive to spend the time teaching her to read, or encouraging mathematical skills? It is true that you may be able to teach her some basic reading before her second birthday. She may be able to say "cat" when you show her the letters C-A-T, and by working extremely hard, you could indeed extend this to quite remarkable lengths. But it really is not worth it – unless impressing other parents is your aim. For this kind of early progress quickly becomes pointless: the real mental benefits of reading will come only when she has sufficient language to read with understanding.

If you can encourage her tendency for make-believe as much as the more "practical" skills, you will be capitalizing on the very essence of childhood, and a key method of developing language skills. When she is pretending, she is picturing things in her mind as she wants them to be. Consider the case of my three-year-old's broomstick horses. Essentially, the broomstick stands in for a horse; and in language, words stand in for real-life objects. When adults think, they manipulate words and pictures in their minds.

COMING TO LIFE
One year on

Procedure Looking back on your childhood, can you remember how you used to pretend your teddy bear was alive? Pretending with your child is a great thrill, and you can encourage her in pretend play. You can help her by playing with her teddy bear yourself: make him walk, go to bed, jump across the room or drink lemonade. Try and include him in daily activities and games. At mealtimes, for instance, put a bib on the bear and give him, and the baby, a spoonful alternately. Always describe what you are doing.

Value
IMAGINATION By helping her to pretend, you are helping her to *think,* to see things as she wants them to be, and to put herself in someone else's shoes. You are also sowing the seeds of the ability to cope with and solve problems.
LANGUAGE By showing her bear "walking" or "eating" or "dancing", you are teaching in a simple and direct way, the meanings of those words.

WET PAINT
20 months on

Procedure If you are decorating, you may find your offspring wants to join in. If so, give her a little bucket of water and a small paint brush and let her paint too. If you cannot find a suitable inside wall, let her paint the outside of the house, or a fence.

Value
ENCOURAGING IMAGINATION She pretends she is decorating, just like you. CONTROL This game furthers her understanding of the relationship between cause and effect. She can say to herself, "I made that mark." VISUAL/MOTOR CO-ORDINATION Wielding a paint brush – dipping it into the water and spreading "paint" on the wall – gives her valuable practice at guiding her hand in simple tasks.

In a similar fashion, a toddler manipulates her pretend world: games are symbols, just like words, and she can move them about in her mind to produce interesting situations.

The beginnings of imagination are indeed the beginnings of thought, and without childish pretending there is no childish thought. When she lets a box stand in for a car, or two chairs stand in for a train, she is mulling over, and solving, a problem just as an adult does.

Another benefit of pretend play is encouraging her to put herself in your place. This is especially relevant now that she can learn by watching how you do things. When she copies you drawing a bus with a crayon, her bus and your bus are very different. Nonetheless she has drawn "like mommy", she will stack blocks "like mommy", mail letters, mow the lawn and do many other things just as you do.

Her developing imagination can also help her cope with her limitations. She can pretend that she can climb trees, that she can really swim, and sometimes that she can run faster than her big brother. She can act out her resentment, and when you say "no", she can be cross with her bear, or she can cuddle it when you pay too much attention to a friend's baby.

Encouraging imagination

Some children live most of their childhood in a world of their own. A shopping trip takes forever because she and her imaginary friends want to look into all the windows. Other children never seem to play imaginative games, and are more likely to be found making things than pretending. You will not make the second child like the first, nor the first like the second, but you can encourage imagination, now, and as the child grows older.

A major toy manufacturer once ran an advertising campaign which said "A toy, a child . . . and a little imagination". Perhaps there is a lesson here: toys should leave room for imagination, not make it redundant. For a long time, there were few toys in our house which could compare with the children's bunk beds. Climb into the top bunk, with a few cushions, and some real or imaginary friends, and it became a train, a bus or a plane. For a trip on a boat, the upper bunk became the deck, the lower bunk the cabin. Another day the bunks became shoe stores, or toy stores, although this could be uncomfortable at bedtime. With the quilts hung over the front, the bunks became a private den for one or two. With the soft toys lined up on the lower bunk, the animals in their cage at the zoo would be fed lettuce and carrots.

At this stage, simple games, simple dolls, simple cars are best for pretending. Anything too elaborate, and the toddler or child

MORNING TEA
14 months on

Procedure What more enchanting way for a child to wake each morning than to find a different scene set out for her to play with? Keep them simple, though, and let her make of them what she will. Here are some suggestions: a little table set for tea with plastic cups and saucers; cars set on a country lane; a shoe store in the corner of the room; a tunnel made with two chairs and a blanket.

Value
IMAGINATION Scenes like these encourage her to play by herself, using her imagination to fill out the details. PRACTICAL You may even earn a little longer to lie in bed while she plays by herself.

will soon lose interest. A three-year-old may be quite happy to use a stick as a telephone, but a toddler in her second year will need something more realistic. At four, she may rock an imaginary baby in her arms, and feed it imaginary food; as she approaches two, she may rock her teddy bear to sleep, but she will not feed him unless he has a spoon. Soft toys – from bears to elephants – come into their own in this context. She can cuddle a bear or put him to bed; later she will take him on journeys, and talk to him. A few toy cups and plates may be acceptable for imaginary meals, or a few pans so that she can pretend to cook. Her make-believe grows out of imitation, so at this age the best pretend toys are those she can use in daily routines: a steering wheel for the car, a paint brush or toy hammer if she sees you working on the house, a wheelbarrow, and a push-along to use as a vacuum cleaner or as a lawn mower.

The under-twos can join in, but they may not know how to start a game, and so you will need to set the scene. Don't expect games to develop in an elaborate way at this early stage. She will not be able to carry ideas through until she is well into her second year, so to start with you will need to stick to very simple actions: pretend to drink from a toy cup, or to phone daddy on her toy phone; gradually, she will copy you, later she will do it without prompting.

If you have given toys roles to play, your child will be used to penguins who pretend to peck tummies, and dolls that give cuddles. Sit a stuffed animal next to her when you have your lunch: a spoonful for teddy, a spoonful for baby. At bedtime, pop her animal in beside her, tuck them both in, and kiss them both goodnight. When you ask a question, ask the animal, too. Books can be useful for starting pretend games even before the second birthday. Pretend to eat up the picture of a cake, or drink the picture of a cup. Pretend to dial on the phone, or stroke the picture of a cat in one of her books.

Another way of stimulating the imagination is simply by talking. Glove puppets can give your efforts a considerable lift – see the margin. Let her experience worlds which she cannot see: talk about going to the park, driving the car, or going on vacation. Take her to visit the zoo, and talk about it when you get home. Talk about the "naughty dog" who jumped in the duck pond. Look out for things which interest her when you are out together, and talk about them at home Give her objects which help her to imitate you. If you have a new baby, let her have one too; if you are doing the housework, give her a duster or a little broom. Don't feel she has to be out of the way while you work: a toddler who has watched you work will often busy herself with "work" too. A child who has seen you sitting down with a book will sit and pretend to read to herself. My eldest son made himself a "university" in the long grass and asked not to be disturbed at a time when I often went into the University in the evenings to write. Her play will reflect your behavior increasingly – and this can be revealing. When you are short-tempered, you may see her shouting at her toys; if you are too busy, she may tell her teddy bear not to bother you just now.

GLOVE PUPPETS
20 months on

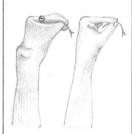

Procedure You can make your own simple glove puppet from an old sock with eyes and lips sewn on. The mouth can be between thumb and fingers – see drawing. Alternatively, buy, or make, a more elaborate glove puppet. Use it to enliven any interludes in your daily routine. Show her what the puppet can do: wave, pick up spoons, clap, pinch noses. Give the puppet a certain character, and stick to it. The way the puppet talks, not what it says, is the important factor: if you can, make the puppet's voice funny.

Value
ENTERTAINMENT She will probably find the transformation of your hand highly amusing in itself.
MAKE-BELIEVE Puppet play provides the steps towards a pretend world, devised by both of you, inhabited by funny people who play their own special roles.

Later progress
Getting to enjoy the glove puppet at this age will help maximize its important later benefits: speech development and eye-hand co-ordination of a fairly high order.

STORY TELLING
Around two years

Procedure Of course books are marvelous for encouraging a child's imagination, but don't ignore the spoken word. By the time a child is two, she may want to hear again and again about "When I was a baby". At about 20 months (depending on her understanding of language), start telling her simple stories about herself. Begin with little snippets, such as "That was your coat when you were a little baby". Or, show her a photograph and say "This is you at the park". Then gradually build up these snippets into a proper story. She will usually stop and listen avidly.

Value
UNDERSTANDING A child finds it difficult to talk about things that are not there in front of her. Telling her stories about herself helps her to understand that this can be done.
MEMORY Talking about events that happened to her helps her to picture the past and use her memory.
LANGUAGE The immediacy of oral story telling is ideal for language development. It also provides the opportunity to introduce verbs in the past tense.

Later progress
Encourage her to remember events for herself, and to tell you stories.

BOOKS FOR BABIES

Parents are often unsure when to introduce books to their children. In spite of television, radio, and computers, books are still the basis of much of our education, and enjoyment. Perhaps you have heard that children are abandoning books for television, and feel, as I did, that if only you could instill the book habit early enough, your own children would continue to read. But when should you start to show her books? Most people feel silly showing a picture book to a six-week-old baby, but, on the other hand, feel equally sure that a child of two who has never seen a book is deprived.

I believe the answer is to be completely relaxed about the timing. Show her books as soon as you feel she may benefit. If you want to start at six weeks, you will not be foolish, and if you wait until six months, that is also a good time. A useful rule of thumb is to wait until you can manage a baby and a book on your knee together. Though at two months books are no more than attractive colors and shapes to them, there is value in sitting quietly together with a book before bed.

In her first year, she will need clear, simple pictures of familiar objects or animals without confusing detail. Look for clear bright colors, and avoid anything that is either fussy or complicated. The success of illustrators like Dick Bruna and Helen Oxenbury is based on the simple, child-like nature of their images. Line drawings are often too detailed, and therefore confusing. Top children's publishers produce large numbers of books showing single animals, cars, or household objects. Some of them, so-called "baby board books", are printed on cardboard, making it possible for her to turn the pages for herself.

I feel that a child's introduction to books should be two-pronged: she looks by herself, and she sits with you at quiet times while you read to her. Although she will not be able to turn the pages of a "proper" book with thin paper pages until she is at least a year, it is worth buying a few because they offer more variety and have many more pictures. Start with one or two of each: two cardboard books for her toy box, and two for you to read. To these you can add books of rhymes and action songs.

Soon after her first birthday, she will begin to enjoy books that depict her daily routines: shopping trips and visits to the park or playground. Later in her second year, she will use these to extend her vocabulary.

By 18 months she will be ready for more complex pictures: she

EARLIEST BOOKS/*Three months on*

You can introduce her to board books with
large, colorful, simple images as soon as she
can focus properly – usually around three
months. If you leave her with books like this
when she goes to bed, or when playing quietly,
she can explore them for herself, and they will
become a natural, familiar part of her world.
But looking at books is also an opportunity for
the two of you to be together; a secure time for
her, and an opportunity for you to develop your
relationship.

*Above, bold but simple
images with strong shapes
can appeal even to a three-
month-old. This one is
from* Family, *a Helen
Oxenbury board book.*

Left, Spot's First Walk
*by Eric Hill is suitable for
babies of six months or
older. The shapes are
large and simple and there
are plenty of familiar
shapes to hold her interest.
Lift-up flaps concealing
further pictures add
enormously to the
excitement and promote
involvement.*

Watch out!

It
was
an
island

They were cold   wet and hungry

Meg at Sea *by Helen
Nicoll and Jan Pienkowski
has the type of simple,
charming story line that
could be considered, if not
followed, by babies from
15 months on. The
delightful humor of the
drawings is simple enough
to be understood, and the
story could pave the way
for later make-believe
games and improvised
story-telling.*

71

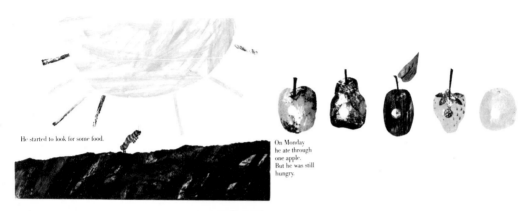

He started to look for some food.

On Monday
he ate through
one apple.
But he was still
hungry.

So one Saturday morning Alfie and Mum went to a big shop in the High Street.

Above, The Very Hungry Caterpillar *by Eric Carle, with its finger-size holes and lift-up flaps, encourages involvement.*

Left, the sketchy style and wealth of detail in Alfie's Feet *by Shirley Hughes would normally be too much even for advanced two-year-olds, but with some help, two-year-olds can find it rewarding to identify subjects among the quite complex detail.*

Cc

Alphabet books such as Helen Oxenbury's ABC of Things *are valuable pre-reading aids, worth introducing at around two years. Though she will not understand the letters, she will become familiar with them. The absurd humor of this book is rightly popular.*

cake
candles
cat
cow
crow

will enjoy animals which hide under flaps or in the branches of trees. As she begins to talk, big picture books, especially picture word-books, provide new objects to point to, and new words to learn.

As soon as you feel she can understand, begin to read her simple stories and rhymes. She will love rhymes with actions, and stories with repetition. *The Three Billy Goats Gruff* is an example of the best of these: you can use different voices for each goat, and stamp your feet as they cross the bridge. All the old traditional stories such as *Goldilocks and the Three Bears* and *The Gingerbread Man* have this element of repetition and rhyme which small children love. Some modern story books use repetition and rhyme in the same way, and these are the ones to look out for.

As far as the child is concerned, there is little need for many different stories: at this age, she will probably want the same book every night. As you read to her she will begin to join in, stamping her feet and saying "my bridge" as the billy goats cross the bridge.

You may well feel that some of the simpler story books are rather dull: children get up, get dressed, and go through a routine day. But small children find them anything but dull because they can identify with what is described. You may even find she enjoys children's clothes catalogues, especially if they contain her overalls, toy catalogues that have pictures of her toys, or photograph albums; above all, she will enjoy a homemade book about her daily life.

At two, her library should contain a good nursery rhyme book, and a book of finger rhymes; some traditional and modern stories which are both simple and repetitive, and a collection of simple picture books. Add a few catalogues and place them all where she can reach them. Books which are out of reach are not used by the child: they are used by you to read aloud. She must learn the pleasures of looking (and later reading) for herself if books are to have a lasting value.

SOUND EFFECTS
Around two years

Procedure You can make story telling much more lively and fun by encouraging her to join in with sound effects at appropriate places. Few stories are written with this in mind, so it is usually best to make your own up. It should work like this: "Farmer John walked down the lane with his . . . dog" (child goes "woof, woof"). "Soon he came to a gate. He opened the gate and went into the field. What do you think he saw in the field? He saw some cows" (child "moos"). This game is quite demanding so keep the number of sounds, and the story, simple, and leave her time to chip in.

Value
LANGUAGE By associating certain sounds with cue words, she will begin to learn the basic call and response nature of conversation – and animal noises encourage her to vocalize, because they are fun.
ANTICIPATION Guessing which sound they must make next.
IMAGINATION Making the sounds will give her a far more definite picture of the scene you are describing.

The
Pre-School Years

TREASURE TROVE
Two years and over

Procedure Simply provide him with a bag or container – preferably one that has taken his fancy. Get him to take this along when you go to the park or woods, or even just out into the garden. Make a game of collecting "treasure" of any kind. He will probably choose to collect just one type of treasure: small round stones, perhaps, or dead leaves. Let him choose, but if he will not, make your own suggestion. Accept his choice, however idiosyncratic, and *see page 90*.

Value
OBSERVATION He learns to look for specific items.
FINE FINGER CONTROL He must not only pick things up, but get them into the bag.
DISCUSSION You talk together about the collection when you arrive home.

NO LONGER A BABY

There is no day on which a toddler becomes a small child. It is both a gradual process and a sudden one. He changes almost imperceptibly from the baby you have to watch each minute to the co-operative, communicative child; from someone you try hard to please to the child who tries hard to please you.

You look at him one day as he sits playing, and you realize he is no longer a baby. He does not even look like a baby: his movements are fluid and confident, and although he still lacks certain skills, he approaches everything with clear intent: he knows what he wants to do, though not perhaps how to do it. You feel he has the confidence to learn, and you begin to realize you no longer have to stop yourself from showing him how everything works.

Although his language is simple, he is beginning to talk like a child. He tells you what he wants, what troubles him and what he is doing. You may even begin to gossip together. He thinks like a child, remembers from day to day and can share the past and look forward to the future with you. The past and future are reflected in his play. He no longer lives from moment to moment, but creates stories to carry his play along.

He no longer learns everything by simple repetitive practice: he is starting to learn indirectly, by watching and listening. Because he understands what you say to him, he begins to realize that you are a source of knowledge, and bombards you with questions: now is the time for "How?" and "What?" and "Why?"

He enjoys predictable stories, and can often say them by rote; he begins to use tools, and, as in the first two years, you will see him practicing new skills over and over. His social and intellectual skills are still learned more or less directly from you, but to widen his exploration of relationships in the adult world, he pretends. He has a make-believe world in which he tells people what to do, just as you do, and he gets cross when they disobey. Toys are naughty, teddy bears become seriously ill – but he can cope; he is in charge. He mimics you, and you will see yourself reflected, sometimes unfavorably, in what he does.

He is still curious and dependent, but even in this you find he is increasingly amenable: he co-operates rather than fights, uses you as a secure base rather than a clinging post. Most of all, he is becoming a social being. You find you enjoy his company, that you can do things together: there is give-and-take in your relationship. You are still the main giver, he the main taker, but he is becoming socially aware of you, and of other children. If there is one feature of his development you notice most at this stage, it is this social awareness. You find, with relief, that he is starting to use language, rather than tantrums, to make demands.

It is now that you may begin to discern his character, at least in broad outline, and observing him playing reveals his personality as well as anything. He may prefer to play with noise and bustle around him, or he may prefer to merge into the background, or he may constantly crave an audience. He may need someone close to him for security, or he may sometimes need to play in peace and quiet away from people. He will always play most when he is happy, so providing conditions in which he can relax will encourage him to play.

You should notice, now, that he talks incessantly while he plays, so that play often seems to be an excuse for speech. As he gossips and chatters, he inhabits a world of his own, where he has dual roles – instructor and pupil. You will hear him instructing himself (just as you instruct him) on building a pile of blocks, then obligingly obeying his own orders. It is as if language has become a means of self-control, an instrument of the self-discipline he must practice in order to learn.

Pre-school children are in this sense ready and eager to learn, but not yet by formal teaching. As parents, we are most effective at this time if we introduce interesting new ideas or variations into games rather than trying to impart knowledge. It is not the time to fill children with facts (unless they ask for them); it is the time to sow the desire to learn. Let them want to find out, and knowledge will follow; let them want to be with people, and the social skills will follow. If play that involves discovering facts and learning how to play with other children gives them pleasure, they will want to take their enjoyment further.

WATERWORKS
Four to five years

Procedure Most young children love helping out around the house. For them, housework is a game, not a chore – particularly if the task involves water. So get him to water plants on the porch, or wash the kitchen table with a wet cloth; or wipe the tiles in the bathroom. Don't expect good results: just let him enjoy playing around. *See pages 78–81.*

Value
TARGETED ACTIVITY Games like these help to develop the idea of working towards an end, and of sustaining an activity until the objective is achieved.
MANIPULATIVE SKILL He will soon learn that to clean surfaces, you need a firm, deliberate stroke and his hand control will improve rapidly.
PRACTICAL He plays in your company, but without you having to drop pressing chores.

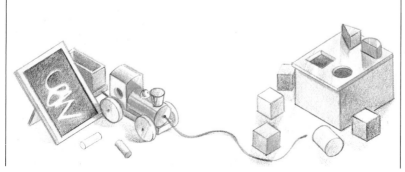

PICTURE PUZZLES
Two to three on

WORK AND PLAY

Procedure You can beneficially introduce simple "picture puzzles" to children as young as two years. You can make your own by mounting magazine pages on sturdy cardboard and then cutting the puzzle into several large shapes. If you use a lot of straight lines, you shouldn't find it too difficult to come up with something that your child will find easy to reassemble. Simplicity is the key here – an overly complicated puzzle will leave a child frustrated and bored. Similarly, if you buy, bear in mind that first puzzles should have only six or seven simple pieces – ten at most – and each piece should, ideally, have a little knob to help the child lift it from the puzzle.

Value
QUIET PLAY A good puzzle will keep a child occupied and will encourage him to experiment and explore by himself.
MANIPULATIVE SKILL Maneuvering the pieces into place demands accurate hand control.
CONCEPTUAL Few games give a child a better understanding of the concept of shape.
EDUCATIONAL As he builds up his puzzle, you can tell stories about each of the elements.

It is easy for adults to make the distinction between work and play: work has an element of drudgery, play is for enjoyment. But children often have different ideas. To him, mopping the floor is as enjoyable as building with blocks, and he considers both behaviors in a similar light: not work, which is something that grown-ups and school children do outside the home, and not necessarily play either, for to him play essentially now means pretending.

When you work, you usually have an end in mind: a clean floor, a bag of groceries. When he "works" for you, he learns to work towards an end, and this is the key to the value of "work" as "play", for he will regard the achieved end of a well-mixed cookie dough in just the same way as a successfully completed jigsaw puzzle – provided it is undertaken playfully. This is clearly beneficial – not just in the sense of learning a positive attitude to household chores. Work does not have to be serious or dull: sometimes it is as exuberant and enjoyable as any play, and not to experience this as a child could be a real deprivation. Remember how much you enjoyed putting on old woolen socks and skating up and down, "polishing" the floor? Or putting on a swimming suit on a warm summer evening and "watering" the garden? This exuberance – even wildness – is highly characteristic of play, and no one knows quite why. If research on animals has any bearing on the play of children, exuberant play seems to be important in the development of flexible social relationships, improbable as that might seem. Animals that play exuberantly are the ones we think of as rather smart: monkeys, foxes, dogs, cats, rats. Animals that do not play in this way we think of as nice, but not very outgoing: rabbits and guinea pigs, for example. As in most folk tales, there is an element of truth here: young rats who are not allowed to play are much less flexible when it comes to learning new tasks. Of course, this may have no bearing on the development of children. Exuberance and glee may be no more than a way of letting off steam; but it might, just might, be good for them.

Until sometime after his second birthday you will need to lead him into exuberant play. It is a social activity, and as yet he has not made friends of his own age. As social relationships with other children develop, he will initiate as well as join in gleeful games. Throughout childhood he will wrestle, chase, jump, push and scream. He will roll down banks, jump up and down on the spot, clap his hands and shout and laugh with delight. As he plays he will carefully watch other children, often matching his behavior to that of the group, and this is of value, but sheer exuberance in its own right is probably just as important.

Playing in this way occurs of its own accord; it is the sort of play that goes naturally with mud and water, grassy banks, garden sprinklers and piles of grass cuttings. Let him get wet and dirty, run about, scream and shout. Few parents today would tell their children that "nice" boys and girls do not play like this, but often the same attitude exists in a subtle form when we wash his face and comb his hair with a vengeance, or tell him to be careful not to rip his shirt as he climbs a tree. With girls the habits and expectations of our culture do much to restrain boisterous play, a problem which is fully discussed on pages 161–163 under the heading "A Question of Sex".

Exuberant play, quiet play and work-play – a balance

He needs the excitement of exuberant play, and the freedom of quieter, organized play. When he pushes his truck, he plans the route for himself, no one imposes a structure upon him. When he makes a nest under the tree for a bird, he tells himself a story. When he builds a tower with his blocks, he practices the skills involved in balancing and placing. Unsupervised, open-ended play is valuable because he learns for himself how things work and why things happen. No matter if he makes mistakes: they must be made if skills are to develop. Quiet play generally provides the opportunities for learning and practicing skills, rather than simply applying them; for exploring, experimenting and creating. It also develops the imagination in a way that work or highly structured play – organized and supervised – cannot.

Some children are much better at playing quietly by themselves than others. Pre-school children are highly social beings, and if your child is reluctant to amuse himself it may be because he does not like being alone. If his play space is in the bedroom, and you spend much of your day in the kitchen, move his toys to the kitchen. There are few rooms in a house where a corner cannot be used for him to play near you: keep a few toys in each room, or buy a toy box that he can wheel from room to room. Talk to him as he plays, if he seems to enjoy your attentions. But be prepared, as he grows older, to leave him to play in peace if that is his choice.

If you find that he needs an unusual degree of encouragement to play by himself, or if he will not play alone at all, the companionship of another child usually helps. At two, they will play in parallel, but by three they will play together.

BIRD PUDDING
Three to five years

Procedure One of the best kitchen games is making a special treat for the birds. Provide him with large quantities of suitable seed, grated suet, scraps of meat, breadcrumbs, nuts and dried fruit. When he has mixed these together in a bowl, YOU add melted lard to bind the mix and let it cool so your child can easily handle it. Once he has kneaded the lard in thoroughly, push a knotted piece of string well into the mix and put the mix into an old yogurt container to harden. When it is hard, turn the treat out of the container and hang it outside for the birds.

Value
FUN Mixing the ingredients is delightfully messy. MANIPULATIVE SKILL TARGETED ACTIVITY This game has a clear objective: feeding the birds in winter. Seeing the birds feed afterwards becomes especially fascinating if he has provided the food himself.

In contrast to quiet playing by himself, "work-play" encourages the carrying out of a planned activity to completion, enabling him to see how his contribution affects the finished result. It is almost a half-way stage to the classroom, for working with you involves picking up information from you rather than learning direct from experience as in independent play. An additional benefit is gaining experience of the adult world. An urban child does not often see work outside the home that has much relevance to his life. He sees the roads swept and the garbage cars emptied, but unlike the country child he rarely hears comments like "there are the cows which produced your milk for breakfast". Helping prepare food, cleaning, washing and gardening go some way towards giving him a wider picture of the world.

When people work together they usually gossip, and gossip can be instructive. If you talk about the coming picnic, he will imagine the day ahead, and if you talk about yesterday's trip, you exercise his ability to remember. When you talk about the funny tree in the next-door garden, you ask him to visualize. At first he will listen to your stories, but soon he will tell you a story of his own, a step which these quiet periods of work-play together does much to encourage. You may find, incidentally, that at three or four he finds it easier to talk about something that happened two or even three days ago; yesterday tends to be a rather blank page.

INDOOR BALL GAMES
Two to six years

Procedure Playing "ball" games with a young child, even if you are confined to a small apartment, can be great fun if you make balls from rolled-up newspaper. Clear all delicate and easily breakable objects from the room. Using a rolled-up newspaper as a bat, you can play "baseball". With more than one child, you can have competitions to see who can throw farthest, or throw the "ball" into a wastepaper basket.

Value
VISUAL-MOTOR SKILLS

PAPER TIGERS
Five years and over

Procedure A couple of children cooped up in a small apartment can let off steam by throwing balls of rolled-up newspaper at each other. Make them each a "fort" from armchairs and start the battle yourself.

Value
VISUAL-MOTOR SKILL Throwing a ball accurately is usually beyond even a five-year-old, but here is useful practice.
EXUBERANT PLAY is an important feature of early childhood – *see pages 78–9.*
PLAYING TOGETHER PRACTICAL Paper fights are safer than pillow fights.

PLAYING IN CONFINED SPACES

The pre-school child needs a varied and challenging environment for her play activities. Providing it is one of the most important things you can do, and this is easy if you have a large house, a backyard and a climate that makes it possible to play outside all year round, but few children grow up in such ideal conditions. So how do you give a small child a challenging physical environment in a small city apartment or house?

Children need space to play, and this problem becomes worse as they grow. You might try confining her, but I have found that this just does not work, even for limited periods. She will creep from her play space into yours, no matter what you do.

Nursery schools often suffer from similar problems as parents with confined living space. Their solution is no more than careful organization: they rarely put all their equipment out each day. You could follow this practice by letting her select just two or three toys at a time; a useful combination could include a physical activity such as a tricycle or a monkey swing, something quieter such as a puzzle or a construction kit, and something to encourage her imagination; for example a sheet over a chair for making a house. Keep the toy box at hand, together with a few favorite odds and ends – a dustpan and brush for sweeping the floor of the house, a teddy bear who visits – and you can elaborate some of the games.

Even in a small apartment, there is room for a physical challenge or exercise. An elastic high-jump takes very little room, and quite an elaborate obstacle course is possible with a little ingenuity. A monkey swing, rope ladder or climbing rope hung from a hook in the ceiling a couple of days a week will be appreciated far more than a permanent fixture. (The hook, which must be screwed into a joist or solid part, can be used for a hanging plant at other times.) A foam camping mattress should be placed under the swing; and this in turn can be used for somersaults and headstands. If she needs encouraging, take a tip from nursery teachers and ask "Are you still jumping?" or say "I didn't know you could get on that swing". The slide you make on the stairs (see page 84) will cause great excitement, whereas the one in the garden may go unheeded for days on end. When not in use, the slide board can double as a shelf. Another strong shelf can be used as a balancing board. Place it between two washing-up bowls (or later two chairs) and let her walk across, or place it over one bowl to make a see-saw to walk over. It will pro-

PHYSICAL GAMES INDOORS/*Two years on*

Young children need to stretch their developing muscles as much as their minds, and robust physical activities are as important as more "intellectual" games. Even if there is nowhere safe outside for him to play, you can turn even the smallest apartment into a temporary activity center with a little ingenuity. Safety precautions are, of course, essential. They are mainly a matter of common sense and careful pre-checking – but make sure climbing surfaces are securely fixed and that there is no furniture that can be pulled over.

Things to hook to ceilings and walls: Young children are light enough for heavy-duty hooks screwed into joists and beams to provide sufficient support for a monkey swing, a rope ladder, and hand rings. Use strong, smooth hemp rope and ensure hooks are mounted securely.

If you have an old but solid chest of drawers, you can build this Tarzan's House on top from chipboard on a pine frame, painted in jungle colors.

If space in the bedroom is sufficient, a climbing frame can provide a versatile physical activity center. Lay foam rubber slabs in case of falls, and always supervise.

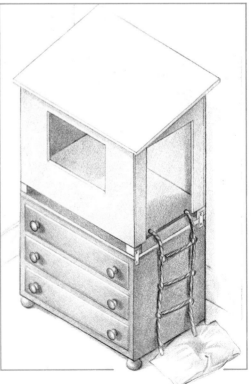

Even the smallest living room can be turned to a challenging obstacle course. The nature of the course depends on what furniture you can make available, but typical obstacles could be: tunnels through the legs of chairs, or through caves made from the cushions of sofas; stepping stones made from cushions; solid tables for cliff faces; low (and solid) bookcases for mountain ledges; a plank resting on very low piles of books for the narrow bridge across a raging torrent; a winding rope laid on the floor as the mysterious trail made by explorers in days gone by; and so on. Mark out the course with big colorful paper arrows.

If he cannot ride outside, make riding indoors more fun with obstacles and a ramp to negotiate.

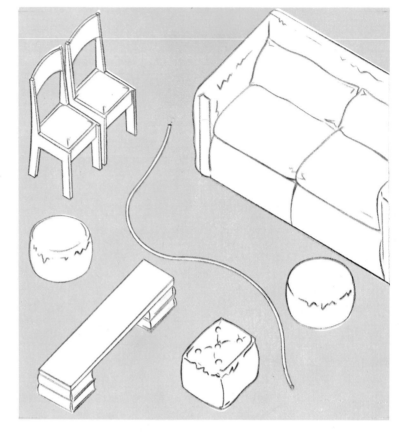

A wooden plank painted in gloss paint can be laid over the bottom of a staircase to make a slide. Children slide down on cushions.

Value
PHYSICAL SKILLS:
BALANCE, CO-
ORDINATION,
STRENGTH; EXUBERANT
FUN

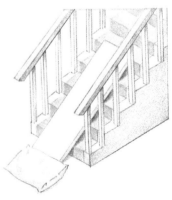

vide a morning's excitement, and later return to its usual function. Even if you have only one child, you might consider a bunk bed for her to use as a climbing frame. Tie a rope ladder to it as an alternative means of climbing to the top bunk. A sleeping platform would be better still. Always supervise such activities.

Apartment dwellers, of course, may have to reconsider some of the noisier activities suggested above.

Messy play

This is difficult in a small space, but just about possible if you confine it to a period when it is safe to share your kitchen, or when you can be on hand to see that the mess does not spread from her corner. Camping ground sheets, or a large sheet of polyethylene, will protect the floor. An easel makes painting possible in a small corner, and an oilcloth spread over a table or cupboard can be used for play-dough. Clay is probably too messy for most small houses – and some big ones. This may seem a regimented approach, but a set hour for sand, water, clay or painting may be the only way to manage these activities in many households: do not worry, your regimentation will be greeted with "Is it messy time yet?" A strong drawer lined with polyethylene can be used as a sand box, and a bowl at the sink is marvelous for water play.

These solutions may help, but none faces up to the reality that a child who is confined to a small apartment just has to run about as fast as she can from time to time. The park, or even jogging round the block together are not always easy solutions. If things become desperate, you can absorb a certain amount of her excess energy by letting her jump into your arms from the table, bouncing on beds, or practicing falls on a floor space spread with cushions or, preferably, outsize bean bags or cushions filled with polystyrene chips.

FOAM FUN
Two to four years

Procedure If you have somewhere children may make a mess or can set up a "messy space" as described in the text, there are few more wonderfully messy substances to give than aerosol foams. Shaving foam is the most readily available, but may sting children's eyes. A more extravagant, but safer and more delightfully *edible* alternative, is aerosol whipped cream. But rather than just squirting randomly, get them to make patterns or draw faces or put ears, eyes, nose and mouth on a balloon. For added realism and fun, you can add food coloring to the cream.

Value
FUN Messy games are always appreciated, especially because they *feel* good.
MANIPULATIVE SKILLS
LANGUAGE As they make each new feature on the balloon-face, children can repeat its name.

MUDLARKS
Two to six years

Procedure Few children fail to appreciate mud. It squidges gloriously through the fingers and toes and can be molded into a convincing range of shapes. What is more, these shapes will often remain intact after the mud dries. If you cannot find a suitable mud hole, why not make one? It may be appreciated as much, if not more, than a sand box. It need be nothing elaborate: just a shallow hole in the ground, lined with polyethylene sheeting and filled with clay-rich mud. In the summer you will probably need to moisten it periodically, and she will love taking off all her clothes in warm weather and just wallowing. Being hosed down afterwards is part of the fun.

Value
DISCOVERY She learns the properties of mud.
TACTILE Mud provides a rich range of sensations.
FUN AND MESS;
EXUBERANT PLAY

WATER AND SAND PLAY

Once, she was happy just to splash in the bath or the wading pool; now she experiments with strainers and water toys (and squirt guns if you allow them). But the main change you will notice in this sort of play during the pre-school period will be the introduction of a story line. Boats do not just float, they sail to an island at the end of the bath; they do not just sink, a large sponge drops out of the sky to obliterate them.

Clean water – and dirty water

Water is wet, water is messy, but it feeds her imagination. You may prefer that she play in a cardboard box rather than in the sink, but if you deny her water play, she will probably find it despite you.

From water she understands wetness and dryness, and learns about warm and cold, movement, flow, volume and shape. But small children often don't distinguish between clean and dirty water, and many are drawn to playing in sewers and in the toilet bowl. You may see clearly that your child is learning from this type of play, but feel unwilling to let it continue. Are you meant to patiently tolerate attempts to clean the lavatory with your toothbrush, all in the name of education?

Most children are messy; many a parent has despaired of a child's future as she takes a cup to the toilet bowl for a drink. But be reassured that most children do change. A child's love of dirt is not an infallible indicator of later interests or habits. Some people have always loved mess and dirt, and always will, but other dirty children grow up to be fairly clean adults. She probably loves dirt for what she can do with it, and for how it feels. A child who experiments with mud may later experiment with paint, or cooking, or science.

As for play in the toilet, it may well be that she is obsessed by it because as parents we encourage this obsession. During toilet training, you try hard to interest her in her urine: she fills her pot and you say "What a clever girl". Then you pour the precious liquid into the toilet – and wonder why she wants to play in there. If you say it is good, it is, as far as she is concerned, good. How can a two- or three-year-old understand that the toilet is good for peeing in, and bad for playing in?

Water is good: good for experimenting with and good for playing in, good for all the reasons the experts say it is. Your problem is not in providing it, but in restricting it to those experiences that are safe. If a child constantly plays in the toilet, is it because she cannot get enough access to water? Make her bath times longer, let her play at the sink every day, and give her a wading pool in the backyard. Plenty of toys in the bath, plenty of cups and jugs at the sink, objects that float and sink in the wading pool, and she may be lured away from the toilet. At the same time, you can make the toilet more inaccessible by fixing her trainer seat to the large seat.

If this does not work, you will just have to wait: the phase rarely lasts. Within the family, the dangers of playing in the toilet are quite small, but if you are worried about infection, flush the toilet twice after use, wiping all surfaces with a small amount of disinfectant between flushes. To the small child, toilet cleaner can be more dangerous than traces of parental urine.

If you have a drain in your driveway or backyard, your child may want to play in it, because water collects there. Before allowing her to play in a drain, be sure it is clean and properly secured. Keep her from the large drains sometimes found in gutters, particularly those cut under the sidewalk, for these can be large enough to be truly dangerous. If your child is inexorably drawn to gutters or drains, set up a wading pool with an inch or two of water in it and some buckets to help carry water to the sand box. This may prove a helpful distraction.

Answering the questions

Water play is bound to raise questions. If she asks you why some things float, or why things get wet, tell her simply, but accurately. Do not try to burden her with complex explanations. You can tell her for example, that the ball pops up from under the water because it is full of air. She may turn to you and say, "and it wants to be with the other air because they are friends". Don't feel obligated to correct her. She is trying to understand her world in her own way. If her explanations are basically correct, why tell her otherwise?

Waterworks

A child's experience of water can also include water work. When she is ready, she will enjoy pouring herself a drink from a jug, or washing her socks at the sink. Show her how to wring out a cloth, and be on hand in case she tips the bowl over, but then let her get on with washing the bathroom floor. Advise her how to improve her efforts, and give her a dry cloth with which to mop up if it gets too wet. Don't clean up after her immediately after she finishes: practice will make perfect, and why discourage a potentially willing helper?

POP-UPS
Two years on

Procedure Ping-pong balls are among the cheapest and most entertaining bath toys. At this age, or even younger, a child will usually be delighted by the way they pop to the surface so vigorously when submerged. Buy 20 or so of the cheapest-quality ping-pong balls and just throw them all into the bath. Or give her a plastic bowl with a flat base and see how many she can trap under the bowl at once.

Value
DISCOVERY
MOTOR SKILL To submerge ping-pong balls under a bowl requires careful control and co-ordination of both hands.
FUN

SAND ART
Three to five years

Procedure Here is an interesting variation on familiar sand games inspired by the sand paintings of the American Indians. Make a large cone of sturdy paper with a tiny hole at the apex and attach string to holes near the mouth of the cone. Suspend the cone apex-down from the edge of a table, or from a shelf, and place a large tray covered in dark paper beneath it. With your finger over the hole, fill the cone with sand. The child can then swing the cone slowly over the paper and make patterns. If she wants to stop at any time, simply put a large saucepan under the cone to catch the sand; refill when she wishes to start again. To make the patterns more interesting, use different-colored sands.

Value
DISCOVERY This is another simple science lesson.
CREATIVITY She can simply let the sand run out into a heap and may for a while be happy to do so, but she will soon start to swing the cone to create patterns.

Sand

She probably took to the sand box in her first year, but now it really comes into its own. She can appreciate, for instance, that wet and dry sand provide quite different sorts of fun. Wet sand is for making long twisting roads down which to drive her cars, mountains for her sheep and goats to graze on, or dangerous passes for her soldiers to defend. It is for shoveling into her wheelbarrow and moving to the far side of the garden, and for making glorious mud by adding water.

Dry sand is altogether different. It is for holding in the hands and quietly slipping through the fingers; for burying toes in and then wriggling them till they just peep out; for watching as it flows from one cup to another, and for wondering why there seems to be more now it is in a new container.

Dry sand is also the ideal medium for building up an understanding of volume: for the realization that something poured from one container to another of a different size remains the same in volume, even if it looks more or less in the new container.

Psychologists call this way of thinking conservation, and it is surprisingly hard for a child to acquire. Just as a baby of less than, say, nine months thinks that objects cease to exist when not looking at them, the child under four years of age does not seem to pay attention to more than one thing at a time. If the sand fills a smaller cup to overflowing, there must be more sand than was in the larger cup; never mind that the cup is smaller. Only later, when she can keep track of more than one thing at a time, does she realize that the cup is smaller and that there is the same amount of sand in the two containers. Actually, children begin to wrestle with these problems before they are four. Use Smarties instead of juice, and she can often distinguish a larger from a smaller number, even when confusingly presented in containers of different sizes. When it is important for her to know, she may well take the necessary step forward.

Clay and play-dough

Ready-mixed clay is surprisingly heavy: although a 50-pound bag sounds a great deal, it is not too much for a child – especially if you yourself are tempted to fashion a few rough pots while he plays. There is nothing quite like the soft, silky feel of wet clay as it is squeezed through the fingers, but of course it is messy. Even when you think you have cleared all signs of the wet clay from the table, you will probably find, as they dry, fine grey or white smears appearing from nowhere. Unless you have a suitable play area indoors, a paved patio or outside modeling area is the best. Children do not really need tools – the pleasure is in handling and molding the material; in creating and destroying. If she likes to keep the things that she makes, you should try one of the clay-like modeling materials that harden as they set. There are too many practical problems with firing clay.

Play-dough is still the ideal modeling material for indoors, but do not overlook real dough. Make a little extra when you bake – or let her make herself a few cookies for afternoon snack. If she is starting from scratch, she will find it easier to manipulate if there is oil rather than shortening in the dough. If she enjoys greasing the cookie snacks for you, she may find a small amount of butter and a baking tray even more fun.

LITTLE CHEF
Four years on

Procedure The preparation of food is one of those magical adult activities that most children would love to join in – particularly as it often has the added bonus of mess and an eatable result. So why not give her a few simple tasks in the kitchen? Powdered instant puddings are perfect. They are so simple that many children can make them – just add milk and whip. Stirring cake mix, squeezing oranges and tearing lettuce are other equally enjoyable kitchen "chores".

Value
MANIPULATIVE SKILL Each task develops a different skill.
DISCOVERY The kitchen is a rich treasure house of different materials.

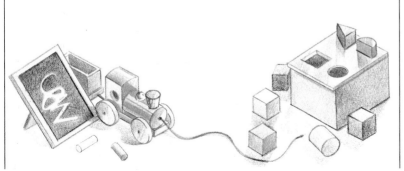

HOSPITAL
Three years and over

Procedure If you remove the hems from old cotton sheets – the older the better – a three-year-old will probably be capable of tearing them up to make pretend bandages. Show her how to make head and arm bandages, and let her practice on her bear, or yourself. Make up a story to explain how the wounds came about.

Value
MANIPULATIVE SKILL
STIMULATING THE
IMAGINATION

AND AGAIN AND AGAIN AND . . .

When children are left to play freely they often choose to repeat the same actions over and over again. The same well-loved story is enjoyed night after night, and games with highly predictable outcomes are greatly enjoyed.

I remember watching my daughter picking berries from the bushes in the garden and putting them into a little shopping bag which was among her favorite possessions at the time. She busied herself for the whole morning going from bush to bush. Another day she collected leaves from the lawn rather than berries, and when the coal had been delivered, she gathered the small pieces. Over quite a long period this gathering of small things to put into containers was her main preoccupation.

I was reminded of my daughter when I visited a Japanese nursery school. One would often see the youngest groups of children, aged between two and three years, learning to use scissors. They sat in groups around tables, each child with a pair of blunt scissors. In the center of each table was a pile of paper strips which the children cut into small bits. Each child had a bowl in which to catch the bits. A production line? That is what I thought at first, but then I remembered my daughter and her shopping bag. Much of what we call play in the very young is simple repetition of a newly learned action. It is how young children develop new skills, and if we believe that children learn through play, we must learn lessons from the ways in which they choose to play. With reasonable supervision, letting children practice with blunt scissors, even in the third year, helps them a great deal with basic skills – provided the activity is kept really simple, and repetitive.

This policy of early introduction could also be used for tearing. Give her a pile of magazines and say "find the pictures you like and tear them out". Start her on tearing out large pictures, then progress to smaller ones, so she can gradually build up the fine hand control required. Only when she can control scissors and tear paper should you be tempted to put the two skills together. She will know when she is ready to try cutting out a picture.

Glue

The same is true for gluing. Once she has acquired a few basic skills, she can use glue to produce elaborate and satisfying collages. Without those skills, sticking can be very frustrating. In fact, if you give her pictures of toys or animals before she's ready

PRODUCTION-LINE SNIPPING/MAKING
COLLAGES/*Two years and over*

Half the joy of scissors is just in cutting, so
why not let even two-year-olds practice? It is
not too early, and the training is valuable for
more complex craftwork later.

Scissors used by this age
group should for safety's
sake be blunt-ended, and
of course, snipping
needs supervision.

*Provide bowls or boxes for
the pieces to land in.
Paper strips should be 12
in (30 cm) long and no
more than ½ in (1.25 cm)
wide for easy handling
and snipping. At first,
thread children's fingers
into the scissors for them.*

Just spreading glue is
fun, and as with
snipping, two years is
not too early to start if
the activity is kept to
bare essentials, with
some adult supervision.

COLLAGE

*Provide sheets of paper or
cardboard and non-toxic
glue in squeeze bottles.
Dress child in smock,
preferably one with
sleeves. Cover a table with
newspaper and put down a
piece of paper for the
child's collage. She can
use paper snippets or
pictures cut from
magazines.*

*Some children may use
just a dab of glue, because
they don't want it on their
fingers. Others will blob
the glue all over the page
and smear their pictures
in it. Encourage both
activities. You can also
provide a stencil, and help
her spread the cut-out
areas with glue. Produce
glitter (or paper confetti
from the production line,
above) and sprinkle. Shake
off excess. Display the
result.*

White school paste, flour
paste or acrylic glues are
right for this age group.
Don't give any other
adhesives, especially not
epoxy resins. A recipe
for home-made paste,
and further information
on other adhesives,
appears on page 110.

Value
UNDERSTANDING THE
MEDIUM

ARTWORK
Two years on

Procedure Many parents give their children just one box of paints and a few brushes for all their early artistic efforts. This is a pity because they will enjoy experimenting with a wide range of materials and trying their hands at a variety of techniques. As well as paints, give them fat, easy-to-hold felt-tipped pens (of the washable kind) or colored chalks. Paint sticks are costly, but excellent for a child confined to bed, or to keep her occupied on a long journey. And you can make up your own thick paints from liquid starch or soap flakes with a little water and food coloring.

Value
PERCEPTION Awareness of color, shape and pattern.
IMAGINATION At first artwork is no more than an enjoyable cause-and-effect game, but as she grows older, she will bring her imagination to bear more and more.
EYE-HAND CO-ORDINATION

to stick on to paper, you may find she puts glue on to the picture side rather than the back.

But why learn to stick and glue?
Certainly, one could manage life quite well without ever making a collage, but the skills we encourage in this sort of activity really are essential. Adults take co-ordination of eye and hand almost entirely for granted – but perhaps we would not if we remembered that this has to be learned from scratch, with an enormous number of subtle variations, for every manual skill we attempt, from carpentry to tennis.

DRAWING: A DEVELOPING SKILL

Give a child of two a crayon or a paint brush and he will scribble; give him a plate of potatoes and gravy, or a cutting board covered with whipped cream, and he will make patterns in it with a spoon or with fingers. His style is rather free, his hand moves to-and-fro, it zigzags or simply moves across the surface. He is not capable of the fine co-ordination needed to draw a man, or to make the elaborate patterns of later years.

A little later you will see that he tends to make circular squiggles, and then that his drawings become a little "quieter": he has found greater control and will produce simple enclosed shapes, almost round or nearly square. By now, too, he can lift the crayon from the paper and make separate lines and crosses. Soon he will put together circles and crosses, triangles and lines, and all manner of shapes. Sometimes his paintings look a little like a rainstorm or a house, but he will not really draw anything that is clearly representational until he is about three. He will draw a thunderstorm – at least he may tell you that is what it is – but even the most doting parent will need a great deal of faith to see it. Very often his interpretation will come after the event: he does not draw a flower, he *sees* that he has drawn one.

Perhaps this is how he sees his first "man". He draws a circle and sees that it looks like daddy, so he adds a few dots for eyes. Since you always admire his work, and look for his meaning, you recognize his man. Thus rewarded, he will practice.

The matchstick men

They have arms and legs coming out of a circular body-head, and he draws them incessantly once he has mastered the art. As they become more complex you will see eyes and smiles appearing, and soon hair, a nose and perhaps even fingers. Sometimes there will be ten fingers on each hand, at other times only two. It is as if knowing there are fingers is enough. He may even draw "jelly fish" men with several little legs coming out of the base of the head. He makes a man, drawing those parts he sees as important – the face, the legs, the fingers; to an adult, the number of legs is important; to him, number is irrelevant, just as it does not matter that the arms come out of the head. The arms come from the biggest part – and if that happens to be the head, so be it.

By four he may be achieving greater accuracy, for example the inclusion of a body and the proper complement of five fingers; there may even be such refinements as chins under their

FLY PAINTING
Two onwards

Procedure At two, children are still at the stage of experimenting with paint rather than creating pictures. So, give him a one-inch household paint brush, some sheets of scrap paper and a jar of water-based paint. Dress him in an apron and set him up in a "messy" corner. Give him a few ideas on how to transfer the paint to the paper: he can brush it on; trickle it on from the jar; dip his fingers in and transfer it by hand. Then leave him to experiment.

Value
DISCOVERY He explores the behavior of liquids.
FUN – a delightful mess.

Procedure An artwork trick that will fascinate many young children is folding paintings. The child simply paints one side of a sheet of fairly thick paper with thick paint. He then folds the paper in half, painted sides together, presses firmly and unfolds to reveal the duplicated image.

Value
DISCOVERY Ask him if the two sides of the unfolded painting are the same. If he does not know, show him how they are similar and then leave him to experiment.

Variations Try folding the painting different ways. Once he is familiar with the technique, show him how he can get a particularly interesting effect by applying a new paint color in a first and a second fold.

mouths or knees half-way down their legs. He now draws things much more as an adult sees them, and the results will be more and more recognizable. The sun usually shines, there are flowers and trees in the garden, and houses resolutely have a window in each corner and a door in the middle. Although your house may have a side entrance, and one large picture window, your child is unlikely to draw it that way. Come to that, whoever saw the sun with rays expanding from it – except in a child's drawing? Even now, the child draws with a child-like vision of his world.

He often draws himself, and will include details such as a wasp sting on his arm, or a cut on his knee. A little girl who yearns for long hair may draw herself with pigtails and ribbons; a new T-shirt may lead to clothes being included for the first time. His life is reflected in his drawings, and so are his interests, and here you may find sex differences reflected. Girls draw people, houses and gardens; boys draw planes, outer space creatures and rocket ships. This is a generalization, of course; but ask at any nursery school and they will tell you it often happens that way.

Why does he draw?
Drawing is important, for it helps him express his feelings, his fears and his fantasies. More mundanely, it is superb practice in hand-eye co-ordination, and in the pencil control he will need for writing. It helps him plan, it helps him to visualize and it helps him to remember things that have happened to him. He draws the plane that took him on vacation, the circus he visited last week and the cake you are to make for his birthday.

Let his drawings progress at their own speed; don't rush him, or tell him people need bodies. Recognize that his drawings reflect what *he* sees as important; he does not think like a scaled-down adult, but as a child, with a child's view of the world. Take pleasure in that view through his language, his stories, his funny sayings and his art.

Trying out
As a parent you can encourage him simply by providing a variety of drawing materials: wax crayons, old lipsticks, chalks or even a thick mixture of water paint to spread over a wipeable table top. At two you will find that he may still prefer to use his hands, and will cope better with paint if it is thickened. Do not be stingy with paper, better to give him plenty of newspaper, unwanted wallpaper, computer print-out or even shopping bags, than a few small scraps of quality paper.

When he seems ready for it, introduce new painting techniques. He will enjoy blowing runny paint across the page

THE ART OF PRINTING/*Three years on*

Use finger paint, starch paint or poster paint for printing. Place paper towels in the bottom of the paint dish to act as a stamping pad.

Young children vary enormously in their ability to handle a paint brush and in their ability to visualize a picture. Printing techniques allow children of all abilities to create attractive and interesting patterns quickly and easily. The simplest and cheapest printing block is a potato. Slice one in half and gouge out a simple shape on the exposed end. The raised parts of the block will print; the valleys will not. The child can rub this printing block in a saucer or shallow pan of paint and then stamp on a large sheet of paper.

Printing blocks can be made from all kinds of materials to create a range of effects.

- Potatoes, green peppers, carrots, apples, half an orange
- Sponges, hair rollers
- Spools of thread
- Keys, jigsaw pieces
- Leaves, bark, flowers

Cut the stamps yourself with a sharp kitchen knife. Keep the shapes as simple as possible. To add variety, give him three stamps, each with a different pattern.

Each painting will yield two or three prints. See if he notices the gradual change in the depth of color with each subsequent print. And that each print is a mirror image.

PRINTS FROM WOOD

Use fingerpaints or mix flour and salt with a little water to make a thin paste like gravy and add food coloring – not red, though, unless you plan to use it alone – it does not mix well with other colors. Dress the child in old clothes or an apron and lay a board on the floor. Show him how to use the paint to make patterns with his hands on the board – using plenty of paint for each dab. Then he makes prints by pressing soft paper down on the board.

Value
USEFUL SKILL; MESSY FUN
CREATIVE; DISCOVERY
FOR ALL ABILITIES

95

BLOW PAINTING
Three years on

Procedure Once he can blow bubbles under water through a straw he can easily use this new skill to make interesting patterns with paint. Simply pour liquid paint on to the paper and give him a drinking straw to blow the paint into place. Once all the paint has soaked into the paper, pour paint of a different color on to the paper and let him blow again. This game must be supervised at first, otherwise he may be tempted to drink paint through the straw – with the paint poured on the paper, there is no danger of this. Make sure the paint is non-toxic.

Value
FUN This is an entertaining way of developing his knowledge of pattern and color.
LANGUAGE Blowing helps develop the breath and mouth control used in speaking.

with a straw, or sprinkling it from a brush: make a thin mixture of paint, get a generous brushful and show him how to dribble it, then try a thicker paint that will make bigger drips. He can even try flicking it, if you have a suitable place for this messy operation. These simple activities will show him how liquids move and flow. It will also show him how to make things that please his eye.

Most children are proud of their creations and derive great satisfaction from new skills, like putting a blob of paint on the page, folding it and spreading it out to make a beautifully symmetrical blot painting. He will like to see his pictures on the wall and to say "I did that".

New techniques mean new skills and new knowledge, and for a while he may be engrossed in these, wanting simply to drip and blow with his paints rather than draw. Showing him new techniques is an obvious way to help him develop his artistic skills; helping his drawing is more difficult, for he does not need interference or advice. He needs your interest and stimulation.

Encouragement
Give him plenty of opportunity to talk about his paintings if he wants to do so, but do not try to guess what they represent. Ask him what the image is, but do not tell him: that horse you are admiring may well be a pig, that tractor a fine sports car. If he finds that his drawings please you, he will be readier to do more. Start as you mean to continue, by discussing his early squiggles and pinning them on the wall. Talking about his work and admiring it is a good habit, but do not overdo it: discuss it when it is finished, or if he looks up for approval, not all the time. As the parent of a small child who constantly asks "Why are you doing that?" or "What is this for?", you must be aware of how distracting constant questions can be.

The best stimulus of all for his drawing is experience. Give your child plenty of interesting activities and occasional surprises and he will want to draw them. If you normally travel by car, a short bus ride or train journey may encourage him to draw buses or stations. A visit to the swimming pool, a large shop, or even a plate of French fries at a restaurant, are experiences that do not happen every day, and that will give him something to talk about and to draw.

Discuss your day as you sit with him at bedtime – a story about himself is something he can draw. But do not be tempted to turn all his activities into words: he needs to draw the picture in his mind, not the stories you tell. You may find, as I have, that the time to draw the station is two or three days after the train journey, not the next morning. It is as if his memories take time to form in his mind, and are clearest days rather than hours after the experience.

Although new experiences stimulate him to start to draw and paint, you may find that his favorite drawings are all on the same theme. One child always draws cars and roads, another makes only patterns. As each child grows older, the drawings of course become more sophisticated, but even as a teenager, one child may draw detailed scenes, while another makes elaborate patterns, perhaps with an occasional still life. My own daughter always draws people; her paintings may include a flower, a bird or even a house, the sun and a few trees; but these are just the background. The foreground is always filled with busy people.

Some children fill every spare moment with drawings, others never voluntarily draw anything at all. For these, it is best to concentrate on the activity rather than the result: get them to use paint rather than pencils, and painting techniques which can be enjoyed for themselves, rather than the finished image. Artwork which is an integral part of something else, such as a birthday or menu card, is probably the best way to encourage them to draw. And do not despair: an eye for design, and fine finger control, can after all come from building and modelling as easily as it can from painting; and he can express himself as well and as fully in words as he can with pictures.

SCRATCH ART
Four to six

Procedure Wax crayons can provide the simple basis for this entertaining artwork game. Cover a sheet of fairly stiff paper with different crayon colors, then crayon over that with black. Your child can then create patterns by scratching through the black to the multi-colored layers below with his fingernail.

Value
CREATIVITY This game helps to develop creative thought more than many art techniques because the child tends to think more about making a pattern than the technique.
MANUAL SKILL

MAGIC PICTURES
Two to six years

Procedure The Indonesian dyeing technique of batik provides the basis of a painting game with a delightful element of magic. Draw a pattern on ordinary paper with a wax candle (do not light it) and then have your child paint the entire sheet with watercolor. The paint will not adhere where there is wax on the paper and so the invisible pattern will be revealed. The child may not realize the connection between the wax pattern and the final picture for some time.

Value
DISCOVERY

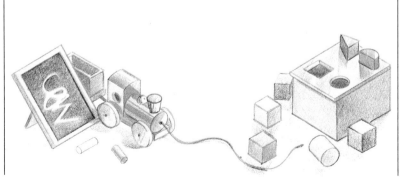

Procedure Little children love inconsequential jokes, and silly word combinations will delight them. For "That's silly", you make up a nonsense sentence such as *"For breakfast today we had: fish with hats on".* He has to reply with something equally silly in the same format, for example *"For lunch today we had: eggs with shoes on".* You reply, *"For supper this evening, we'll have: teddy bears on toast",* and so on.

Value
LANGUAGE Although the language is silly, the game encourages him to think about word combinations – and shows that language can be fun.
TURN-TAKING The alternation in this game is a useful building block for social interaction and basic conversation. *See page 35.*
PRACTICAL This is an invaluable game for keeping little children occupied in the doctor's waiting room, waiting for a bus or on a long car journey.

LANGUAGE

One of the most endearing features of your child's chatter is the way it reveals his thought processes. Language reflects the way in which a child sees the world, and the first words and ideas expressed by children, whether English, Russian or Kenyan, have much in common.

Children see the world in simple terms, so it is not surprising that first words are often concerned with simple actions: they tell us what they and other people are doing: "Mommy sit down" or "Car brrm". They talk of possessions, especially their own possessions, "My car", "My coat", "Mommy shoe", and they find words to discuss their current obsessions, such as putting one object inside another. Events at meal times account, perhaps, for them asking for more and telling us food has "All gone". Finally they use "this", "that" or their baby language equivalents to label or emphasize another word.

By two, most children will say about 50 words and understand many more, but before he can express ideas and relationships, he must acquire grammar – the rules of language. No one gives grammar classes for two-year-olds, but you will notice rudimentary rules governing his language as soon as he starts putting words together. In some languages the subject and object of a sentence are indicated by an ending or a tag word, but in English word order is frequently used for the purpose. Take the sentence "The dog bites the man": the subject "dog" goes before the verb, and the object "man" after it. Transpose the order and the sentence takes on a radically different meaning. When English-speaking children begin to form sentences they usually obey this rule. They say "Eat dinner", not "Dinner eat". You would expect him to have picked up this correct grammar from listening to you – but it is not the entire explanation: he is quite capable of using ungrammatical word combinations such as "Bye-bye hot" and "All gone sticky". Basic grammatical ability seems at least in part to be programmed in, and it develops on several fronts: very soon he will use word order to indicate possession: "My brother's dog" could easily be muddled by a child into "My dog's brother", but likely as not he will get this order right; he's much more likely to say "Mommy dress" than "Dress mommy", too.

Pivots
He will have a few select words that he uses rather like verbs, and all of his sentences will contain one such word. The technical

term for these is pivots, and the rest of his vocabulary is described as "open class" words, all of which can be combined with the pivots. He says "Bye-bye bus", "Bye-bye dog" and "Bye-bye daddy", or "All gone bus" or "All gone dinner". It is interesting that he usually uses pivots in the same place in each sentence: that is, they obey grammatical rules. This shows that he is developing a grammar right from the start, and that he is not just simplifying what he hears.

This means, of course, that you can assist his language development simply by speaking to him often. The quantity of speech to which he is exposed, rather than the content, is the key factor although it will help if you can simplify what you say – something you will in any case tend to do naturally. In fact, so inborn is the knack of simplifying that even a four-year-old will speak in simple terms to a younger child.

His errors of language reveal a great deal about the way he learns. After a visit to the zoo he tells you with great excitement "I goed to the sheeps" – a sentence you know he has never heard you say, but which, in its way, is quite clever. If "sheep" took a regular plural, and "go" a regular past tense, the sentence could have been grammatically correct. The error tells us that he knows how to form the plural by adding an s, and the past tense by adding -ed: that he has learned the grammar, but not yet its exceptions. From such "clever" errors it has been established that in the early learning stages children use the past tense -ed for activities of brief duration that have a definite end, as in "dropped", and "jumped", and only later use them for activities such as "walked". We know, too, that once he learns the rule he can apply it to new words: tell him his bear is "wumping" and he can tell you that he just wumped.

Take a step further
English-speaking children develop these rules in a certain order: first they learn the regular plural ending of s and the progressive -ing on verbs. Then "in" and "on" begin to appear, together with the articles "a" and "the". The past tense follows, but it is some time before children can use "is", "was", "were" and "are" correctly. This is not surprising, for they must know about the past and about plurals before they can solve this problem.

Obviously, he cannot express ideas he does not have; his language must reflect his current understanding. He will use the plural as his numerical sense develops, "in" and "on" as he becomes interested in the relationship between objects, and the past tense as his memory and interest in past events develop.

His span of attention is still relatively short, and this limits the

SMALL AS A PIN
Three to five years

Procedure There is a popular story for children by Ruth Ainsworth about when Charles "was as small as a pin" which you can use as a basis for a creative talking game in quiet moments. Like "That's silly", it depends on nonsense word combinations. You start by saying *"When I was as small as a pin: my bed was . . . a matchbox".* Or *"When I was as small as a pin: I used to live in a shoe box".* The eventual aim is for him to reply in a similar way, for example *"When I was as big as a house . . ."* – but taking turns in this way is difficult, and you will need to lead him for probably quite a while.

Value
LANGUAGE Putting new word combinations together makes him think about meaning. CONCEPTUAL He will develop a better understanding of big and small. STIMULATING THE IMAGINATION

RHYME OUT
Three to five years

Procedure Once a child becomes thoroughly familiar with simple nursery rhymes and can repeat them confidently, say a rhyme through, but substitute silly words here and there. His job is to correct you.

Value
LANGUAGE Breaking the familiar pattern makes him listen closely.

MR CAT AND MR BEAR
Three to five years

Procedure You ask him, *"Find me . . . a blue car . . ., Mr Cat".* He points to a blue car (or whatever object you have asked for) and says, *"Look over there, Mr Bear!"* Then it is his turn to say, *"Find me . . . a red bus . . ., Mr Bear",* and you reply, *"Look at that, Mr Cat!"* Make it as easy as possible to find the object you ask for – look towards it as you ask. If he finds the reply a little hard at first, just ask him to point.

Value
VISUAL
LANGUAGE
TURN-TAKING
SHORT-TERM MEMORY

length of his sentences. He cannot organize a long sentence because he cannot hold it all in his mind at once. However, he can often circumvent this problem by using two or three short utterances. Instead of "This car is going to the store" he will say "This car", "car go", "go store". If this seems odd, think how much easier it is to follow short sentences than complex ones. As his span of attention increases, he will be able to hold more information in his mind at any one time and his sentence will lengthen. As he grows better at planning in general, he will be better able to plan his speech and his language will become more complex. By the time he is five, he will speak at length and almost completely grammatically.

He will learn much simply from listening to your speech, but several underlying factors such as memory and attention span will also govern his progress, and these must develop in parallel with language. Anything that assists their development will help him now, and this means games that challenge his memory and rhymes that stretch his span of attention. So, too, will anything that encourages him to think in a logical way. In observing a grammar he is looking for rules, and rules apply to so many things that he does. Let him explore and discover the laws that govern the world about him, let him learn to classify objects into categories, such as smooth or rough, and their names will follow.

Memory games are actually very simple to play wherever you happen to be – excellent fillers for dull moments. You may perhaps find them dull, but he will not. Probably the most valuable and serviceable basic memory game is to lay out a selection of say half a dozen objects on a flat surface and ask him to examine them for as long as he likes. Then ask him to shut his eyes while you remove one object. When he opens his eyes, he tries to guess what is missing. To start with, you will probably have to help him with clues, but as his memory improves, you can increase the number of objects, shorten the time given for memorizing, and indeed remove more than one object simultaneously. Some children start responding to this game at three years, some even earlier; others will not do so – for the best of reasons – until the fifth year, or later. As with any form of game that you perceive as being important and challenging for his mental development, avoid putting him under pressure. Make it a game, not an exam; even if you are disappointed in his progress, don't show him your disappointment. Relaxation and hilarity should take their place, as with any other form of play.

Rhymes, songs and books now play a specific role not only in developing but in elaborating his language. When you read him a simple story, he follows the train of your thought, which encourages him to stretch his span of attention. After, he will want to hold the information in his mind in an organized fashion, and that means exercising his memory. If he can do that, he can re-live the story in his make-believe world, re-creating it in his own way, just as he does the adult speech he hears from hour to hour.

In the pre-school years, all play is accompanied by language, and nursery school teachers often regard organized games as an excuse for talking. But pretense must be the supreme example of how language and play combines: for a game of make-believe cannot help but have a structure and few children play these games without speaking to themselves and others. Above all else, encourage him to pretend, for in doing so he can practice language; sort out the rules that govern relationships; organize his thoughts; seek, at his own pace, for reasons, and deal in abstractions.

SPOT THE DIFFERENCE
Three to five years

Procedure There are many different observation games, but this is one of the most valuable. To play, draw a simple picture – trace it from a child's coloring book if you cannot draw. Then trace this drawing to make another copy, but alter one detail. Ask him to spot the difference between the two drawings. Make the difference very obvious at first, for this game is less easy for children than it might seem.

Value
READING Appreciation of detail provides valuable grounding for his first efforts at reading.

Later progress To foster the development of reading skills at a later stage, try drawing two lines of big, bold letters (perhaps six in each) with one letter different. He will have no idea of what the letters mean, nor is it important. But this will help him to become familiar with letters and to look for the differences between them.

SIMON SAYS
Two to four years

Procedure "Simon says" is an old favorite usually played with slightly older children, but in simplified form, the two-to-four age group may, in fact, enjoy it more and learn more from it. It is an ideal game for groups. You start by saying *"Simon says, put your hands on your head"*, and demonstrate. The children must copy. You then repeat for other actions. Let all the children have a turn at being Simon, and let them use their own name instead.

Value
OBSERVATION Each child must watch Simon closely.
LEARNING By copying closely, a child develops an important learning technique.
LANGUAGE Describing each action and helping the child perform it helps language development.

MAKE-BELIEVE

The pre-school years are the years of make-believe. Nothing is as it seems, and even she may not be the person you think she is. The main arguments in my household are about pretending: "I don't want it to be a boat" or "Lions *can* climb trees" are the cries to which we wake some mornings. But more often we eavesdrop on games that go on from morning to morning. Typical of them is boats and beds. Quite why children with perfectly good beds should want to get up at six to make "pretend" beds with chair cushions and bits of old carpet is not clear, nor why they should then immediately get into these beds and pretend to go to sleep: but they do. Of course, the game does not stop here: at three and five years of age their pretend is elaborate. They leave their beds to go shopping, to make breakfast, and sit solemnly drinking tea and eating pretend toast and talking in "grown-up" ways.

For some children, pretend play is social play, and it never occurs when they are playing alone. Other children live in their own world from morning to night: a world that other children can enter in most cases, but sometimes an exclusive world. I once watched a small girl play the most elaborate game with mattresses and pillows. The pillows were horses, cars, shopping bags and friends. She cooked meals and read books to them. She even tucked the pillows up in bed. She did not shun other children, but would always escape quite quickly to her own world. I watched her for the best part of a week, and in all this time her make-believe world was never shared. But she was, I think, unusual in this respect, an only child who suffered badly from asthma. She was obviously used to amusing herself; many children share their worlds with others if they can. But you should not worry if your child seems to prefer playing in this way alone. It is unlikely to be an indication of anxiety or disturbance unless you have noticed other symptoms as well.

Why do they do it? No one is sure, but there are clues. Children begin to pretend as they begin to speak, their pretense elaborating as their language (and thought) becomes more elaborate, reaching a peak in the late pre-school years. Pretense then begins to decline, so that by the time she is eight or nine it plays a minor role. Children from deprived backgrounds often speak much later than other children, and their pretend play is similarly delayed, peaking at about seven or eight, but whether or not there is a relationship between language development and pretense is far from proven. It seems more likely, however, that

MY HOUSE
Two to four years

Procedure Pretend houses usually figure large in a child's pretend play at this stage. She will probably build her own in due course, but you ought to have ideas up your sleeve to help her on her way.

Value
MAKE-BELIEVE
CONSTRUCTION SKILLS
SECURITY Her house is a barrier against the outside world.

WALK LIKE A MONKEY
Four to six years

Procedure This is another game ideal either for single children or large groups. The idea is to imitate the way various animals move. For a monkey, they walk on all fours with straight arms; a frog hops on all fours; a crab crawls sideways; a penguin has arms stiff and feet turned out; a kangaroo jumps forward, legs together and upper arms tucked in; and so on.

Value
STIMULATING THE
IMAGINATION
LEARNING Copying is a valuable learning technique.
FUN – particularly if you make appropriate noises as well.

pretense is related to thought processes that progress in parallel with language. As she pretends, she is manipulating – playing experimentally with – ideas, thoughts and emotions, and acting out her relationships with others.

Some children use pretense to work through emotional problems, others to sort out relationships with parents and friends, but it would be foolish to read too much into most children's pretend games. They will usually reflect not much more than current interests, what is happening at home and at school, and the way the child looks at the world.

Dressing up

Children pretend to be cars or trains, dogs and cats, but most of all they pretend to be "grown up". A cowboy suit or a policeman's hat may help with this illusion, but the best dressing-up clothes are adult cast-offs. I find most of ours at garage sales. You can always spot mothers of small children at garage sales – they are the ones who grab the gold shoes and sequinned tube tops, and hunt for the lace curtains and flared skirts to make into capes.

Capes of any description are among the best dressing-up clothes and can transform a child in a moment, into a bride, superman, or a princess. For the small child there is nothing quite like hats. The smallest child is capable of putting them on and taking them off, and adult hats are big enough to enclose a child in her own world. In my experience, Indian feathers and policemen's helmets have never been as successful as old wedding veils, or ancient furs. I can still remember the joy of possessing, as a child, an ancient fox collar.

Clothes are of course the main props for being grown up, but an old razor (without the blade) and a shaving brush will help the role of "daddy", and a handbag and some high-heeled shoes will assist the role of "mommy". (No matter that you go around in flat shoes with a backpack; children are great believers in stereotypes.) If you habitually carry a briefcase or shopping basket, make sure there is one in the dressing-up box, together with any other props she will need to be "you".

Nursery school teachers find that many children hate dressing-up clothes that have to be pulled over their heads, and that outfits that they can slip into, such as cloaks and aprons, are in much greater demand than dresses. If you make dressing-up clothes, bear this in mind and remember that Velcro fastenings are the easiest for small hands. And don't forget the potential of the humble carton: the photograph on page 114 is an example of what can be done with very little trouble.

Props for pretend

The weekend shopping is always eagerly awaited in our house: a shopping spree means two or three cardboard cartons, and even quite small children like sitting in cartons, or crawling through the tunnel you can make if the bottom is opened. Cartons can have windows and doors cut into them, but just plain boxes have great potential.

Next to boxes, dining chairs are probably the best props for pretend play. A row of chairs makes a boat, train or even a plane in which to ride away to another world. Rugs are often used for vehicles too, and for islands and camps. Big, deep chairs and settees make camps and castles, or forts from which to start a war. Children often fish for crocodiles, or keep a look-out from their boats in shark-infested water.

House play

Home is something that children understand, and the routines of living are so universal that even children who do not know each other well can share in play that mimics them. A child playing alone may even take each role in turn, changing voices as she is in turn mommy, daddy and the baby herself.

A single corner is space enough for playing house. A house is protection from the outside world, and her play house must offer this same protection. A blanket or a curtain will do, a screen would be better. In my experience, most of the cardboard play houses on the market are rather too small for satisfying house play.

As you watch them in this type of pretend play, you may notice that girls are sometimes surer of the feminine role than boys of the masculine one. Perhaps this is because many mothers still have a clearer role inside the home than fathers, either in real life or in television. I remember being told by my four-year-old that only daddies went to work. When I pointed out to him that I had worked since he was a baby, he seemed genuinely surprised, as if it had only just struck him that women are not always at home.

Friends

My young son had two well-loved friends Gilla and Gulla who went everywhere with him. Both friends always wanted what he wanted and were often extremely naughty when no one was looking. They were scapegoats – the ones who had helped themselves to cookies or apples behind my back – but they were also his companions while his sister was temporarily at nursery school. He had always played with her and probably did not know how to play without friends – so he created them. As soon as he had his

MY SHOP
Three years on

Procedure Most young children love to play at being adult, and doing adult jobs in a make-believe shop will keep her occupied for hours. Save all the empty packages you can for her grocery store – but let her build up her own stock too. Provide her with a large box for a counter and an egg-carton to hold all the money – later on, you can buy a toy cash register if she enjoys playing shop. Give her some loose change to put in the "register" – plastic money is no cheaper in the long run, and real money has an attractive authenticity. Call on the shop every now and then: no shop can function without customers.

Value
MAKE BELIEVE The precise value of make-believe games is still to be firmly established (see text), but it is thought that they encourage conceptual development – that is, the growth of ideas.
CONSTRUCTIVE Building and arranging the display of stock provides experience of practical creative skills.
MATHEMATICAL Exchanging money gives the opportunity to demonstrate counting – but see pages 146–151.

Variations She can build all kinds of different shops with different props – shoes for shoe shops, dough cakes for cake shops, old Christmas cards for card shops, and so on.

CARDBOARD
CASTLES
Four years on

Procedure Rubbish can
have greater appeal to
children as a
construction material
than manufactured kits.
Cardboard boxes are
perhaps the best
appreciated of all. With
a range of cardboard
boxes, some strong
masking tape, paste and
paint, a child can make
tractors, trains, boats,
cars, spaceships and
anything else you can
think of. An element of
make-believe can add an
extra dimension to these
models and it is well
worth making up a story
to go with one. For a
group, a medieval castle
has almost unlimited
potential. Set the scene
by relating how the King
has been kidnapped by
the Black Prince and
imprisoned in the grim
Castle of Doom. The
children must then make
their suits of armor and
build the castle, before
laying siege to it and, at
last, knocking it down.
Remember to assign a
specific role to each
child.

Value
CONSTRUCTIVE Making
the armor and the castle
demands both ingenuity
and manual skill.
MAKE-BELIEVE Each
child has to act out his or
her role.
FUN The final
destruction of the castle
will be riotous.

sister to play with all day again his friends "got squashed by a truck" and were never mentioned again.

Dolls and teddy bears

Some children of this age have imaginary friends who share their play, others have dolls or teddy bears. For some children a doll or bear might also become a comfort object, something to cuddle when sad, to hold close when nervous, to lie with in bed at night; for some, a blanket, towel or cloth diaper may have the same function. However, the most creative role of doll- or bear-play is in developing the relationship between child and the adult world. At three, this means between her and her parents, but when she starts day care or school it will include her teachers too.

In real life, a child's role is nearly always one of being told what she can or cannot do, but in this world of play, *she* makes the rules. There are many things she does not understand about adult relationships: people quarrel, pay attention to others rather than her, or talk on the phone when she wants a drink. To compensate, she puts herself in control of her dolls: she loves them, she is cross with them, and she makes them go to bed before they have finished their game. In doing so, she investigates what it is like to feel and to act as you do, and so to learn about – and come to terms with – relationships.

Guns

I know a child who was not allowed to have a gun, so he built one out of Lego, and Sunday walks in the local woods became a search for gun-shaped sticks. In the end, his mother lifted the ban and bought a gun and some caps for him: within three weeks the obsession was over and he rarely played with guns after that.

Children learn pretend-play involving guns from watching other children, and if your child is exposed to it there is nothing you can do. Children are great conformists, taking more and more of their values from their peers as they grow up. This is as it should be: we cannot dominate their thinking. Early gun-play does not reflect any real violence: "bang-bang – you're dead" is a fantasy game; the child is no more dead than there are crocodiles in the bath. Abhorrence of this type of play is, however, still a powerful reaction in many parents, and if you feel like this it may be worth reflecting that gun-play is, at least, a game of trust. One child shouts "You're dead", and the child usually falls down; but if he calls back "You missed", there is usually no argument. The shooter accepts that his aim was bad. Trust is an important element in the social play of children. Play can be rough – but rarely too rough. If one child wants to stop playing roughly, it

STAR WARS/*Four years on*

This game involves making an "asteroid gun" to fire ping-pong balls at a night sky of paper plate planets, guided only by a flashlight. The idea is to hit the DOOMWORLD of the evil red dwarf "Deadly" Sirius III. Although this involves a degree of gun play, the essence of the game is in the making, and in building up a story to create a complete space fantasy. The excitement of playing by flashlight provides a suitable climax.

Materials

● For asteroid gun: ping-pong balls, 1¾-in (4.4-cm) plastic pipe, strong rubber band, old pencil, pen light.
● For the night sky: old wallpaper, paper plates, glitter, egg carton
● For spacesuit and ship: strong cardboard box, foil, cocoa tin lids, egg cartons.
● Glue, fluorescent acrylic paints (to be used *only* by parents), non-toxic poster paints (for children), scissors, cotton.

A child can make the asteroids by dipping ping-pong balls in a bowl of poster paint. They can then be dried on a rack made from strands of cotton strung tightly about ½ in (1.25 cm) apart across an old can. The planets are paper plates painted by parents with fluorescent paints and dangled against a dark blue or black background on cotton threads. He can paint the sky and create stars and galaxies by sprinkling it with glitter while the paint is still wet and splashing tiny spots of white paint from the end of a brush.
Doomworld is simply a paper plate with the trays from egg cartons stuck on and painted red and black.

Value

IMAGINATIVE FORM OF GUN PLAY; CREATIVE; MANUAL AND CRAFT SKILLS; HAND-EYE CO-ORDINATION; FUN

The asteroid gun should be made by parents and the child together. Cut a ping-pong ball-sized loading hole about 4 in (10 cm) from one end of 1¾-in (4.4-cm) diameter plastic pipe. Make a plunger with a ping-pong ball stuck on an old ball-point pen tube, guided by a narrow aperture in a disc of cardboard stuck to the end of the pipe. A strong rubber band provides the propulsion. Paint in bright colors.

The spaceship can be made by a child as simply or elaborately as he wishes, starting with a strong wooden or card box, and using silver foil, cocoa tin lids, egg cartons and paint to make it look as much like a spacecraft as possible.

The final assault:

when all is complete, switch off all lights except the pen-light strapped to the asteroid gun. The goal is to hit Doomworld with a succession of asteroids, but this will be a challenge for a child of five, so the other planets must be hung close together (and close to the spaceship) so that there is a good chance of hitting them instead.

TIGER HUNT
Four to six years

Procedure This is an elaborate make-believe game best played with a small group, though you can play with just one child. The idea is to mime a hunt for a ferocious man-eating tiger – it must be netted and brought back to the zoo. You really need a fairly large room, or, better still, a backyard. You lead the expedition and describe what you are doing and the children must follow. A good hunt might involve: climbing a hill; hacking your way through the jungle; swinging across a crocodile-infested river on a rope; spotting the tiger; crawling through the long grass; stalking the tiger; netting it; and marching home again. When they get the hang of it, let the children take turns leading.

Value
MAKE-BELIEVE
MUSCULAR CONTROL
The children begin to think about exactly what their bodies are doing and exert precise control.

usually stops without question. If an older child plays a rough game with a smaller child, he will usually handicap himself to make it fair. If you watch a mother cat playing with her kittens, or a father boxing with his son, you will see exactly the same thing happening.

It was not so much the violence of gun-play that bothered me, but the divisive underlying ethos of goodies and baddies, of "us" and "them". But experience of three children has taught me that this is not much more than a child's way of expressing emotion. They have friends they love, and peers they hate; even the plants in our garden are divided radically between "good" plants and "horrid" weeds, and the insects between "good" bees, worms and ladybirds, and "horrible" wasps, slugs and mosquitoes.

And the fact remains that in children's war games, both sides remain friends: if only adults played in this way.

BUILDING

Three or more years of near-constant practice have given him hands that are able to do much of what he wishes them to do, but there is still plenty to learn. Quality construction toys will now further develop the use of hands, fingers and eyes *together*. Remember they are *his* hands and *his* eyes and only he can learn to co-ordinate them. In this context your role is relatively effortless. You simply encourage him – and this means providing the toys, the environment and occasional praise. He will not need detailed instruction. If he does not like to play alone, better to work, read, or play beside him than tell him what to do; occasional help, though, is obviously in order. Key operations – twisting and turning, screwing and unscrewing, pushing together and pulling apart, placing and balancing – are quickly and simply demonstrated. In building play he will absorb many simple scientific and mathematical principles, but without understanding them in any formal sense. He does not understand mechanics or the principles of squaring and cubing numbers, but he can tell you that round shapes roll and square ones stay where he puts them. He may even know that if he replaces a square block measuring 2×2 in with others 1×1 in, he will need four to cover the same surface area and eight to cover the same volume. If asked why, he will look puzzled; understanding the principles will come later, but they will come more easily if he is simply introduced now to area, volume and gravity in action.

Building blocks

For the pre-school years, color is less important than shape and size; extend his original set so that he has about 60 blocks, including some pillars and arches. Check that the blocks fit together well: they should all be to scale so that the large blocks are multiples of the small, and arches and pillars can be matched in height with other blocks. This not only makes building less frustrating but teaches him about volume, size and elementary multiplication. If you intend to make your own blocks, bear this in mind: quality wooden blocks are expensive because they are made in carefully planned sizes, with smooth surfaces and accurate angles.

Store blocks in their own container, perhaps a strong wastepaper basket or a draw-string bag, not in a general toy box, where they tend to get lost. A small drawer, or box on wheels, would be even better: 60 wooden blocks are quite heavy.

TOWER BLOCK
Two to six years

Procedure Building towers with wooden blocks is of course a perennial activity for children. Don't let its apparent simplicity fool you into underestimating its value. Use the right blocks (see text) and don't start a child off with too many. Three or four is plenty for first experiments. Show him how to put one block on top of another and, once in a while, build up a tall tower so that he can have the fun of knocking it over. Leave him to experiment with the three or four blocks, and don't expect much progress – unless the child happens to have an exceptional aptitude for building.

Much more sophisticated building is done by three-year-olds, who are capable of building entire cities if they have enough blocks. Dolls and creatures are often added at this point as well.

Value
MANIPULATIVE SKILL
CONCEPTUAL The awareness that a new object can be created by building from a number of units is a major discovery.
IMAGINATION

GLUES AND PASTES
Two on

Types of glue The best type of commercially available glue is white glue. This is non-toxic, easy to use and is clear when dry. More important, it is easy to sponge off most surfaces when newly applied. When dry, it can usually be peeled off. If it gets on woollens, put the garment in the freezer overnight; the glue can be picked off the next morning. Use cold water to wipe it off, not hot, and keep it cold. Hot water simply sets it.

A cheap home-made paste can be made according to the following recipe.
One handful of flour
Add water until gooey
Add a pinch of salt
Alternatively, for boiled paste:
½ cup flour
Add water until it is as thick as light cream
Simmer and stir for five minutes
Add food coloring
Store in a refrigerator in airtight jar

Brushes Never use paint brushes for gluing; they are wasteful of glue and impossible to clean properly. Proper glue brushes are better, but glue in bottles with screw-top applicator spouts are better still.

At two he will simply pile up the blocks, but by four he will have a definite structure in mind. That structure will be vague, and will probably change as he builds, but as he grows older this visualization of what he wants to build becomes more precise, and elaborate. He will become more skilled at placing blocks and will know at once which shapes fit together. If quality blocks are essential for these games, so is the right building surface. He will, ideally, need a flat surface both to build on and on which to lay out his blocks. The floor is ideal, but not if it is carpeted – the longer the pile, the more unsuitable it is. A table is the obvious answer, but an area of floor with a fairly smooth close-piled carpet may give him more scope. If conditions are less than ideal, supply a sheet of plywood – but remember too that not all children mind if their buildings fall over, and most children will make them fall on purpose.

Nursery schools often have sets of very large building blocks which can be made into extra-large constructions. Excellent for enclosures and walls for hiding behind, they seem to stimulate social and imaginative play more than building for its own sake. Unfortunately they are expensive; there are large cardboard blocks, which cost considerably less – though they are still not cheap.

There is nothing quite like an enclosure for stimulating imaginative play. Perhaps the wall between his world and the real world gives him a sense of security.

Left to their own devices, many children find ample building materials in a normal household. If you provide glue (see margin) and tape, he will make use of furniture, rugs, cans and grocery boxes. You may even find he makes roads and hills out of his food at meal times. Household goods of various sorts make excellent construction kits: spring clothes pins can be put together in interesting ways, and monsters can be made with a few slices of potato and a box of tooth picks. If you are thinking of buying him a construction kit, try him with those first: the wrong kit at the wrong time can be an expensive mistake.

Construction kits

Construction kits come in a bewildering variety of types and sizes, and different kits open up different realms of fantasy. The rods and discs of Tinker Toy encourage one sort of fantasy, the blocks and wheels of Lego another. Some make very large models and others can be used on a tabletop. The middle-sized kit is usually the best with which to start. Be guided by the age range on the box, and don't be tempted to buy kits too soon: the ages given are rarely conservative. If you guess wrongly and find he

PIPE-CLEANER PEOPLE
Four to six years

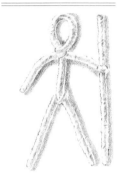

Procedure Pipe cleaners can be an excellent substitute for simpler construction kits. They can be bought in a range of different colors and twisted together to make little men and women – or even animals, trees, cars, or houses. Give the game a structure by using the models to tell a story about a visit to the circus or zoo – the models can be made accordingly.

Value
MANIPULATIVE SKILL DISCOVERY This simple form of sculpture teaches him about the shape of the object he models.

Variation
See STRAW DOGS, *page 115.*

shows little interest, put the kit away for later use: a new toy can be enormously stimulating if he is ready for it, but may be classified as dull if it hangs around gathering dust on the shelf.

Many manufacturers sell kits that the child is supposed to build in a particular order. Often this is a marketing gimmick to encourage parents to buy additional sets at regular intervals. This is of course fairly harmless if the child has a basic set of that particular brand. But remember that few pre-school children can follow the instructions for a model of more than ten pieces. Some kits are designed to make one particular car or truck; sometimes the parts cannot be used with other kits, but such "one-shot" models are generally much easier for a four-year-old to make, and the final products often impressive. Most such kits come complete with special hammers, screwdrivers and wrenches, and involve building in a specified sequence. This suits some children better than others. If he is frustrated by his inability to execute the models of his dreams, these "one-shot" kits are probably the answer, and even if he is happy with his own building abilities, he may enjoy using tools "like grown-ups". The models make excellent toys when assembled, too. Following the instructions will be difficult without your help, but it is a skill well worth acquiring. Later he can progress to making complex models such as battleships and airliners.

Ultimately, your view of construction kits could well be crystallized by cost. They are expensive if you start a child on them when young, but if a child takes to them, the cost per hour of play may turn out to be negligible. I don't think a child would be very much deprived if he never played with a commercially-made construction kit, provided similar opportunities were presented in different forms.

You don't have to be particularly ingenious. I know a child of two and a half whose father gave him an old motorcycle engine and a set of wrenches to play with while he repaired the aging family car. The mother thought her husband was mad and neither parent expected the boy to show real interest beyond pretending to mend his engine. They were both wrong: for weeks the boy rushed to the garage as soon as breakfast was over to do his "work". His father would loosen the bolts a little, and made sure nothing heavy could land on his feet, and watched him slowly but surely take the engine apart.

Children like to mimic adults. If you type, they will want to learn too; if you spend hours on the phone, so will they – and if you make pots, mend engines, or build tables and chairs, they will want to copy your skills. Don't underestimate how well they may do it. The corny old saying about children following in their parents' footsteps has more than a measure of truth, largely because they grow interested in their parents' skills when playing at their feet.

Models from odds and ends

A collection of household odds and ends, a bottle of glue, a quiet corner and the average three- or four-year-old will create some weird and wonderful things. Many of us have seen children leaving nursery school proudly carrying creations made from boxes, trays and cardboard tubing. Many a child who avoids construction kits will readily make such models.

Constructing from odds and ends practices rather different skills from simple building. The child does not have to fit things together with quite the same precision – the glue and tape will allow him to make structures that would be impossible with blocks. In other ways he has to be more precise: he has to fit and hold the sticky surfaces together, and to put on tape without getting it tied into knots. The manual skills are quite as challenging, but he will not learn about half sizes, or quarters, in the way that he intuitively does when building with blocks or construction kits.

Most models will not stay together without being glued, and as a result require more visualization than block and construction kit creations. He will find it helpful to clearly visualize his final structure before beginning, although many children prefer to build as they go without a final product in mind.

Try to make collecting the odds and ends an enjoyable exercise in itself. You may find your children start earmarking boxes or other items before they are even empty. Have a special carton to collect such useful rubbish, label it clearly and give it special status, thereby adding to the mystique of model-making.

Modeling from odds and ends is a substitute for building with blocks or simple construction kits; making useful, or at any rate usable, objects from rubbish is similar to putting together kits which require a child to follow a set of instructions. The first is "free play", the second is "work" – or at least in principle: few children keep strictly to an agreed plan and, however detailed your instructions, they will be distracted by the nature of their materials in building other objects.

There are literally hundreds of items a child can make with boxes and tubes. Some, such as threading tubes on to a string to make a snake, are simple enough for the three-year-old to complete with little guidance. Others, such as building a house from boxes, are obviously much more complex. Until he can follow instructions, and often even after that, he will need help. Before

CORKERS
Four years on

Procedure If you are a wine-drinker, don't throw the corks away: they are a useful modeling material. Sliced into discs, they can be wheels for cars; painted, they can make a set of checkers; pierced and threaded, they can make "fun" jewelry. Perhaps best of all, they can be made into little boats: cut a sail from sturdy paper and use a toothpick for the mast. Weight the underside with clay. Then, you can play *Corkers*. You need a bowlful of water, placed on a waterproof surface, some plastic straws and the boats. The boats are propelled by blowing through the tubes and the idea is to see who can blow their boat across the bowl and back first.

Value
MANUAL SKILL He helps you make the boats.
FUN

you start, discuss with him what he might make with the bits and pieces you have assembled. Let him enter into the plans; tell him quite simply what the possibilities are and how you would start. Encourage his questions as you proceed.

Making things together can be highly enjoyable, and he can often start on a process such as threading while you see to other more complex tasks. Part of the value of these activities is that he works *with* you, so do not be tempted to do it all by yourself. Sitting together for an extended period, it is easy to see the right moment to tell him the name of a shape, or how something works. With practice you will recognize the moments when a little extra information will be absorbed to best effect.

Don't confuse the value of following instructions with the value of modeling. If he sees possibilities in the materials that you hadn't thought of – or consider unproductive – let him follow his whim. After all, he can follow instructions as you tell him how to wash-up; the experience of making things and handling materials is valuable, whether or not it leads to a recognizable finished product.

STRAW DOGS
Four to six years

Procedure Straws can be used, like pipe cleaners (*see page 112*), to make models of animals, people and things. The bendy straws with accordion sections are ideal for modeling. For more elaborate shapes, straws can be joined together with a two-inch (5-cm) length of pipe cleaner. Pieces of card and dried canneloni threaded on to the straws will increase the scope even further.

Value
MANIPULATIVE SKILL
DISCOVERY

115

OUTDOOR PHYSICAL ACTIVITIES/*Three years on*

As a child grows more confident in his body, it is essential that he gets the chance to exercise developing muscles: at this age, muscle growth accounts for 75 per cent of weight gain. These games are best played in the open air: an enclosed space with a patch of grass is ideal.

Tie a series of objects at different heights along a line between two trees or posts. The child must jump up and touch each one in turn.

A rope tied between two sticks about nine inches (23 cm) from the ground is fun for crawling under or jumping over.

Jumping rope is the old but effective (and social) way of developing jumping and balance skills.

Mark two parallel lines to represent a stream to be leapt over. Increase the width in steps to provide a continuing challenge.

Walking along a rope laid on the ground is a useful way of developing balance. As her balance improves, let her try walking along a log a few inches high.

Props, right, is a fun balancing game The idea is to support yourself on all kinds of different parts of the body – say, two hands and a foot, shoulders and one leg, back only, and so on.

Hopalong, left, is a version of hopscotch (see page 199) for very young children. The child simply hops or runs from one hoop to the next.

Stepthrough entails clasping hands together and stepping through them and back.

Children are not always aware of their own movements. One way, right, of developing this awareness and improving muscular control is playing "mirrors". You and your child face each other. One leads with very slow movements; the other must mirror every move exactly. Take turns leading this activity.

Value
PHYSICAL SKILLS:
BALANCE, CO-
ORDINATION, MUSCULAR
STRENGTH

117

LEARNING TO
THROW

BALL GAMES/*Two years on*

Ball games and childhood are almost inseparable. A child starts to throw and catch things while still in the cradle, but the ability to throw and catch a ball properly develops in stages – illustrated in the margins. Without encouragement, children may make slow progress – and sexual stereotyping sometimes means some girls never get beyond the second stage of throwing.

First stage: *Child stands feet together, holding the ball behind his ear. He then flings it downwards.*

Older children play "hockey" with a squash racket and tennis ball. The player who is "it" uses the racquet to stop the ball from touching his shins. She is not allowed to move her feet, while the others must throw the ball from where it lands. A catch puts the batsman out. For very young children, you can draw a large square on a wall to act as a "goal", and provide a large, soft ball and tennis racket.

Second stage: *Feet are still together, but the hand goes back behind the head and the child twists.*

When a child learns to throw, he can improve his accuracy by a simple version of bowling. Suspend a ball from a tree branch and arrange nine plastic bowling pins in a diamond pattern beneath the ball, but just to one side. The idea is to knock down as many pins as possible in three throws.

Third stage: *He stands sideways; the arm goes right back and he transfers his weight.*

Value
MOTOR SKILLS; SIMPLE
FUN

LEARNING TO CATCH

First stage: *Child stands arms straight out, palms up and tries to clap his hands to catch.*

Second stage: *Soon children learn to bend their arms and clasp a ball to their chests.*

Third stage: *Arms and hands ready to catch; catching with hands alone; bending to absorb its impact.*

A simple game for children at the very earliest throwing and catching stages, this involves you and the child just throwing the ball to each other through a suspended hoop.

Splash: an exuberant game for a hot day. The children stand round a pool and simply try to make each other as wet as possible by throwing the ball hard at the water.

119

SPOT THE MOUSE
Two to four years

Procedure Some adults love to look for the little mouse or other tiny distinguishing mark that certain artists put in all their pictures and you can make this hunt into an entertaining children's game. Some illustrators deliberately include such repeated motifs in children's books, but you can still play with books that do not have such motifs. As you read the book with her, you can get her to look, for instance, at the shoes everyone in the pictures is wearing, or spot all the lights, or the church on the horizon – in other words, the details you would normally ignore.

Value
VISUAL The close scrutiny needed to "spot the mouse" develops her awareness of detail. READING An appreciation of detail provides valuable grounding for her first attempts at reading.

BOOKS FOR TWO- TO SIX-YEAR-OLDS

For the under-twos, books are chosen for their patterns, their sounds, their colors and for the close shared activity they bring. They are for teaching a child that there is pleasure in conversation, and pleasure in reading: they are not yet sources of information. But although two is obviously too young to look up some fact in a book, it is not too young to begin to learn that books are sources of information: after all, this is an essential aspect of printed matter. Let her see you consulting reference books, and in time she will consult them, too. Everyone looks up the odd recipe, or checks telephone numbers. At first your example need be no more than this, but later you can buy her information books to look at as well as stories. She needs facts as well as fantasy for a well-rounded development.

At two, she will still enjoy her baby books, the simple pictures, the catalogues and the rhymes. She will make more and more of the conversational opportunities they offer – no need to coax her now.

The pattern of sounds
She will still enjoy the pattern and rhythm of language, even though she can only partially understand it, and may listen as you sit and read her epic poems – especially if you emphasize the meter: try Victorian parlor poetry as a change from nursery rhymes. Soon she will have enough understanding of language to enjoy very simple stories if they are supported by the right kind of pictures, and by three she will be ready for rather more complex stories and rhymes.

At two, the language of her stories should be simple and predictable, and the pictures should support the stories, helping rather than hindering her understanding. If she cannot follow the story, she will follow a catch phrase: she will "huff and puff" to blow the house down, or join in with the Gingerbread Man to shout "Run, run as fast as you can, you can't catch me, I'm the Gingerbread Man". Each verse in Nadine Bernard Westcott's version of *I Know An Old Lady Who Swallowed a Fly*[1] ends in the same satisfying way:

"I know an old lady who swallowed a fly.
I don't know why she swallowed a fly.
Perhaps she'll die."

In Margaret Wise Brown's gentle masterpiece, *Goodnight Moon*[2] the objects in the room are named in simple repetition and rhyme:

"Goodnight kittens
Goodnight mittens
Goodnight clocks
And goodnight socks."
And in Wanda Gag's *Millions of Cats*[3] the story is enhanced by a delightful catch phrase:
"Hundreds of cats,
Thousands of cats,
Millions and billions and trillions of cats."
(The numbers after each title are a reference guide for the list of publishers given on page 124.) Stories such as this, which repeat phrases again and again, are excellent because she can listen to the pattern even if she misses the thread of the story. Margaret Wise Brown's *The Runaway Bunny*,[4] Bernard Most's *If the Dinosaurs Came Back*[5] and Pat Hutchins' *Good Night Owl*[6] and *Titch*[7] are modern books that use this technique; or try some of the simple classics such as *Chicken Licken*[8] or *Little Red Hen*.[9]

Books in verse
Some parents enjoy reading books written in verse, and others loathe them. They are popular with many two- and three-year-olds. I have a friend who spent three weeks in a hotel room in Brazil with only *Bunny Fluff's Moving Day*[10] to read. Her two small children were delighted, as mine were when she passed the book on to me, although it is not a book I would have selected myself. A few readings and you find (to your horror) that you can say it off by heart. Many of the Dr Seuss books have this same compulsive rhythm (and some appalling rhymes); but the formula works well for most children – at least with the earlier books. Even if you are not very keen on verse, you may like Beatrix Potter's *Apply Dapply's Nursery Rhymes*[11] and *The Wind Blew*[12] by Pat Hutchins.

It is obviously much easier to read stories that you enjoy, but in the long run a child must, and will, choose books that give her pleasure. You will find as she gets older that your tastes do not always coincide. Often, a successful author has found a formula that suits children rather more than their parents. Adults have sometimes disparaged Harry Allard's Stupid series, and the humorous tales about Stanley Q. Stupid and his family have often appeared on the list of banned books compiled by the American Library Association. Yet *The Stupids Step Out*,[13] *The Stupids Die*[14] (because when the lights go out in their house they figure they must be dead), and *The Stupids Have a Ball*[15] are appealing and fun for children. Other authors hit upon a formula that pleases parents but not children.

ACTION RHYMES
Two to five years

Procedure Other games have shown how acting out stories can bring them to life, but with nursery rhymes you can add another dimension. Nursery rhymes depend for their effect on their simple, regular rhythm. If you tie actions in to this rhythm, the child can create a controlled sequence of dance-like actions. Start with the familiar spoken rhyme such as "Humpty Dumpty sat on a wall" and then progress to the simple action songs, such as "Here we go round the Mulberry Bush". Make sure the child or children sing the words with you; it will help them to keep the rhythm.

Value
MUSCULAR CONTROL Moving to a rhythm helps develop muscle control.
SEQUENCING Following a set order of actions helps children become familiar with sequences, an essential pre-requisite for reading and counting.
LANGUAGE The rhythmic repetition of words and phrases increases a child's confidence with language.

At the beginning of her second year, her stories need to be simple with a large proportion of picture to words. To her, the pictures are still the most important part of the book, and you may find that she expects you to turn the page as soon as she has looked at them. She likes you to read, but cannot always follow the story. Each page must therefore be understandable by itself (as many good picture books are), or the story simple and familiar. The Out-and-About series by Helen Oxenbury, with titles such as *The Birthday Party*[16] and *The Check-Up*,[17] uses simple, predictable language to describe ordinary situations in a child's life.

Two- and three-year-olds seem to enjoy having naughty children in their books: this is part of the appeal of Dr Seuss's *The Cat in the Hat*[18] or *Green Eggs and Ham*.[19] H.A. Rey's *Curious George*[20] books, which concern the antics of a monkey who continually gets into trouble, have been perennially popular. *Rotten Ralph*,[21] and others in the series by Jack Gantos, describe the behavior of a truly bad cat and are also easy for children to identify with. A recent survey of children's own top ten books suggests that this fascination continues throughout childhood. At three you will often find that her dolls and teddy bears have done the most outrageously naughty things and have to be spanked and sent to bed. (Even if you do not believe in spanking, she may.)

Looking by herself
Once she can turn thin paper pages by herself, she will almost certainly like to look at more factual books. Zoo and farm animals are popular themes, so are road-making, cars and trucks: Richard Scarry's *Hop Aboard, Here We Go*[23] or *Busy Busy World*[24] must be among the best-known examples. Look, too, for the Usborne picture-word books: words and pictures are often presented in comic-book fashion, naturally encouraging the child to move her eyes back and forth across the page in the correct sequence for reading.

The story gains importance
Gradually, she will begin to follow the train of rather more complex stories: one or two sentences per picture would be a rough rule of thumb, and at this stage a wide choice of excellent books becomes available. Let her help you make the choice.

If you are lucky enough to have a children's book shop, visit it together. Unfortunately, not all book shops let the children handle books, but most libraries let the child choose for herself.

Everyone has their own favorites in this category, but Gene Zion's *Harry the Dirty Dog*[25] or *Corduroy*[26] by Don Freeman, and Arnold Lobel's *Frog and Toad are Friends*[27] must be on many

PUBLISHERS
of books mentioned on pages 120–124; where both hardcover and paperback editions are available, the hardback is given first.

1 Atlantic Monthly Press/Little Brown; 2 Harper and Row; 3 Coward, McCann/ Putnam Publishing Group; 4 Harper and Row; 5 Harcourt Brace Jovanovich; 6, 7 MacMillan; 8, 9, 10 Ladybird Stories Series; 11 Warne; 12 MacMillan; 13, 14, 15 Houghton Mifflin; 16, 17 Dial Books for Young Readers/E.P. Dutton; 18, 19 Beginner; 20, 21, 22 Houghton Mifflin; 23, 24 Western Publishing; 25 Harper and Row; 26 Viking/Penguin Picture Puffin Series; 27 Harper and Row; 28 Viking/Penguin; 29 Houghton Mifflin; 30, 31 Doubleday; 32 Prentice-Hall; 33 Harper and Row; 34, 35, 36 Houghton Mifflin; 37 Harper and Row; 38 Faber and Faber; 39 Harper and Row; 40 Random House; 41 Harper and Row; 42 Dell; 43 Dover; 44 Dutton/Dell; 45 Sierra Club/Knopf; 46 Random House

Books mentioned on page 145: 47 Charles Scribner's Sons; 48 Shambhala/Random House; 49 Firefly Press; 50 Dial Books for Young Readers

parents' private lists. For the slightly older child, try the *Madeline*[28] series by Ludwig Bemelmans and Ruth Bornstein's *Little Gorilla*.[29] Phyllis Krasilovsky's *The Cow Who Fell Into The Canal*[30] and *The Very Little Girl*[31] are both charming, with story lines pitched at just the right level. Look out, too, for books by Ezra Jack Keats and Maurice Sendak, which always have marvelous illustrations, as do Shirley Hughes' simple reassuring stories of childhood.

You will find in time that the story becomes as important as the pictures: even before her fourth birthday she will listen happily to a story on a record or tape. These are invaluable for the car and for times when she needs (or you need) to sit quietly. There is now a very wide selection of commercially made tapes, but remember you can make them yourself.

By five or six, the story is the most important part of a book. If you have not yet read Shirley Hughes' *David and Dog*,[32] Russell Hoben's *A Baby Sister for Frances*[33], Bernard Weber's *Ira Sleeps Over*,[34] or Virginia Lee Burton's *The Little House*[35] and *Mike Mulligan and His Steam Shovel*,[36] try now.

Books with few pictures – or none

At five she will probably sit and listen as you read from books with just a few line drawings to occasionally stimulate her interest. Try starting with a anthologies such as *The Three Bears and Fifteen Other Stories*[37] edited by Anne Rockwell or the Corrins' *Stories for Five-year-olds and Other Readers*.[38] Then move on to single authors.

Sooner or later, you will find you can read a chapter from a longer story each night. Jeff Brown's *Flat Stanley*[39] about a boy who was "four feet tall, about a foot wide, and only half an inch thick" delighted my elder son. Norman Juster's *The Phantom Tollbooth*,[40] illustrated by Jules Feiffer, is a good bet. Other favorites include E.B. White's *Charlotte's Web*,[41] Kenneth Grahame's *The Wind in the Willows*,[42] *The Wonderful Wizard of Oz*,[43] by L. Frank Baum (along with the entire series that follows), and of course A.A. Milne's *Winnie-the-Pooh*.[44]

By now she will be ready, too, for some more factual books. Sierra Club books, such as *Otter Swims* or *Panda Climbs*,[45] are a sound first buy: they are small, simple, and beautifully illustrated. The Step-Up Series, with titles such as *Animals Do the Strangest Things*,[46] is aimed at slightly older children who are sophisticated enough to appreciate the truly surprising collection of biological oddities each book presents.

TOYS FOR FOUR- TO SIX-YEAR-OLDS

Between two and six, a child passes through many stages, but they are less clearly defined than the stages of babyhood. It is possible to say with confidence that a baby of four months will put out her hand to touch and that one of seven months will put objects in her mouth; but one cannot say with nearly the same certainty that the four-year-old will enjoy simple board games or be able to ride a bike with pedals. However, you will know your child, and as she gets older and as time passes you will of course be in an increasingly better position to help her choose.

The general principles of toy choice remain: match the toy to the child and her current interests, and make sure that the toy leaves her room to expand her game: if play is to be creative there must be something to create. By the time she is six she will have firm ideas of her own, fed by advertisements she has seen, and the opinions of her friends, and sometimes she must have her heart's desire, even though it is unsuitable.

Unfortunately, the toys with the most immediate appeal often have no lasting play value, and this is why you should be in no doubt about drawing the line somewhere, though you should ask yourself whether you are putting the child's interests after your personal prejudices. One can give a gun against one's better judgement, but perhaps not a truly aggressive – and sometimes dangerous – toy such as a machine gun that fires "real" bullets. Some parents would draw the line – on feminist grounds – at those highly popular dolls' heads that come complete with make-up and hair-dressing kits; but they can, for the child who is good with the hands, be highly stimulating. If you wish to take a firm hand, it is probably easier to do so now than later: the real problems arise with older children who spend all day playing next door with toys you have discouraged, but which your neighbor has not.

By four, a child will have matured both physically and mentally. By six she will think much more like an adult, and much of that childish excitement about little things will have been lost. Between four and six, children become much less dependent upon you and far more dependent upon their peers; ready to enter those mysterious middle years where children are often heard but rarely seen, except when they are bored.

Many of the toys for two- to three-year-olds will still be enjoyed. If she enjoys building and constructing, these are the years when she will fill every spare minute making things and where,

SIMPLE STILTS
Five to six years

Procedure Simple stilts, made from paint cans with cord attached (or bought ready-made), are, for this age group, a feasible alternative to full-scale stilts. You can help sustain interest in using the stilts by organizing, for two or more children, simple races back and forth across a room: to complete the course, the child must temporarily hold both cords in one hand and touch a wall before continuing.

Value
DEVELOPING BALANCE EXERCISE in a confined space.

Variation
Place a pile (or piles) of coins on a shelf or other surface which is just within reach when the child or children are on their stilts. The coins have to be removed *one by one* and placed in a container on the other side of the room.

STATUES
Four to six years

Procedure Try this game when you need to quiet a group of noisy children. When you say "freeze", they must stay absolutely still and silent in their last position. They will giggle, of course, but they can only "melt" when you give the word. Anyone who melts too soon is "out". Continue freezing and melting until only one child is left, or until they begin to tire.

Value
MUSCULAR CONTROL Freezing is more demanding than moving. SELF-AWARENESS The children become conscious of their bodies. REACTIONS Freezing demands a rapid, controlled response.

Variations Statues can also provide the basis for an energetic and popular tag game. One child is "it" and must catch the others. When touched, each child must freeze until melted – released – by the touch of another child. Change the child who is "it" frequently.

for the right child, money spent on construction kits is not wasted. They are the years when she can progress from puzzles of a few pieces to jigsaws that may initially challenge an adult. If she shows the aptitude for puzzles, do not wait for a birthday before giving her a more difficult one. The ability to concentrate on a task in hand is a priceless asset for a child approaching school age. Feed and cherish it: your money will be well-used.

Now is also a time when she is never quite what she seems, when the dressing-up box is in daily use, and face paints, wigs and gold shoes will often be in evidence. She will be bored without company, but mature enough to be set up with paints, play-dough or modeling materials and left to play. Doll houses, road systems, railways and villages will be spread across the room. Blankets to make houses and dens will be dragged from drawers and cupboards. She will play without adult supervision, but not always sensibly: as a child I broke all the cut glass vases my mother had won in athletics competitions, by using them to weight down blankets in a den.

From four to six are years when cupboards and drawers often fill with unwanted toys, and parents are perhaps best advised to put their money into a few big toys: a proper bicycle, if it is safe to ride it, or a jungle gym in the backyard. She may never be so imaginative again, so let her improvise as much as possible.

Probably the only really new development is her ability to play simple games with explicit rules. Although some children can play simple games before four, they often lack concentration: they take ten minutes at their turn, and wander off while you take yours. The more educational of these games are discussed on page 151, but if she is not keen on these, try some of the games that have been designed just for fun. They will teach her to take turns, to win, and to lose: important skills for any child who is to pass happily through the highly social middle-childhood years. Other children are not, after all, as tolerant as you might be of a child who "doesn't know how to play properly". Try to remember some of the games you played as a child (or look ahead in the next section of this book). Traditional games are free, and have been chosen by children themselves for their play value: *Hopscotch, Tag,* or *Statues* will teach her to play just as well as any store-bought game.

EXPLORATIONS

I have a clear childhood memory of watching my small sister poking her fingers into piles of cow manure and pronouncing them "hard" or "soft". She must have been about three, for I was certainly old enough to have no desire to join in. Much of childhood is devoted to exploring things – from manure to feelings.

As they grow, children tend to push themselves more and more towards extremes. Do you remember turning round and round until you were so dizzy that the ground seemed to come up to meet you, or rolling down grassy banks so fast that it was hard to stop? Do you remember the urgent but enjoyable sensation of panic as you threw your senses off balance? So prevalent are these games among children all over the world that some theorists have categorized them as a special sort of play – "vertigo". A similar form of play is the business of provoking in oneself feelings of dread or horror. Folklore the world over is full of masked festivals, ghosts and bogeymen, and of children's games that push children to the limits of their strength and endurance. The fact that all children play in this way suggests that such games are important, but exactly why no one really knows. It seems likely, though, that these games are a form of exploration – of investigating danger while remaining safe.

Musical exploration

Vertigo is one form of exploration that you will not need to encourage; simply understanding its significance is enough. Music, by contrast, requires an organized approach.

All children are born with a fascination for sounds: small babies like music and will often lie quietly if you put on a record. But whether or not this early interest develops into a love of music and a desire to produce it depends to some extent on encouragement.

On one of my children's records (*My own ABC* by Ernest and Rosemary Burden), M is for music, and the song that goes with it has an important message:

"When a blackbird sings: it's music,

When a telephone rings: it's music,

When you hear the rain, on the window pane, it's a happy melody,

Music is all around: whatever the sound may be."

The message is that one should listen, for its own sake, even when there are no obvious sounds. You could even suggest

LISTEN TO THE WORLD

Three years

Procedure Even if your child's hearing is perfect, you can help develop his "ear" for different sounds. It is well worth setting aside quiet times when you and he can sit and listen to the world and discuss what you hear. See who can identify all the sounds from outside and who can hear the softest sound. If you can afford it, buy him a simple-to-operate child's cassette tape recorder and encourage him to make his own experiments with sound. Encourage him also to take the recorder with you and make recordings when you go to the zoo or into town. Discuss the recordings when you get home or, if you can, incorporate the sound effects into a story.

Value
AUDITORY DISCRIMINATION does not come naturally, but must be developed.

MAKING MUSIC/ *Three years on*

Children are not born with an ear for music; they develop it gradually by listening. Research suggests that the years up to the age of six are crucial in this learning process. Thereafter, learning to differentiate sounds may be more difficult and it could become much harder to learn to recognize variations in pitch and tone. So it makes sense to provide him with a rich array of musical experiences to carry into those later years.

The best first musical instrument is likely to be a xylophone and it is worth spending a little extra for a quality instrument, preferably with bars of hard wood. Quality is important because any inaccuracies in pitch (and harmonics) will hamper his development – after all, he cannot compensate for a poor instrument's deficiencies if he has never heard the tone of anything better.

The relationship between pitch and the bars on the xylophone may seem obvious to an adult, but it is far from obvious to a child. He will learn plenty from his own experiments, but a few structured games will give them impetus.

1 With the child watching closely, hit a note on the xylophone slowly and deliberately. Ask him to point out the note you struck. If he finds this hard, try removing all but a few of the bars from the xylophone. Get him to strike the same note as you. The best note to start on is Middle C.

2 Now strike a higher note and see if he can point out this note. Ask him if the two notes sounded different – play the notes again to help him. Then repeat the process for other pairs of notes – but no more than four at a time.

3 Once he can point out individual notes confidently, you can introduce him to the idea of the musical scale as a series of stairs. If you can, build a small set of stairs, with eight steps, each step big enough to seat a bear or some other favorite toy. (Wooden school blocks are good to use for this.) Get him to move the bear up the stairs, a step at a time, as you play a rising scale, one note at a time. Repeat this a few times and then try the same, running down the scale. Finally, try jumping, with the bear, from top to bottom, and vice versa.

4 The final, and hardest, stage of this game is for him to put the bear on the step that corresponds to the note you hit. This is difficult even though he can see which note you hit, and you should not be surprised if he is not successful at first. Painting the steps and xylophone bars in corresponding colors, or providing matching pictures, may help. Don't let him do the work all the time – let him test you as well. To add to the fun, try to hum the notes you play.

Learning to distinguish sound quality is as important as learning pitch and the xylophone can help here too if you help him to make a variety of hammers from all kinds of materials – wood, cork, rubber, Plasticine, metal and so on. Some ideas are given on the right. With these hammers, you can take turns guessing which hammer the other hits the xylophone with.

Children soon begin to learn how different materials and objects make different sounds when hit with a xylophone hammer. At six or older, they may be able to make a "symphony" from the various sounds in a room, using a tape recorder to test different variations. Give them different structures to work with, such as a highly simplified version of the basic classical symphonic structure: a loud section followed by a quiet, slow section, then a fast, jolly section and finishing with another loud, dramatic section.

HOME-MADE INSTRUMENTS
Five or six years on

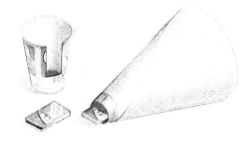

There are as many different ways of making musical sounds as there are different materials in the world. Here are just a few musical instruments that older children can make for themselves.

Toot-toot Yogurt cartons make surprisingly good reeds if you cut two small, matching oblongs and bind them together with tape at one end, face to face. This reed can then be mounted in a cardboard cone or a tube, or indeed any suitable resonator.

Bubble o'heaven is not very musical, but it is fun. Just fill a large, light metal pan with water and let him hum under water through a straw. Better still, give him a length of rubber hose or plastic pipe and let him do it in the bath.

Paper and comb may be an old idea, but most young childen still love it. Remember, they should hum, not blow the comb.

Paper tambourine Punch holes in soda-bottle caps with a nail and then let him string pairs of them in a ring around the edge of a paper plate.

Value
AUDITORY DISCRIMINATION; MUSCULAR CONTROL

RHYTHM KING
Three to five years

Procedure Children at this age are not, of course, fully co-ordinated and cannot dance properly until they are older. But you can usefully start certain rhythmic movement games at three years or younger. An old clock with a loud tick, or a metronome, will help considerably. Start with simple marching games. Let him pretend to march up and down like a soldier in a definite one-two time. Then ask him to be a clock and shake his head rhythmically from side to side, "tick, tock". For three-four time, he could be Long John Silver walking with his wooden leg. Get him to move as many different parts of his body as he can in these rhythms, first singly, then all together.

Value
MUSCULAR CONTROL

listening to silence: sit quietly together, and wait for the usually unheard sound. He will probably giggle or shout after a minute or two, but he may also tell you that the clock ticked, that he could hear the sound of the wind rattling the loose window, and that a car went by. This is not, of course, what you mean by music, but if a child is to make and enjoy music, he must learn to listen first.

When children start to play music in school or at a play group, they usually do so with a percussion band: tambourines, triangles and drums. Listening and making rhythm – and nothing else – is the accepted way to introduce music. Like music, rhythm is everywhere, and he just needs you to point it out to him. So, when you read him verses, emphasize the beat by jiggling him on your knee, or patting his back in time. Rock him to the beat of a song. Later, let him do this himself, and show him how to tap his fingers on the table, or click his tongue in time to the music. Let him dance. Many children will dance without inhibition, especially if you dance along with them: just put on a record and let him dance and clap with you. If he enjoys himself, you might think of taking him to dancing classes.

Once he is aware of the pattern of sounds, see if he can reproduce them. Beat out the first line of *Ba-ba Blacksheep* and ask him to copy it. Remember his memory span is short – so no more than the one line at first. Now give him a can with dried beans in it, or a drum made from a large instant coffee tin, and let him replay the sounds to you.

Since you are so often his model, just singing (even if you are not perfectly in tune) is probably the best next step. Some children seem to take to singing easily and can hold a tune as early as three, others will not be tuneful until much later, and some never will.

There are many toy instruments you can buy, from harmonicas to recorders, but you will need care in selecting them. For a two- or three-year-old, true notes are less important than the variety of sounds produced: he is learning to hear differences at this stage, not to play tunes. By three or four, a good xylophone, or a small electric organ, will allow him to experiment, to discover which sounds blend together, to recognize the similarity of notes an octave apart, and to make his own tunes.

If music looks like becoming a major interest, a real musical instrument is the next stage. The Japanese Suzuki method teaches the violin to children as young as two, essentially by getting them to play simplest tunes over and over again right from the start, with no preliminary attempt to teach musical theory or sight reading. It is no coincidence that the violin is the instrument of the Suzuki method. Violins sound excellent played in concert, however simple the melody, whereas the piano is essentially a solo instrument, impractical for group music-making. The children find that making music together is highly entertaining and satisfying; mutual encouragement, not a little of the herd instinct, and perhaps even competition play an important part in motivating them to master the essential skills.

The lesson is clearly that a young musical talent can be stifled by being pushed into formal lessons too early, and by being confined for long periods with an adult, forced to concentrate relentlessly. Of course, if he positively wants formal lessons, he should have them; but you could do worse than to encourage free experimentation with the chosen instrument. Before he can make music, he must discover for himself what he thinks it is.

MUSICAL JARS
Three to six years

Procedure Even adults are fascinated by the musical effects of tapping a spoon on a glass of water. Young children probably enjoy it even more both for the noise and the thrill of discovery. But if you give a child a range of ten or 12 identical bottles (milk bottles or jam jars), a selection of different "drumsticks" and a jug of water, he can make his own systematic experiments in different pitches produced by filling the bottles to different levels. Drops of food coloring in the liquid will add to the pleasure of the game.

Value
AUDITORY DISCRIMINATION He is encouraged to listen for fine differences in pitch.

NATURE CASTS
Three to five years

NATURE

Procedure Clay and play-dough can be used not only for molding into different shapes (see pages 88–9) but also for making casts. A lump of clay pressed against the bark of a tree, for example, will record all the minute detail of its surface texture. Suggest he make a collection of bark casts from all the trees in the garden or park. If there are no trees anywhere nearby, make casts from various types of brickwork and concrete.

Value
DISCOVERY The casts reveal the rich variety of textures in nature.

City-bred children need not be completely cut off from nature. It's easy to make the assumption that the countryside teems with wildlife, while cities are natural deserts, but nothing could be further from the truth. I know a family that lived for two years in the heart of the countryside without their children learning to recognize anything except dogs, cats and horses: another family who lived in downtown Montreal observed squirrels on their balcony, and spotted chipmunks and skunk within half a mile of their apartment building. Badgers raided the trash cans of our Durham suburb, and we heard a fox call to its mate from our front lawn. Even in London, an owl sometimes sits on our chimney at night, and we regularly remove frogs from the cellar. Of course, city children need to be shown where and how to look for wildlife – and in this lies a rich potential for play. Many parents think that special natural history knowledge is essential to promote this kind of interest, but this is not so: children, even at this age, are so keenly imitative of their parents that they will concern themselves with anything in which you show an interest – from football to the Spanish flea. Simply let them hear you wondering about the identity of the new arrival at the bird feeder, or see you looking it up in a field guide, and you significantly improve the chances of their becoming aware, if not actually interested in, the natural world.

At the pre-school stage, you can hardly do better than limit your explorations to humble insects, worms, snails and woodlice: they move slowly – a great advantage for the younger child who takes time to respond to your whispers of "look over there".

Obviously there are parts of the world where it would be dangerous to encourage children to search for insects, but unless this is the case, an insect hunt in a city, suburban or country garden is an enduringly useful form of play. Once found, an insect can be carefully brought to you, the supervisor, and put into jars along with greenery for examining with a magnifying glass or, better still, a magnifying box, which confines the creature without damaging it. These are modestly priced and available from quality toy manufacturers. Don't allow the exercise to become any more formal than that: the value is in searching, pausing to examine, however superficially, and perhaps in handling or labeling the creatures.

If you have a natural dislike of insects, don't let it stand in the way of a child who has the urge to keep them as pets. At three or

CATCHING INSECTS/*Four to six years*

Children find insects fascinating – and they require a minimum of attention. After a few days, they can be returned to the garden, usually with no harm done. But avoid butterflies: many species are endangered, and all will suffer from being cooped up. Also avoid stinging insects such as bees and ants. Crawling insects or grasshoppers are best.

Go hunting with a screw-top jam jar and a postcard – the postcard is a simple but effective way of scooping the insects into the jar.

Sometimes you can cut off the stem of a plant with the insect on it. To catch a large number of insects at once, you can lay a sheet under a bush – preferably a white sheet to show up the insects clearly. Then beat the bush with a stick to knock insects on to the sheet.

To observe how snails move, place a sheet of lucite on piles of books. Put the snail on and watch the way it moves from under.

Value
DISCOVERY
SUSTAINED ACTIVITY
CARING

KEEPING INSECTS AND WORMS

The simplest home for an insect is a jam jar with holes punched in the lid. Put sand or soil in the bottom, and a few small stones, leaves and twigs from the plant you found the insect on, for this probably provides its food supply. You can also buy ready-made insect homes in certain toy shops.

Make a wormery in a large glass jar: at the bottom put a layer of soil, then a layer of sand, a layer of peat and finally leaves. Add a worm and wrap paper around the jar. After a few days, remove the paper and notice how the layers have been mixed up: as worms move, they pass material through their bodies, and in this way stir up the different layers.

133

WEATHER DIARY/*Four to six years*

Weather tends only to be of interest to children of this age when rain stops them from going out to play. But if you keep a daily meteorological record, even rain can be fascinating. A child may have no idea of the cause of the weather, but weather games will help her to realize that weather does not just happen – particularly if she listens to the weather forecaster on TV as well.

Value
DISCOVERY; SUSTAINED ACTIVITY
READING Learning to use symbols and colors to represent events in the world parallels some of the demands that reading will make.

DIARY

Buy a large diary with generous room for daily entries – a whole page is not too much. Record the weather after breakfast and after the evening meal every day, using symbols for sunny, rainy, cloudy and windy. Invent the symbols yourselves, or adapt ones you may have seen on TV weather maps. It does not matter that she can neither read nor understand the day or the date; you make the daily entries to start with, with her helping. It is an ideal opportunity for you to do something constructive together. Use different colors for the symbols, and make the diary look attractive. As the project continues, she may eventually learn to fill in the diary by herself.

RAIN GAUGE

If the game is a success, make a simple rain gauge, and add rain readings to the diary. For the gauge, you need a tall, thin jar and a wide funnel. The funnel ensures that quite small amounts of rainfall register in the collecting jar. Mark regular intervals on the jar. At this stage, don't worry about marking it with inches of rainfall; instead, make the marks in splashes of paint of different colors. Remember to give zero rainfall a color of its own – a child must be motivated to record this as well as actual rainfall. It is best to start such records in a season of changeable weather – the variation will help to keep him interested.

four years she is too young to give a more sophisticated animal the attention that it needs, but she can watch insects lovingly for two or three days, and then return them to their normal habitat.

The exercise will promote respect for the creature's own way of life, and an awareness of its environment. The search for new insect pets is also an excellent way to train her powers of observation, and encourages her to pay attention to detail; however, I suspect the greatest benefit is the pleasure a simple awareness of the natural world can bring in later years.

Pets

Taking care of a living thing is an important lesson; watching gerbils eating, or caring for their tiny, bald offspring, is a wonderful experience – but try to keep it until she is old enough to significantly participate in looking after the pet. Even if you are prepared to see that she feeds and waters an animal each day, there is the danger that she will literally love a hamster or other small animal to death – in this age range children have little concept of their own strength, unless taught. Anyway, if you do most of the work associated with caring for the pet, she will tend to take it too much for granted; much of the value of pets lies in promoting a sense of responsibility outside oneself.

If she keeps pestering you for an animal, you could suggest a practice run with some "pet seedlings": this will demonstrate the degree of regular care and attention required to sustain any living thing. If she remains interested in the seedlings, you could then progress to a pet: and as her contribution to its care, you might reasonably expect a five- or six-year-old to regularly check its water; fill the water bowl; tear up lettuce for its food; but not to actually fill the feeder or food bowls, or to clean out the cage.

Growing things

There is always room for a child to have her own garden, even if it is a flower pot on the window sill, or a pie plate in the kitchen. A two-year-old will expect something to happen as soon as she waters the seeds, so choose seeds that germinate quickly. This information is usually on the seed packet. Bean sprouts are especially satisfying. She can make her own bean sprout sandwiches within three to five days of planting the seeds, and radishes grown outside can be harvested in a month.

In all your dealings with an inquisitive, impatient child, it pays to have a card up your sleeve, and in the case of nature experiments you may find it essential. Perhaps she is not impressed with the bean sprout jar – and you are wondering whether to abandon all growing experiments. Of course, it is a

PUNK POTATO
Four to six years

Procedure This is an amusing variation on seed-growing activities that will delight many children. Find a large, smooth potato and scoop some of the pulp out from one end. Then cut a slice from the other end so that it will stand upright. You will probably need to do this yourself, although some six-year-olds may manage; the rest she can do herself. Moisten a cotton ball and place it in the scooped out hole at the top of the potato. Sprinkle with grass or beans for sprouting. Place in a saucer surrounded by water. Make sure that the cotton wool stays moist. After a few days, the potato will sprout green hair and she can stick in drawing pins or buttons on pins to make a face.

Value
HAND-EYE CO-ORDINATION DISCOVERY Like all seed-growing activities, growing a punk potato teaches her about natural growth, but the touch of humor sustains her interest longer than usual.

GROWING PLANTS/*Four years on*

Growing plants can be such a rewarding activity for a young child that it is worth getting a book on the subject, not only to give you ideas, but to help you diagnose problems – she will be disappointed if her plant wilts and dies. Some of the more common problems are identified in the margin (*opposite*).

Older children in the age group will be fascinated by the way that plants grow. Here are three techniques you can try to show how plants "work".

A plant needs water
Fill a jam jar with water and add bright red food coloring. Cut across the bottom of a stick of celery or a carrot and let her see you place it in the jar. Leave it until the end of the day and then cut across the celery or carrot with a knife. Show her how the celery or carrot has taken on a bright red color by drinking the dyed water.

A plant needs light
Wet two small bath sponges and sprinkle with grass seed. Place on a windowsill and cover with clear glass dishes. Soon the seeds will send up green shoots. Then cover one sponge with an opaque dish. Show him how the grass dies.

Roots and shoots
Soak a few dried mung beans in water overnight. Moisten a wad of cotton balls and place at the bottom of a jam jar over the drained beans. In a few days, she can see the roots curling round the bottom of the jar and the shoots pushing up through the cotton balls.

Growing vegetables
Cut the top off a carrot, parsnip or beetroot and place in a shallow saucer of water. It should send out green shoots in a few days if left in a sunny place. You could also try putting three toothpicks in an onion and suspending it in a glass of water so that the bottom of the onion is submerged. It should first sprout leaves and then flower.

DIAGNOSING SICK PLANTS

Too little water
Leaves turn yellow or brown and may wilt and fall off.

Too much water
Dark, soggy soil, stems dark and bloated-looking, leaves curling and limp.

Too little light Long,
straggling stems and few leaves as plant tries to reach the light.

Too much light
Leaves are small and curl under.

Too warm Leaf edges
turn brown and dry, or whole leaf goes yellow and wilts.

Aphids Tiny insects on
the underside of the leaves and new growth. Remove them by wiping with a damp cloth and then spray the plant with water containing a little detergent.

Value
DISCOVERY
SUSTAINED ACTIVITY
CARING

Garden pie *Children as young as three will enjoy making a simple garden in a tin plate with moss, soil and a few small plants. A mirror makes an acceptable pond.*

pity to give up, so keep in reserve the fact that the big plants have a special fascination, especially if they grow rapidly. A sunflower soon grows taller than she is, and annual climbers such as morning glory grow at a furious rate. Both plants will reward her with flowers later in the season.

For the two-year-old, the fact that plants grow at all is magic; at first, she may want to see more, so again, keep some experiments in reserve: you will give her plenty of food for thought if you demonstrate how a plant drinks, or what will happen if a plant is deprived of light.

Don't forget the corny old flower games – the ones that pass from generation to generation. Their continuity almost certainly underlines their value, despite their simplicity. Making a daisy chain will, apart from testing manual dexterity, introduce a child to many interesting properties and aspects of plant anatomy; putting honeysuckle or rhododendron flowers on the fingers and running around with them for half an hour will make her far more aware of the nature of the flowers, and the passing of the seasons, than just looking at them, or being told about them.

PEBBLE DASH
Two to three years

Procedure When you go to the beach, encourage her to look for pebbles of all shapes, sizes and colors. To help her on her way, involve her in a "pebble dash": ask her, "How quickly can you find me a round stone?" Then ask for, say, a big stone and a little stone, a red stone and a white stone, a wet stone and a dry stone, and so on. Let her take the stones home if she wants to; they will probably be greatly treasured, and even if not she can have great fun painting them.

Value
DISCOVERY She explores shapes, textures and weights.
VISUAL

IN THE MOOD
Three to five years

Procedure Children of three and four are really too young to participate in a proper game of charades. Instead, you can all take it in turns making faces while the rest of the players guess the mood. You need a "chairman" to whisper the type of face you must pull when your turn comes. All the chairman needs to say is "Make me a happy face", or "make me a sad face", or an angry face, and so on.

Value
COMMUNICATION The game reinforces a child's growing understanding of facial expressions and non-verbal communication.

SELF-DISCOVERY

North American and European mothers talk incessantly to their children, and so from a very early age a mother's voice is an important part of her presence. Sometimes her voice is soft, sometimes it leads her baby, toddler or child into excitement. At other times it is sharp, signaling danger or anger; but always it is there. The voices of the father and other caregivers vary in the same ways, and from listening to them the child learns to predict the moods and intentions of her family and friends, and almost certainly begins to understand her own social identity. By contrasting her behavior with that of others she begins to understand herself. Like everything else she learns, social skills need practice: while engaged in the quest to understand herself, she will do a great deal of playing with words and emotions.

Different cultures, different games
Of course, she does not understand the feelings and intentions of others by words alone. Even as a product of our very verbal western culture, she must understand that postures, facial expressions and ways of moving can indicate mood and meaning. In cultures where words are less important, voices probably play a smaller role in her perception of others. In Japan, for example, mothers speak much less to their children. This does not mean they do not communicate: simply that they communicate in different ways. To eyes and ears tuned to western child care, it is fascinating to observe the differences.

I took part in some experiments in Japan that looked at communication between mothers and children. Mother and child sat in a room full of marvelous toys, which the children were not allowed to touch. Japanese mothers sat in complete silence, but nevertheless managed to keep their children from touching the toys for up to 20 minutes at a time. I only managed ten minutes with my smallest child – and had to talk non-stop to do so. I was never sure how the Japanese mothers kept control – but perhaps it was by postures and facial expressions. Certainly they used a very different technique from mine. But there was no doubt that the children understood. One girl even hit her mother in her frustration at not being able to touch.

The bond between mother and small child is extremely close in Japan. Traditionally, babies rarely leave their mothers' sides day or night; baby sitters are rarely used – even for the odd half-hour – before the second birthday. Japanese child psychologists claim, almost certainly correctly, that the relationship between mother and child is so close that words are unnecessary.

The play of Japanese children is very much quieter than that of American or European children: it is as if they do not need to practice the verbal signals that western parents use on their off-spring. As anyone who has passed a school at play-time will know, nursery schools and playgrounds are noisy places in western communities, and children are, on the whole, both seen and heard. This is not surprising, for if a child is to learn about the feelings and intentions of others through their voices, her play – her practice – will include speech. When signals are silent, play can be much quieter, since the practice is silent too.

The Japanese children's play differed in one other way which also reflects cultural differences. When our children manage to make a tower of blocks, we praise and comment, and often instruct: we may smile, but more often we use words: "That's good", "Isn't that high", "Show me how you did it". Consequently, as our children play, they often instruct themselves, or give themselves encouragement. "I think I'll put that there", they mutter to themselves, or "I'll paint that green", they say to no one in particular.

In many hours of observation I did not hear Japanese children talking to themselves in this way, although I was assured that some children do so. Probably most children use the sorts of gestures and silent instructions that their own mothers use.

It seems fairly certain, then, that children practice the communication skills required by their own culture, and come to understand the intentions of others through their play.

By the time a child is three, she reflects in her voice not only her own feelings but also a sensitivity to the feelings of others. She whispers when she should be quiet, speaks soothingly to anyone who is upset, and will raise the pitch of her voice and speak more slowly to a younger child. You will also hear her practicing these skills in her interactions with her toys.

Playing up

A child knows herself partly because she knows others. And if she knows them by the way they speak, she will surely understand herself partly by verbal experimentation. From two to six she becomes an increasingly social being, so don't be surprised if you find yourself the brunt of her social experiments.

"I have decided to be naughty all day", my sister's three-year-old once told her, adding "and there is nothing you can do about it". While she may not tell you in so many words, we all know of days when a child seems determined to make us angry, or when

SSSHH!
Four to six years

Procedure You sit with your back to her and your eyes shut guarding the treasure (which can be a cookie). Starting off from the far side of the room, she must tiptoe up and steal the treasure, which simply lies beside you on the floor, without you hearing. If she makes any sound, you can turn round and open your eyes. But if she is frozen completely still, she is "invisible" and can carry on again as soon as you shut your eyes and turn round again.

Value
MUSCLE CONTROL
REACTION
PRACTICAL She learns the value of quietness, and the game may help calm her down when overexcited.

PASS THE PRESENT
Three to six years

Procedure "Pass the present" is a very old and well-known party game, but it is also a surprisingly effective way of encouraging children's willingness to share. The idea is to wrap a little present in many layers of paper, each sealed with tape – not too much, or tiny fingers may find it hard to break. The children then take turns unwrapping while you play some lively music. As soon as you stop the music, the child must pass it on. As the last layer approaches, turns get shorter and shorter. In order to avoid ruffled feelings, make sure that you have enough presents for everyone on hand.

Value
SHARING Children find it much harder than you may think to share their toys, and during the game the present seems the most desirable toy in the world. Passing the present demands that their innate selfishness give way to social rules. Provided they do not seem to lose out ultimately – give every child a present later on – it will help them to share.
MANIPULATIVE SKILL The urgency required to unwrap the parcel will teach finger control.

she seems to have set out to do exactly the opposite to everything we ask.

Squabbles

Falling out is very much a part of early friendships. "I hate Sam" he will tell you after a morning at play school, or "Simon says he will never play with me again". We hate to hear it, or to see him hurt, but he must learn to be sad, to be angry – and to control his anger – in the same way that he must learn to love and to control his affections. It is all part of his early social learning: and as with all learning, some children do better than others.

Some children have an easy social manner, while others have difficulties, just as some are good climbers and others not. It takes practice, and the best practice is obviously with other children of about the same age, for they will rarely treat him as a special case in the way his parents do. But even with all the social stimulation in the world, some children prefer their own company – just as some adults prefer to live and work alone. If it does not bother him, on the whole there is no reason for it to bother you.

Take six small children, and within half an hour there will be a disagreement. But then, if you take six adults having a few drinks together, there will probably be some minor difference of opinion. It is just a matter of degree: we are unlikely to fight over the ownership of a glass of beer; they are unlikely to disagree about who buys the next round, or how to vote in the coming election.

Rational argument supported by acceptable evidence is a highly valued social skill: it is the way we fondly believe that we solve social and political problems, and the aim of much of our education. It is an ideal, something to be attained. The quarrels of young children are not, of course, rational, and will not be until adolescence (if then), but this does not mean disagreements, and how they are resolved, are not important. Many people believe that mature argument is achieved through a child's interactions with others, and their attempts to co-ordinate activities and solve differences.

At two, he will scream and hold on tight if there are any disputes over ownership of a toy, but by three he will have taken his first steps towards rational argument. He will begin to give reasons when faced with a conflict. "No because it's mine" or "No I want it" are typical early examples. Gradually, these reasons will become more complex and he will learn the techniques and strategies necessary to resolve a conflict. He will learn, for example, to compromise, to say "Let's take turns", or to lay down conditions when he gives way, "You can have this car if I can borrow your bike". He will learn to give reasons for his needs, or to distract his opponent. "I need that car to drive to the store" or "You have this fast bike and I'll have the car".

As the child grows older, these squabbles will often become more abstract and more playful. "My daddy is bigger than your daddy", or "My car is faster than yours" are familiar taunts, and so are the outlandish claims of children: "My uncle is so rich he has 500 cars – all painted with real gold". To which another child might reply "And my uncle has 500 cars MADE of gold".

This bragging, like the name-calling of older children, is a ritual game of one-upmanship, a childish game perhaps, but one with a long history. In the past, verbal dueling was a common adult pastime, and in some communities verbal taunts still continue into adolescence and adulthood in the form of ritualized spoken – or sung – duels.

The "soundings" of young black Americans and West Indians are usually obscene insults and invective in which duelists try to go "one better". Their origins are probably the verbal duels still found in some West African communities. Although no longer common in much of Europe, similar duels still occur in Turkey, Malta and Sardinia, as well as Fiji and Mexico.

Therapeutic play

Children also use games to allay fears. Encourage a group of children to play fishing and you will find them fishing for crocodiles or snakes. Make them a camp in the garden, and you may find the backyard is inhabited by giant spiders, lions or terrible monsters.

The child who happily plays monsters by day may scream with fright in bed at night. He may spend happy hours fishing for crocodiles and fearful nights waiting to be eaten. Three- and four-year-olds often worry about death, or about how they could have been "nothing" before birth. Yet he will happily play at dying, and kill his toys off with gay abandon. Later he will ask you quite tearfully if you will still be alive when he is a "very old man". He will tell his sister she is "not even thought of yet", then worry about what he was before birth – and how he might return to nothing. Some parent may find these questions just about possible to deal with, and can often gently set his mind at rest. If you cannot do this, don't worry, he usually finds his own solution in play.

His insistence upon playing with ideas that frighten him is not as contradictory as it seems: the child is, after all, using many of the techniques that psychologists have developed (and borrowed) for treating irrational fears in adults. In behavior therapy, for example, the patient is exposed to the feared object in a relaxed

MASQUERADE
Four to six years

Procedure Faces hold a deep fascination for children almost from the moment they are born, and masks combine this fascination with an element of make-believe. You can buy masks, but it is more fun for children to make their own. Younger children can make simple masks from a large paper bag – you must put the bag over his head, mark where the eye holes are to be, and let him decorate at will with a felt-tipped pen. (Bear in mind that some children do not like things put over their heads.) Older children can make more elaborate masks from cardboard tied on with string. If the mask is big enough, you can make eye holes in the mouth and draw in fake eyes higher up – this makes the mask much bigger and more impressive. Make masks for yourself and all the family as well, so that it becomes a shared game. Suggest themes for the masks: happy face, sad face, angry face, clown, monster animals.

Value
MANUAL
SOCIAL Drawing the faces and acting out the part increases his understanding of the way people express themselves.
THERAPEUTIC This can be an effective way of making certain moods and faces seem less frightening.

environment, and in psychodrama he acts out his fears. This, in essence, is what the child is doing when he plays games with death or monsters.

Stories and books can also help him to allay his fears. Modern classics like Maurice Sendak's *Where the Wild Things Are* or *The Night Kitchen,* or indeed traditional stories with trolls and wicked wolves, do not seriously frighten children: for whatever the terrors, it all comes out right in the end.

I have found that many of the classic children's stories, especially those involving small children, such as *Babes in the Wood* or *Red Riding Hood,* are quite frightening for three- to four-year-olds in their original versions. Your child is, after all, little, and he may indeed feel he might get lost and eaten. But since he is not as wicked as the big bad wolf, nor as silly as Chicken Licken, he is not worried by wolves in boiling water, nor indeed by Chicken Licken being eaten; though he may think Chicken Licken's fate is sad and unfair.

Many of the classic stories were more appropriate to a time when it was felt necessary to put children in fear of hell and damnation if they disobeyed their parents. While, of course, children should not be shielded from death, nor the fact that terrible things do happen, I am not sure that being eaten by a wolf because you stopped to talk to a stranger gives the right conception of values for today.

There are less frightening versions of the old fairy tales, and some excellent folk tales which can involve the child without fear. *Stone Soup*[47] is a story children always enjoy, and *Russian Folk Tales*[48] offer several good stories. Modern stories can provide an enticing combination of traditional elements and modern values, as in *The Paperback Princess*[49] by R. Munsch, a modern fairy tale in which the princess saves the prince.

If your child has a particular fear, you will almost certainly find a book in which the monster or snake or some other creature that he fears so much is rendered loveable. Mercer Mayer's *There's a Nightmare in My Closet*[50] is a classic of this sort. You will find, too, that there are many stories in which a timid character overcomes his fears to become a hero.

GHOST HUNT
Three to six years

Procedure This is a hide-and-seek game with a difference – it is played in complete (or almost complete) darkness. One person plays the ghost, with an old white sheet draped over his head, holes cut for eyes and mouth. With all the lights out, the ghost goes off to another room to hide. The ghost-hunters, in turn accompanied by an adult, must then "catch" the ghost – by snapping on a flashlight and shining it directly at the ghost. If a flashlight misses, it must be switched off again immediately. When a child is confident alone in the dark, he can play the ghost.

Value
THERAPEUTIC There are few better ways of conquering fear of the dark than by playing in it.
FUN Switching off all the lights is an unusual experience and most children will find it exciting, particularly if the ghost makes suitable wails now and then.

ONE FOR ME, ONE
FOR YOU
Two to five years

HOW MANY?

Procedure Counting
need not begin with
numbers, but with
numerical concepts
introduced at an early
age. When distributing
blocks for a building
game, or crayons for an
art session, don't just
hand him his portion;
make a big thing of the
distribution, saying "One
for me, one for you"
slowly and deliberately
and letting him see what
you are doing. Better
still, let him share out
the items under your
direction. Give him a set
of colored buttons and
encourage him to play
this game himself,
sharing with his teddy
bear.

Value
COUNTING Distribution
is a simple binary form
of counting. If you share
with a third person (or
teddy bear) it is the
equivalent of counting to
three – one for me (one),
one for you (two) and
one for teddy (three).
Naming the numbers
will come later.

Children as young as three may reel off an impressive string of
numbers, but there is more to numbers than their names. To start
with, "one-two-three-four" is much the same as "eeney, meany,
miney, mo", a rhyme to say while pointing. Playful ways of con-
verting these labels into a real understanding of number – the
"twoness" of two, and so on – will be of great value in giving him
a sound basic numerical understanding that will make formal
mathematics much less daunting.

My elder son could not count to ten until after he started
school, but at three he understood what numbers meant and,
from a game we played together, developed his own system of
counting. Whenever I gave him something to hold I said "one for
that hand". If there were two objects I said "two, that's one for
each hand", and if there were more I said, "One, two, oh dear
there are too many". As you might imagine, there were three
numbers in his counting system: one, two, and too many. Only as
he understood what a number meant did he begin to separate
"too many": three was "one for all the family"; four was "two for
each hand"; five was "two for each hand and one over".

One of the problems children have in understanding numbers
is, in fact, that they cannot easily perceive the "fiveness" of five.
If some pebbles are thrown on to the ground, an adult instantly
sees, without counting, that there are four or five, but if there are
as many as 10 or 11, he cannot say whether there are 10 or 11
without counting, – unless they fall in a simple pattern.
Psychologists call this ability to instantly perceive number the
"span of attention". For an adult, the average span of attention is
between five and nine items, but it is much smaller in children:
about three at three years, rising to four or five by the child's
sixth birthday. Obviously, if his span of attention is three or four,
he certainly will not see the "fiveness" of five. He will develop his
understanding of number from those numbers within his span, so
start by concentrating on one and two, and gradually including
three and then four. Forget all about numbers over five for the
time being.

It is perhaps easier to understand the child's second difficulty
if you consider how he uses words. One of the earliest words
many children learn to say is "daddy". At first he uses "daddy"
only for the appropriate person, but gradually he forms a concept
of "men"; and "daddy" becomes a name for all men. My
daughter used her little brother's name to mean baby in just this

way. Calves were "Tom cows" and puppies "Tom dogs". This pattern of specific use followed by over-generalization is highly characteristic of the younger child's thinking. So, you can help him with numbers by associating ready-established concepts with different figures. Mommy and daddy are *two*; he has *one* younger sister making *three*; the cat makes *four*, and so on. He must somehow extract the concept of larger numbers from the many examples of sets and groups he now encounters. You can help him a great deal by looking out for examples.

Matching

Mathematical understanding develops more gradually than you may remember from your own childhood. If you look at the mathematics books your child is likely to use when he starts school, you will find they practice certain skills over and over again: matching similar objects, sorting them into sets, arranging them in order, and matching sets of the same number. Unlike learning to use scissors, where the child must practice the same movements, learning to think requires a flexible approach: endless practice, but plenty of variation, too.

Children enjoy matching and sorting, whether at work or play. Through these activities he will begin to understand that things of the same kind may differ in size, shape and color. At school he will be taught to call these groups of similar items "sets", and will learn how to compare and manipulate them. He will learn that sometimes it is possible to make sets with the same number of items. Simple games played with you at home will assist this development, as will introducing him to the word "sets" at an early age. But tread cautiously: a game is not a game unless he enjoys it. Nursery schools provide a wide choice of games so that a child can choose to avoid activities that for entirely idiosyncratic reasons do not appeal.

He will need quite a few odds and ends to match and sort. Miniature cars or plastic farm animals usually hold a child's attention as well as anything. For a two-year-old, the simplest task is to match two identical objects. Ask him to find you another can of baked beans from the cupboard, or another red block from his pile. He may well have more difficulty understanding the instructions than doing the task, so use your ingenuity. Remember actions often speak louder than words: show him what you mean. With my own daughter I found that showing her "one red block", and then, "two red blocks" worked quite well – but I had to ask her to "find the two": not very grammatical, but the point was understood, and there is plenty of time to worry about grammar later on.

LAYING THE TABLE
Three to four years

Procedure A simple and useful way of introducing him to the concept of one-to-one matching or "pairing" is to get him to lay out either the spoons and forks (save the knives until later) or the cups and saucers for mealtimes. It is his job to make sure everyone has one of each – make sure you give him the right numbers of each item.

Value
PAIRING The idea of one-to-one correspondence provides the basis for understanding number.

Later progress You can deliberately miss one knife or one saucer to introduce him to the concepts of "more than" and "less than".

Variations The story of "Goldilocks and the Three Bears" is a parable in pairing, with chairs, bowls and so on to match each of the three bears. Let him act it out with three bears or dolls as you tell the story.

147

MATCHPLAY
Three to five years

Procedure You can introduce him to proper playing cards through a form of lotto. Sort out five pairs of cards (different numbers from the same suits of two packs) and lay down one of each pair. Ask him to lay down the five remaining cards with their pair. When he can do this, give him all ten cards and ask him to lay out five cards for you. Ask if they are all different.

Value
PAIRING This game is an advanced form of pairing. Although he may not be "counting" the numbers on the cards, he matches a whole range of numbers visually and this will undoubtedly help him to *count* later on.

Gradually you can introduce more complex matching. Introduce another species of animal, or make of car, and ask him to find "another cow". A tower of two or three blocks can be copied, or colored beads put on to a string in a certain order. Always remember to praise him, even if he gets it wrong: say "That's a nice little pig, is there a cow in there too?", rather than "Silly, you've put a cow in with the pig". Shape sorters encourage matching, particularly if they use color as well as shape.

Some of the perennial children's games and pastimes are no more or less than mathematical matching contests: *Old Maid*, *Crazy Eights*, *War* and the three-year-olds' favorite, *Go Fish*. Don't dismiss them as worthless because they are so old-fashioned.

If this is his first card game, show him how to turn the cards over and how to hold them. Two- and three-year-olds find it difficult to follow or remember instructions, so it is best for them to play *Go Fish* (or any other game) with people who know how to play, so they can pick up the rules as they play. Let him win, of course – and unless you want to spend the rest of his childhood losing games, let him lose, too. Color cards are surprisingly versatile, and can be used for a number of games (see margin). Whenever buying cards, it is worth buying a decent pack. Pictures should be clear and the board stiff enough for small hands to turn.

The essence of these games is to find pairs, but pairs do not have to be cards. Shoes can be sorted and so can socks. Try instituting a bag into which all the odd socks are stored. Every couple of weeks the children can go through the bag, sorting them into pairs.

Matching numbers

One-to-one correspondence is basic to his understanding of number. Matching objects to hands in a one-to-one relationship is the most universal method of showing this, but shoes can be matched with feet, gloves with hands and so on. A three-year-old can lay the table, cups matched with saucers, knives with forks. Afterwards, give him the saucepans to play with and suggest he puts a lid on each one. Make a collection of large and small animals, then ask him to give each "mommy a baby".

From sets to sequences

Seeing how and why things go together is a basic skill, necessary for language, logical thought and understanding. By the time he is three, sorting is likely to have become one of his regular occupations, both in "work" and play. While "working" he will learn to use categories, for example pairs for knives and forks; while playing at sorting he will learn to form them.

His sorting systems probably have a logic of their own: he might put acorns with leaves because squirrels like them, and then add red petals because they look nice. However weird the categories may seem, they are extremely useful to him: bear in mind that you often solve problems by sudden jumps in imagination, and that he too is as likely to learn by realizing why something should not be in a collection, as by realizing why it should.

Simple sorting teaches the child how to form sets, but in more complex sorting he learns to "abstract" a common property. Kitchen implements can be sorted from toy animals, coins of various values from different sorts of bottletops. His task is to see what each set of objects has in common. Once he can do this he will be well on the way to understanding that what three cats and three spoons have in common is "three-ness". Later he will use the same kinds of skills to understand far more complex relationships.

A little earlier, shoes and socks were used for sorting into simple pairs. Soon he can progress to sorting the white clothes from the colored pieces for a machine-wash, or separating cans from boxes in the weekly shopping or cars from other types of vehicle in the toy box.

Big and little

You have probably forgotten that it was relatively easy, as a child, to see if something was colored, or packed in a can, but not always so simple to see that it was big. It is true that to your preschool child a skyscraper will always be big, but he may not appreciate that an elephant and an ant are different sizes – especially when he sees them reproduced roughly the same size, in isolation, in a picture book. Understanding *relative* size is essential to the development of his mathematical and logical thinking, so give him plenty of concrete examples to work on simply by talking about sizes whenever the opportunity arises. Start with simple ranges of size, such as you, him, and his baby sister, with him in the middle; he will easily understand that he is smaller than you, but bigger than her.

Many household items can be arranged in order of size: plates, spoons, shoes and socks are obvious examples, and now may be the time to do a size demonstration with Russian dolls or any other toy that works on the principle of several similar items fitting inside each other.

"More" and "less" rarely present problems, especially if

LOTTO
2½ to five years

Procedure Lotto is an old and popular game – and with good reason: it is the best of all pairing games. The idea is simply to fill up spaces on a board by turning over cards to match. There are many different versions of the game on the market and most are worthwhile. But for younger children, make sure the pictures are bold and clear.

Value
PAIRING This game reinforces the idea of one-to-one correspondence vital for a grasp of number.

THREE HOOPS/*Five years on*

"Set theory" is a fundamental concept in mathematics and its value in early math skills is increasingly widely accepted. The matching and sorting games that provide the groundwork for counting all derive from set theory. "Three hoops" takes the process of sorting into sets a step further. A complex game that will stretch children to the limits, it not only entails sorting objects into three sets, but also identifying common elements. Because it is difficult, it is better to start with just three sets of objects with three different properties and two different colors.

Materials
You need three hoops and three sets of objects with three clearly different properties. You could, for instance, use balls, cylinders and blocks; paint in two different colors. If attempting a more complex set-up, draw yourself a table of the properties and colors, and check them off as you paint the shapes.

First, overlap the three hoops as shown right. The idea is then to place the objects in the areas created in appropriate sets. If they find it difficult to begin, start placing a few of the objects yourself so that they get the right idea. Next, progress to painting three different shapes in three different colors or patterns, and try to work out which piece belongs in the central space created by all three hoops overlapping.

Value
MATH SKILL: SORTING, COUNTING

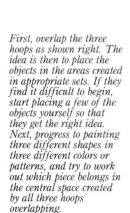

children have siblings, as you will have experienced when giving two young children their candy.

Counting

Many children can count up to ten by the time they are three, but have little understanding of quantity beyond two or three. By four they can count to 20 and understand numbers up to four or five. When he can manage the numbers one to six, he will be ready for simple counting games using a dice. There are many from which to choose: *Chutes and Ladders* and *Candy Land* are tried and tested old favorites, but keep them for children over four; simple racing games or dominoes, or modern games such as *Ladybird,* are better for younger children. Most *Chutes and Ladders* boards are difficult because players must move in a zigzag course, and considerations of direction confuse the counting process. Even at five or six, you may have to remind them that they do not start counting again when they reach a new *Chutes and Ladders* line. When selecting games for the youngest age groups remember that they lose interest quickly, and work out ways to simplify the rules and shorten the game. Whatever the rules say, using a complicated method of deciding who will have the first turn is an infallible way of ensuring that a pre-school child loses interest from the start.

A child who has played with play-dough, sand, water and blocks will gradually have become aware of volume and shape; mosaics (especially the sort that he can nail on to a board with a hammer) will take the understanding of basic geometry a stage further. Some children enjoy looking for circles or squares about the house: plates and tables are easily found, but the round screw heads on his bed, or circles on the wallpaper, are more difficult. These quests can easily be turned into games, and looking for hidden figures means he must examine an object in detail – excellent pre-reading exercise.

ONE FOR EACH HAND
Two to five years

Procedure When you give him two snacks, ask "Is there one for each eye? . . . One for each hand? . . . One for each tooth?" He will soon get the idea and laugh when you ask a silly question. Later you can build on this by asking whether there are *more* teeth or *more* sweets. Cookies are ideal for discussing "more" or "less": most children know what more cookies means.

Value
PAIRING This is an amusing pairs game, building up his familiarity with one-to-one correspondences.
COUNTING It also takes him on to the concept of order.

SHAPING UP
Three to five years

Procedure Picking out blocks of the same shape for building is one skill; understanding shapes on paper is altogether more difficult. You can help the process by using the flat face of an eraser or a cut vegetable as a printing block. Simply dip it in paint and encourage him to print a pattern on paper.

Value
MATCHING Comparing the shape of the printing surface with the pattern it makes is relevant to mathematical skills to be learned later at school.

Procedure This is a simple, fast-moving turn-taking game which needs four or five players. Every player is given a number and also a distinctive set of cards. To play, every player lays a card from his pack on a central pile in turn: player one goes first, followed by player two, and so on; each shouts out her number as she does so. Any player who plays too early or late misses a "turn". The winner is the first to lay out all her cards. The game should be played slowly at first, until the youngest child has grasped when she is to play her card. But you should eventually play it as fast as possible.

Value
SEQUENCING Learning to take her turn in a fast-moving game improves her awareness of sequences, a useful pre-reading skill.
NAMING NUMBERS Although she is not actually counting when she shouts out her number – she is simply following a cue – the repetition will result in the number being memorized. She will know it exists, not what it means, and as long as she also plays games which reinforce the meaning of numbers, the game will be constructive.

PREPARING TO READ

Finding math difficult is considered relatively normal; not being able to read is very different. Even if today reading difficulties are much better understood, and managed, than say two decades ago, a child still knows she ought to be able to read, and people still assume she is not very bright if she cannot. Seven is too young to realize that you are considered a failure. So try and adopt the attitude that whether she reads at three or at seven is immaterial: why should your pride be hurt if she does not read before she starts school? She stands to lose much more if you make her feel she has failed. If she has problems, your faith in her will be essential. Tread cautiously.

Of course, it would be foolish not to show her words, or to discourage her from reading if she begins to recognize them. But take your cues, as in all things to do with her education, from her. If she recognizes one or two words, she will recognize nine or ten just as easily. If she enjoys "pretending" to read, she will, one day, enjoy real reading, so do not hold her back.

If she shows no interest in reading, concentrate on pre-reading skills, and on showing her, by your own interest in books, that reading is something that will give her pleasure. Read to her, show her picture books, and in time she will want to read to herself. Do no worry about her lack of reading skills. Most children cannot read at all before they go to school.

Left to right
In English we read from left to right: this, I know, was part of my own reading problem. Always inclined to start on the right and move to the left, I was badly flustered when corrected. I still cannot locate my right hand without moving it first, and when I took my driving test, I took the tester on a completely unplanned course because I turned left and right quite randomly.

Parents need to be aware that eyes do not automatically scan from left to right. Years of reading practice make this automatic for adults, but it is difficult to teach a child to move her eyes from left to right before she starts to read because there is simply no reason for her to do so.

Pre-reading books suggest exercises that involve drawing from left to right – for example, joining a baby animal on the left to its mother on the right. That is fine if you have the kind of child who likes that sort of exercise, but it is hard to know what to do if she shows no interest in such activity.

COMIC STRIP/*Four years on*

Comic strips are much derided, but despite their popularity with children, they can be an excellent way of developing pre-reading skills. Reading depends on a particular pattern of eye movement, from left to right and down the page; comic strips help a child to learn this pattern. A child will find a strip particularly easy to follow if the story and pictures are already familiar, so why not make your own comic strip, showing a familiar routine? Take half a dozen or so photographs to illustrate a story about going shopping, or walking to school. Make prints and mount them in sequence on a piece of card. Write very simple captions to each picture and hang it in an honored place on a bedroom wall. Don't underestimate the "comic" value of what seems to you amazingly banal.

GOING TO SCHOOL

Matthew and Lucy go out of the door.

They walk down the road. They see Emily.

Matthew and Lucy call at Jane's house.

Jane mails a letter.

They cross the railway bridge.

They all swing on the school gate.

BUS STOP
Three to five years

Procedure This is a matching game that promotes the pattern of eye movement needed for reading. Lay out all the cards from a picture pack in parallel rows, leaving a gap sufficiently wide to drive a toy bus down. On a sheet of paper, draw a seating plan for the bus with card-sized seating areas. Eight seats is enough. Next, make up a sequence in which she must pick up the passengers, and show her how to drive along the rows, from left to right, stopping at the appropriate cards and saying "On you get Mr. Giraffe" (or whatever image appears on the card). She then picks up the card, places it on the seating plan and continues the journey. She must fill the whole bus with the passengers you have named, and if she misses any, she must drive back to the proper row and proceed along it from left to right to pick up the missing card. (To start with, four rows with say ten cards in each will probably be enough.)

Value
READING The eye movement required for reading – following a straight line from left to right – is not innate and has to be learned. Reinforcing the correct pattern with exercises will help when it comes to reading at school.

Tracing her finger along the line of words as you read may help, and so may some of the matching games in which she has to tally a card on the left with a series of cards on the right. But a general awareness of the need to practice scanning is probably as efficient as anything. If you give her peanuts or raisins as a treat, lay them out in a line, counting from *her* left. Lay her clothes out along the bed in the order that she puts them on: pants on the left, shoes on the right. Make or buy picture friezes that have a story line that develops from left to right.

I suspect one of the best pre-reading aids is the comic strip. Comics and comic-books are much maligned, with some justice as far as older childen are concerned, but they are really excellent at this stage. In a well-devised comic strip, the pictures tell a complete story. As the child follows it, she automatically moves her eyes in the correct way from left to right along one line, then diagonally down from upper right to lower left to start the next line. Unfortunately it is not always easy to find comic books that appeal to three-year-olds, but there are a few books for young children written in comic form. Fortunately, comic-books are easy to make at home (see page 153), and if they tell the story of a favorite outing or a regular routine, your child will be able to "read" them without your help.

Looking for detail
Words differ in subtle ways. To tell them apart, a child must pay attention to detail, a skill she can develop gradually in the pre-school years. Books are one of the most obvious aids: by two, she probably looks carefully at the pictures in her books if she is encouraged: you can make a game out of pointing out a particular character or animal on every page. Many children's books incorporate some diminutive, partly hidden creature in each illustration with this game in mind. In some books the pictures move a little faster than the words, so that the child says "Look, there is the goat" before it enters the story: since children soon know their stories by heart, this is useful. There are also books that deliberately hide figures in each picture and ask the children to find them, and others that give so much familiar domestic detail that it is easy to play this game more informally. Large picture word books, illustrated dictionaries, and books about cars, planes or animals can easily serve the same purpose.

Jigsaws
These are another way of making a child concentrate on detail, and at this stage their greatest value is probably in practicing pre-reading skills. Of course they seem simple to you – especially

STRANGE TALE
Three to five years

Procedure Unlike adults, most children love to hear their favorite stories again and again. Some stories they want to be told repeatedly, even once they know them by heart. They will enjoy anticipating and beating you to the most exciting parts. You can use this familiarity to play a number of games. First of all, with a group, you can act out the story, giving a different role to each child. But you can also vary the story, changing the way it ends, changing the characters or the setting or altering the sequence of events, saying "But this time . . ." With older children, you can even try acting out the story backwards, doing all the actions in reverse.

Value
SEQUENCING is a useful pre-reading exercise, and may help with counting, too.

when the child only has to fit, say, three very different shapes into three very different holes. The reason why your three- or four-year-old can find them so difficult is that they require three inter-related but distinct skills: selecting the correct shape, putting it in the correct place and orientating it properly. Fail on any one of these and the puzzle cannot be completed.

Often, a child gets the right piece but cannot find the correct orientation, and if this is a problem, geometric form boards, which simply present circles, regular triangles and squares, are your answer. She will not need to worry about the orientation of the pieces, and when she can do these puzzles she can move on to the simplest tray puzzles, where more complex shapes fit into specific holes. Once she can do these, she will be well on her way to proper jigsaws, but do not rush ahead. The key to puzzling is to move in small steps, not large bounds, and all the while she will be developing useful pre-reading skills. Try to gradually increase the difficulty of the tray puzzle, perhaps by looking for puzzles in which a number of different objects fit into a general picture. Next should come the simplest interlocking puzzles, where five or six pieces make a picture. They are still not true jigsaws, since each piece completes a whole section of the picture, but soon she can move on to more complex tray puzzles where only some of the pieces are whole pictures, and finally traditional interlocking jigsaw puzzles with four or six pieces.

From then onwards you can try a steady progression of increasingly difficult jigsaw puzzles. Look at the pieces as well as the picture before you buy: a good jigsaw should have a recognizable image (or portion of an image) on each piece; the pieces need to be large enough to manipulate, preferably made of wood or thick cardboard; and the picture revealed by the completed puzzle should be a type that appeals – criteria for which are similar to those discussed in the section on books for this age range, page 122. This is much more important than the number of pieces: children can have far more difficulty with a badly designed 20-piece jigsaw than with a well-designed one with five times as many pieces.

The age ranges given on puzzles serves as only an approximate guide to their difficulty, and some children manage puzzles intended for much older children, and vice versa. In any case, you will have to introduce her to more difficult puzzles yourself, helping build up her skill – be sensitive to how much help different children need, however: my sons always wanted help; my daughter would start the puzzle again if I put in a piece without asking her first.

In my experience, children never start with the edges of a

jigsaw puzzle as an adult would, nor do they seem to know that edges have a special place in the puzzle: perhaps this is because there are no edges on the pieces of tray puzzles. I have usually found that suggesting that "We should look for the pig's tail" or quietly pushing the next piece where she can see it helps if she is beginning to lose interest; equally that a break for a drink may lead to renewed enthusiasm. For an interested child, it is worth taking this much trouble with jigsaws: they really encourage concentration on detail and improve the spatial skills: visualizing, matching and seeing how things can fit together.

Alternatives to jigsaws

Like it or not, some children just do not enjoy jigsaws. It is unlikely, however, that a child will not have some alternative, special interest, which will serve the same purpose. When my brother was about three, he regularly amazed my mother by naming each car as it came down the road: he was matching them to his collection of toy cars. This sort of expertise requires attention to detail, whether it involves 30 different cars or 30 different breeds of dog. If he is happier searching for his initials on car number plates, or looking out for packages he recognizes in the supermarket, so be it.

Recognizing words

Many children learn to read purely by looking at a word and saying its name, and most children rely on this method to some extent. Parents (and particularly grandparents) sometimes think this is not really reading: that children can only read when they have learned to spell out. Only part of the story, of course: early reading involves plenty of memory, plenty of guesswork, and plenty of help from pictures. Only gradually do children begin to recognize the words completely out of context. There are games that help the child to match word and picture, but nothing is better for this purpose than a book. Making her generally aware of words will help, too: she might enjoy looking out for the letters in her name on shop fronts, or for the name of a favorite food on advertising billboards.

Learning letters

Although these days children do not learn to read by spelling out words, they begin to recognize words by looking at their initial letters. Even after they can read quite well, some children still have difficulty with mirror images, such as p and q, or d and b, so do not despair if she cannot tell these letters apart. A set of magnetic letters on the refrigerator, or an alphabet sorting tray

ALPHABET SOUP
Three years on

Procedure The letters of the alphabet need not simply be parts of words that must be learned; they can be fun shapes with which to play. Cookies can be cut into the shape of letters, then baked and eaten. Cheap magnetic letters can be slapped on to the refrigerator. Letter stencils can be painted on to paper. Plastic letters can be arranged into patterns. Rub-on letters can be bought in a wide range of sizes and colors from art shops. At first, the child need have no appreciation of what letters mean, but you can gradually arrange them into words and show her what they mean.

Value
READING Familiarity with even just the shapes of letters will help her when she starts to read.
WRITING Arranging letters to form words is the first step to writing.

157

Procedure You can play this game with commercially made cards, but it is much better to make up your own using favorite characters or animals. Draw them yourself or cut them from comics and stick them on stiff cardboard. Write names on separate cards for each character in clear letters. Lay out all the name cards, from left to right, and then lay out the picture cards, each by its appropriate name card, making sure that she is watching. Next, slowly turn all the picture cards face down. Then ask her "Who's hiding here?" – she must guess the character on the turned-down card. She will, of course, rely on memory to start with, but as you increase the number of cards in the game, she will find it is worth trying to recognize the names on the word cards in order to improve her chances of winning.

Value
WORD RECOGNITION The game provides an incentive to learn to recognize words and gives her plenty of practice at associating the pattern words make on paper with pictures and sounds.

will help, but again there is really nothing better than a book. Most children's book shops stock ABC books with illustrations in at least a dozen different varieties, from simple animals to weird and wonderful monsters. You can find friezes, sheets, duvet covers and even dresses with the alphabet written all over, likewise, handkerchiefs, towels and tee-shirts can all have her initials printed on them. Choose lower case (small) letters since these are the ones she will use in reading – many otherwise excellent toys and books are spoiled because they use upper case (capital) letters.

Once she knows her letters, games like *I spy* and filling her treasure bag with objects beginning with a certain letter, will reinforce the skill. Finding the initial letter is the first step towards "spelling out" words, but few children will be proficient at this before they start school.

Rhymes

Do not overlook rhymes at this stage: eventually she must learn to spell out words, and when she does, nursery rhymes and her ability to rhyme words will stand her in good stead. A game of "what rhymes with cat?" can pass the time on a long journey; and can be elaborated into producing verse of rhyming couplets as the child grows older. A comprehensive collection of nursery rhymes really is an excellent investment – whether on records or in books. Many children find their familiarity comforting. Reading a few favorite rhymes or dancing to a record of nursery songs before bed is a useful way to relax a child, especially if her routine has been disturbed.

At three, she will probably recite or sing parts of many rhymes, and by the time she is four she will probably be able to sing whole songs to herself. Do not forget that actions help her to remember and to enjoy songs. Ask her to sing to you and the actions will be included with great seriousness: many a nursery school class has stolen the school show with a display of action rhymes.

Writing skills

Writing needs a steady hand and fine co-ordination between hand and eye, and although there is no need for a child to write before she goes to school, some four- or five-year-olds will like to write their names on their paintings. Other children will like to copy words you have written for them, and to write their own birthday cards and invitations. If your child shows an interest in writing, write the words she wants and let her copy them. Hold her hand at the beginning if she cannot quite form the letters, but wants to.

LETTERS/*Four years on*

Writing is a surprisingly difficult manual skill to learn and early practice pays dividends – provided a child is not pushed. Start her off by writing her name in bold letters in felt-tip pen. Get her to draw over the top.

Basic letters should be drawn by moving the pen in the way shown by the arrows, starting at the dots and finishing at the triangles.

ON THE TRAIL
Five years on

Procedure If she can read a few words in one of the simple word-and-picture books, you can try this game. Hide a treat somewhere in the room and then lay a trail of one-word clues to help lead her to it. Explain that the clues will be found in books. Starting at the door, say, you could leave a book open at the page showing a chair. When she reaches the chair, she could find another book open at "table", and so on. Always make sure she finds the treat – help her if necessary.

Value
READING

There are also a large number of early work books that show how writing will be taught in school, but many children want to play at writing and prefer not to follow detailed instructions at this point. Simply copying a few words is interesting enough.

If she does not want to write just yet (and most children show no interest in writing before school), remember that writing is a sensory motor skill, and that anything that helps the co-ordination of hand and eye will help her to write when the time comes. Threading, drawing and building are all excellent practice, so are peg boards and trains that hook together. Mazes are excellent, especially if the child traces them with a pencil.

Make some simple dot-to-dot pictures, and let her trace from dot to dot to form an entire image. You might even ask her to draw around simple templates or stencils: either task requires quite advanced pencil control, so don't expect the average five-year-old to be accurate.

Coloring books practice similar skills. Both coloring books and stencils have been much maligned by those who feel that children should be allowed to develop artistic skills freely. The criticism is not totally fair: coloring in simple pictures and drawing around stencils are no substitute for artistic endeavors – but nor are they meant to be. They are activities in their own right, which develop entirely separate skills.

A QUESTION OF SEX?

All children are different: they develop at different rates, have different interests and play different games. Some children are noisy and out-going, others quiet and self-contained, some are reckless, others cautious, and all these differences can be seen in their play. Look around a play group, and you will see not only large noisy groups outside on bikes but also children quietly involved in complex activity. Even in the play house or at the paint table, behavior differs. For some children the play house is a home where cooking and caring for families takes place, for others it is a resting place for the gang. Some children paint people, houses, and flowers, others paint planes and monsters.

Often, the gang on the bikes or in the play house are all boys, while the smaller group looking after pretend families, or making puppets at the table, are all girls. Parents may feel they have treated their sons and daughters in the same way, and wonder why their daughters are gentle and their sons rough – or vice-versa. Others may want to know if it is possible to put an end to this division between the sexes. Is it really natural?

The causes of sex differences

Much has been written about sex differences in recent years: some of the principal – and most controversial – claims center on the view that boys and girls are born different, have different in-born abilities and even different brains. It is hard for the average parent to know how much of this is to be believed, or how inevitable, or significant, these differences really are. If she is always busy with her dolls, is it because she was born that way, or because her culture has shaped her in this fashion?

An unanswerable question, of course: it is never possible to separate a child from the influences around him, indeed without these influences he – or she – would not be a child at all. As I have tried to show, the child reaches out to the world from the moment he is born, and that is exactly why the parent's role is such an important one. As often as not, a girl reaching out is treated in one way, a boy another. Looking for inborn qualities in any child is like looking for the flour in a cake after it is baked. The original ingredients are in there all right, but changed beyond recognition. In fact, those ingredients are changed even before the child is born, for it is not the genes that make a girl or boy, but the action of hormones. Nature will make a girl from any fetus unless told by the presence of the male hormone testosterone, in the

ROLE PLAY
Four years on

Procedure Role-playing games are one of the best ways of breaking down sexual stereotypes because they make each role more accessible and help children to see both girls and boys in roles traditionally reserved for one or the other. Playing "doctors and patients" is an old game, but perfect for this, provided the roles are swapped freely. Rather than buying a doctor's outfit, though, help the children make their own using old shirts for coats, sheets for bandages and so on. This stimulates the imagination a little more. A prop worth buying, however, is a real stethoscope (second-hand from an army surplus store). It can become a marvelous focus for the make-believe.

Value
SEX EQUALITY The particular value of this game is that it encourages caring in boys as well as allowing girls to play a traditionally male role.
DISCOVERY Children are often astounded to hear a heart beat through a stethoscope.

ROLL OVER
Five years on

Procedure To develop physically, girls should have as much chance from an early age as boys to play "rough" games that build up confidence in their own strength and physical games skills. *Roll Over* is a trial-of-strength game for either sex. To play, two children lie on their backs side to side in opposite directions. Each then raises the right leg (or left leg if they are lying to the left of each other) and hooks it behind the other's knee. Once the grip is firm, each player must then try to roll the other over on his or her side, using the hooked leg only. *It does not matter who wins.*

Value
SEX EQUALITY Research has shown that many girls are already lagging behind boys in muscular development by the age of eight – partly for physiological reasons but perhaps too because they are encouraged to play "quiet" games. Played at an early age, this game, along with other "rough" games, may help to restore the balance.
FUN The silly position takes the seriousness out of this trial-of-strength.

weeks following conception, to make a boy. A boy is a baby who experienced testosterone; a girl is a baby who did not.

These then are the stereotypes: not the realities. Sex differences may exist: but they are never large, and looked at against the enormous range in children's abilities, are quite insignificant. However, people are still curious to know if boys' and girls' brains are different. Obviously in some ways they are: women menstruate, and menstruation is controlled by the brain. But difference in ability is a more contentious issue.

Some people argue that a boy's upbringing is more likely to encourage his spatial abilities, while a girl's upbringing encourages verbal skills, and that these small differences in the way parents treat children produce differences in abilities. Others believe that the differences are much more fundamental: that girls are born with a tendency to be more verbal, and so enjoy playing verbal games; that boys are born with an interest in things spatial, and so enjoy constructing and building. It is impossible to say who is right. The small differences researchers observe are in grown men and women: by then the cake is cooked, and who can tell whether it was the eggs or the soda that made it rise? More to the point, does it matter? Both spatial and verbal skills should be encouraged in the games you play with your children.

When most of us talk of sex differences, we are not thinking of verbal and spatial abilities, but about the roles culture has traditionally imposed on men and women: women in the home, men out to work, women gentle and caring, men tough and strong.

It is easy to see how these stereotypes arose: without the ability to control her fertility, a woman of childbearing age would always be either pregnant or lactating. Naturally she cared for children, and did other jobs which she could temporarily put aside in order to feed children or retrieve them from danger. Hunting and fighting are obviously incompatible with pregnancy and feeding babies.

Today, women no longer spend most of their adult life bearing and breast feeding children. The traditional sex roles make little sense in modern society: and our culture is gradually changing to accept this. Already we can say with truth that both men and women tend houses and care for babies, and that both sexes leave the home to work. In many instances, children's play already reflects this new interchangeability of sex roles, for play inevitably reflects what children see.

If you feel strongly that your children should not grow up believing in the traditional roles of men and women, you will need to do more than simply encourage your daughters to take on male roles. Girls have always been more flexible in the roles they take up, and there have always been tomboys, and girls who climbed trees better than all the boys in the neighborhood. Young boys, though, are often great conformists: they find it difficult to shake the idea that boys who play with dolls are sissies, however young. My older son was horrified when his 16-month-old brother took a doll and pram for a walk to the park. There was no way that I could induce him to accompany us. Yet, like most of his friends, he responded warmly to his young brother and sister, and at three, he too had enjoyed playing with dolls.

As children enter middle childhood, the peer group pressure increases, and parental influence lessens. The division of the sexes is never greater than between six and ten: if you hope to influence your child's attitude to sex roles it is probably best to try before six or after 14. Better still, let him learn from the example of his family and friends.

SCIENCE MAGIC
Five years on

Procedure Science is traditionally a male pursuit and girls are rarely encouraged to take an interest until it is too late. You can help counter this bias if you know a few simple "science tricks". One is to make huge piles of bubbles by mixing vinegar and bicarbonate of soda. Another is to put a small bottle into the freezer for five minutes and then spread petroleum jelly around the rim. Lay a coin on the rim and begin to warm the bottle by rubbing it. As the air in the bottle heats up, it expands and soon the coin will suddenly pop up, much to the delight of both girls and boys.

Value
SEX EQUALITY
SIMPLE SCIENCE

Variations More simple science tricks are shown on pages 166 and 167. In the same way as girls can be encouraged to take an interest in science, boys can be encouraged to cook. If you approach cooking as applied science – which is, after all, just what it is – some of the "sissy" stigma may be dispelled.

From Six
to Ten Years

MIDDLE CHILDHOOD

Procedure Few things seem to feed a child's growing curiosity than simple scientific experiments, and this one has a nice element of "magic". Stir a little salt and pepper together and then ask a child to separate them with a spoon. It is of course impossible to do so with any real effect. The secret is to rub the spoon against a sweater – preferably one made of man-made fiber – and hold it just above the mixture. Pepper is light and the static electricity on the spoon will lift it free from the salt.

Value
SIMPLE SCIENCE This is a simple and effective demonstration of static electricity. For younger children it is sheer magic!
SORTING For children, the obvious difference between salt and pepper is the color; this game shows how there can be other more subtle distinctions.

Starting school is obviously one of the great landmarks in a child's life, and despite the fact that children enter school at widely differing ages according to nationality, and sometimes income group, the beginning of formal education is a useful departure point for the final section of a book about play. School will, in due course, radically affect the way your child plays, even if not at present. Indeed, at five or six, you will see him playing very much as he did at four.

He still enjoys his sand box, bath toys, and playing with water at the sink. He may have progressed to a bike with two wheels, and a full-size climbing frame with a monkey swing, but apart from his increased agility, you may well see little difference in the way he interacts with his toys. School may color his fantasy world, but will not suppress it. Toy manufacturers, who are obviously aware of how children play, frequently mark toys as being suitable from three to seven years, or four to eight years: a clear reflection that much play does not substantially change in character until about seven.

A child who has enjoyed construction kits will continue to build, mastering more and more complex projects; the puzzler will tackle jigsaws with more and more pieces. A child who enjoys playing *Picture Lotto* may progress to *Chutes and Ladders* or *Uncle Wiggily,* but he will not yet be ready for games of skill or strategy; and although he may enter more into the spirit of the game, he may still be unable to handle losing.

Practice with a pencil will have improved his fine finger control, and he will draw and write with increasing precision. He may fasten buttons, thread laces and beads, and even tie his shoes. His hands could be skilled enough to draw around a template or sew with a large needle. By the time he reaches ten, he may sew and knit, build complex model ships, cook an evening meal, or paint and draw with increasing skill.

His fantasy world is still much in evidence, but the forms it takes may be different now, reflecting his new life at school and the increasing influence of his peer group. He may play Superman, cowboys or monsters: games based on TV characters which have caught the imagination of the group (perhaps an older group) and which may alter at little notice.

These changes are obviously superficial, but there are other, more subtle, differences. At three it was *he* who played the role of "daddy", he who rode the horse, or drove the car; now, he is often the *organizer* of a fantasy world. He gallops the toy horses across the fields of his farm or he takes little people for rides in their cars. He manipulates the pieces and in turn takes all the parts in these miniature worlds: he is not just a single character but the means by which all the characters of his story come to life. At four you may have seen the beginning of this sort of play, by six it was probably more common, but by eight or nine it constitutes a large proportion of his fantasy world. Dolls' houses, trains, forts and battlefields are the classic toys of this era of childhood: racing cars, model villages and space stations are modern alternatives.

Growing up

Although school-age children see themselves as grown-up, it is not always possible to give them extra freedom outside the home. While six may be old enough to play out on a housing development, or in a very small town, it is too young to be out alone on a town or city street, or to go alone to the park, crossing busy roads. But he will need to express his new maturity in some way: it may be possible to take a trip to the mail box, to go alone to a local shop, or simply to telephone a friend or help with the household chores.

Some children learn to read in their first year at school, but few of them are able, or willing, to sit down and read a story to themselves. They will still look at pictures, and need you to read, for some time yet. That jump between having stories read and reading books happens after they can read competently, say between seven and nine years of age.

Seven

Seven marks much more of a watershed in intellectual development than five or six, and in physical and social development too. At about seven, children experience a growth spurt and a slight change in the shape of their bodies. Boys become a little broader in the shoulder, girls a little broader in the hip, and there is a slight change in the hair line. (The changes are produced by the release of very small amounts of the sex hormones, testosterone and estrogen, and will be greatly increased at puberty, when these hormones are released in much larger amounts.) Between the growth spurt at seven and the later, and much larger one, that signals the onset of puberty, there is a steady improvement in muscular balance and hand-eye co-ordination. Most six-year-olds can kick a ball, many can catch one, but few of them show any real skill until they are eight or nine.

At six he may still be very close to you, but by eight there will probably be a change in your relationship. He may no longer

SECRET CODES
Seven to nine years

Procedure During these secretive years, children love codes, invisible ink and secret passwords. There are an infinite number of codes they can try, and children will probably make up their own, but a good starting point is to make a code based on their names. The first letters of the alphabet can be coded as the letters of their name; the remaining letters can be counted off from there on. Thus if his name is Daniel, the code word would be "Daniel" and the code would be as follows:

Letter: A B C D E F
Code: D A N I E L
Letter: G H I J K . . .
Code: B C F G H . . .

The code letter for I must be F because D and E are already encoded in DANIEL. They can, of course, make a similar code based on any code word they choose – the less people who know it the better. Codes need not be written, though, and two of the best known "visual" codes, morse and semaphore, are shown on page 169.

Value
INDEPENDENCE It is important and natural for children of this age to show their independence by creating their own secret worlds with their friends.
NUMERACY AND LITERACY. To make codes work, children must be logical and precise in their counting. Codes also encourage children to play with words.

INVISIBLE INK
Seven to nine years

Procedure Like codes, invisible ink is a wonderful prop for the secret games of these years. One of the simplest invisible inks is potato juice. To make a potato inkwell, cut off both ends of a large potato, stand it up, and scoop out a hole. Scrape and squeeze into the hole juice from the top of the potato. To write, dip a used matchstick into the hole. The ink becomes invisible when it dries and the message only appears again when the paper is warmed near a lightbulb. Lemon juice, onion juice and Coca-Cola will all work in the same way.

Value
DISCOVERY
SOCIAL
FUN

Variations Wax can also be used for secret writing. Wax some paper by rubbing with a candle. Then lay the paper wax side down on a fresh sheet. Write the message firmly so that it is printed on to the paper beneath. The secret message can be read by sprinkling with any colored powder, such as instant coffee.

enjoy sitting and talking to you as much, and the warm involvement of early childhood may have gone: he may confide in you less, show less affection, and may even seem a stranger in your home: as you ask about his day he moves impatiently from foot to foot, longing for the time he can run through the door to his friends. He could become withdrawn from the family, where once he was open and talkative. His friends are now his confidants and the leaders of his play. More often than not you will be uncertain where he is, for now he escapes with his friends to a world you cannot enter: the secret world of middle childhood.

At six his friendships are fleeting things; he is attracted to a group by the games they play rather than the children who are playing, and may change friends from week to week. Six-year-old boys and girls still play together in school and at home, but by eight the sexes are more separate than at any other time in their lives. Although school playgrounds are mixed, boys and girls play almost entirely separately, unless the school is very small. At home there may be more mixing: but many children have no friends of the opposite sex. In both sexes, friendships can be firm and lasting by eight.

These are the years of pranks: of ringing door bells and running away, of telephoning people with odd names. They are the years of secret clubs, codes and passwords, of climbing high into trees and paddling in streams. They are the years in which there is every point in possessing 250 keyrings or a sweater exactly like every other child in the neighborhood.

Parents sometimes look back with nostalgia at their offspring's early childhood. Through the rosy glow of the child's funny ways and childish talk they forget the worry and the lack of sleep. But when adults look back on their own childhoods, it is surely these carefree middle childhood years of new-found independence that they savor most. Certainly, when people write of childhood, those are the years most often recalled.

So when you find it increasingly difficult to get a child to play in ways you see as constructive, and wonder whether all those years of patient supervision have been wasted, don't despair, and think back on your own enjoyment of middle childhood. All these new departures, even negative ones like being bullied, or excluded from the gang, are as integral to development as play, which once depended on your presence or inspiration.

For your role now gradually passes from that of executive director to chairman. You can understand, if not actually know, what is going on; you can steer, rather than intervene; and when he tires of his own devices, or other children's, or suddenly sees the futility of a new craze, you can, at least, be a source of ideas.

CODES/*Seven to nine years*

If your children like secret codes, try introducing them to the classic signalling codes, morse and semaphore – real codes used by the navy, coastguards and many others.

Morse can be signalled indoors by tapping on pipes or, outdoors on sunny days, by flashing a mirror towards the message taker. After dark, a flashlight can be flashed by simply passing a hand across the beam.

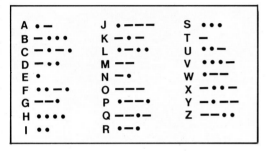

A	• —	J	• — — —	S	• • •
B	— • • •	K	— • —	T	—
C	— • — •	L	• — • •	U	• • —
D	— • •	M	— —	V	• • • —
E	•	N	— •	W	• — —
F	• • — •	O	— — —	X	— • • —
G	— — •	P	• — — •	Y	— • — —
H	• • • •	Q	— — • —	Z	— — • •
I	• •	R	• — •		

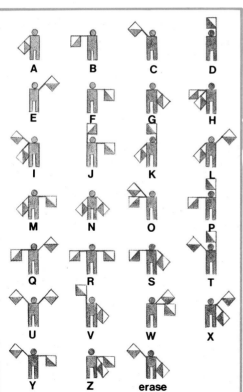

Semaphore signals can be sent with a pair of brightly colored handkerchiefs, but signals are clearer if these are attached to sticks.

Value
APPEALS TO SENSE OF SECRECY

SCALE DRAWING
Seven years on

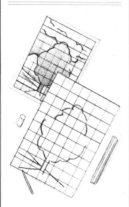

Procedure Children whose artistic skill is limited can still make successful drawings by using a grid to copy another picture. Lay a sheet of tracing paper over the original and draw a grid with lines half an inch (1.25 cm) apart. On a fresh sheet of paper, draw a grid of any size, but consisting of the same number of squares. Then copy the original on to the fresh sheet using the grid as a guide. If the grid is in pencil, it can be erased out when the drawing is finished.

Value
MOTOR SKILL
USEFUL SKILL The ability to scale up and down using grids may prove invaluable.
QUIET PLAY
SPATIAL ABILITY

THE AGE OF REASON

A four-year-old tends to talk as if she believes that when two things happen at the same time they must be related. Listen to the things she says and you can hear the way she thinks. At four she might say:

"It can't be bedtime because I haven't had my bath yet."
"I think I need a drink because my knee hurts."

But an eight-year-old does not talk like this. Part of the joy of small children is listening to their childish reasoning. It is not that they lack logic, nor that their logic is fundamentally at fault. If I hit a ball and it moves, I am logically correct in concluding that my hitting caused it to move; but when a child applies the same rule to the relationship between bedtime and bath, her application of logic is wrong.

From the start, children have a scheme of things, and they fit the information they gather into this scheme. Their schemes are simple, one might even say primitive, ways of making sense of the world. But children are not static, their knowledge and abilities grow day by day, and naturally they begin to see the limitations of their way of thinking. As they grow and develop, they change and restructure their view of the world. Such changes are always gradual, and they happen more than once during childhood.

One such change occurred at only about nine months, when the baby's developing memory made it possible for her to see that things exist even when she is not looking. Another came at about 14 months, when she began to use words and actions to stand in for objects. At about six or seven, perhaps earlier, the key change is that she begins to extract general principles from her individual experiences and you will notice this now that she has the language to express her discoveries.

Intuitive to inductive reasoning

The early "childish" type of reasoning, where, if two things happen at the same time, one causes the other, could be called intuitive. At six or seven, this gradually becomes inductive reasoning.

Consider this example: your four-year-old has just come back from day care and is telling you about her morning. She begins by asking "Did you see Zoë's new shoes?" She has not forgotten that her grandmother always picks her up from day care, rather than you, but she takes it for granted that you share her experience. When you tell her you are not sure who Zoë is, she answers, "You know, the girl I was playing in the boat with."

An eight-year-old's thinking, by contrast, has progressed to the extent that she can put herself in your place: to realizing that since you were not at the school, you need further information in order to make sense of what she says. She is likely to start, "You know that girl whose mother drives the red sports car . . ." Indeed, even five-year-olds will start an anecdote with "You know me, well . . ."

Piaget, whose theories of child development have had so much influence on the way we view children's thinking, called the childish inability to put oneself in another's position "egocentrism". The child sees things through her own perspective, and does not always take account of other views. Put like that, it is clear that egocentrism is not confined to young children. How often have you talked too fast for a foreigner with little English to understand you? On the other hand, what of the four-year-old who simplifies her speech and raises the pitch of her voice when she talks to a younger child, or a baby doll?

Clearly, egocentrism is a matter of degree. We are all egocentric sometimes, but for the pre-school child, egocentrism is more likely to be the rule than the exception. She may not even realize that when you sit on opposite sides of the kitchen table, she can see out of the window, but you cannot.

Five may seem rather late to realize that people do not have eyes in the back of their heads; but learning that her own point of view is different from yours is more complex than it seems to you. First, she has to learn the properties of objects: that they have tops and bottoms, backs and fronts. Second, she has to learn that other people have different perspectives: they look at things from different angles to her; and third she has to realize what that perspective is. Learning to appreciate another's view does not only apply to what we see but to what we feel and think as well, and these skills can be broken down in similar ways. In effect, this crucial development away from egocentrism is simply a matter of putting herself in your position; or, taking your role. So role-playing and pretending still assume great importance in your child's development.

The ability to realize that other minds have other views and that these views may not coincide with her own is not only sophisticated but probably essential: there is even evidence that its development correlates well with reading skill: a child who learns the other point of view early on is likely to read early; one who learns later, to read later.

Mastering the other point of view will be partly learned from

BENDY BONES
Six years on

Procedure Children of this age are fascinated by the world around them and simple science tricks are very popular. To make bones bendy, take a clean stiff chicken bone with no cracks. Place it in a bowl overnight, completely covered with vinegar. The next morning the bone will be pliable and soft.

Value
SIMPLE SCIENCE This experiment shows that the acid in the vinegar dissolves the calcium which makes the bones rigid.
SUSTAINED ACTIVITY

FLYING CORKS
Six years on

Procedure Another fun experiment is to put two spoonfuls of bicarbonate of soda into a wine bottle. Then mix four spoonfuls of vinegar and four of water and pour into the bottle. Push the cork in very gently a little way and point the bottle in a SAFE direction. Carbon dioxide will soon send the cork shooting out. For safety's sake, children must always be supervised.

Value
SIMPLE SCIENCE
FUN

ON THE MAP
Seven years on

Procedure Learning to map-read is an activity that nicely complements the growing independence of middle childhood. You can introduce her to maps step by step by making a game of locating places. Start with a simple map, and ask her to find a certain street or certain town for you. When she becomes adept at this try: "What towns do I pass through if I go to . . .?" Remember, you have to play too, or it simply becomes hard work for her. Draw a map of the area immediately around your house, showing only the familiar roads, and see if she can recognize features. See if she can go out and find the house you mark on the map.

Value
USEFUL SKILL; LOCAL KNOWLEDGE; INDEPENDENCE; DISCOVERY

Later progress Teach her how to make her own maps of places she knows.

you, of course. If you allow that she has views and opinions that differ from yours, she is more likely to see that the reverse is also true. Suppose she is busy painting, but has left her blocks all over the floor. You could insist that she leaves her painting and picks up the blocks at once. Or you could insist that she does so as soon as she finishes. In the first case you do not allow for her point of view; in the second you do. Adding that next time she will have to pick up the blocks before she starts painting because you could trip over them allows her to see your view, too. If you attend to her view, she will learn to attend to yours. When your child looks tearful as you read a sad story, or comes and hugs you when you are feeling down, you will know that she is learning.

From the immediate to the operational

The third major feature of the pre-schooler's way of thinking is also related to her egocentrism, indeed it probably explains it in part: she finds it difficult to take more than one relatively simple concept into account at the same time.

Give her two identical balls of play dough and she will tell you that they are the same. Now flatten one, and she will not appreciate that they still contain the same amount of dough. Her attention is caught by the change of shape, and she cannot keep in mind how things were before. This failure to go back a step in her mind has an obvious consequence: if she finds it difficult to appreciate that the flat play dough was once round, she will probably also find it hard to work out that the operation can be reversed – that a flat ball of play dough can be returned to its round shape. Indeed, she does not think at all in terms of operating on – modifying – substances, or indeed operations generally. She thinks in terms of here and now; of immediate causes and immediate effects.

These new skills will develop so gradually that you can hardly detect them. However, you can see how she is progressing if you try this simple experiment. Make two lines of five buttons – she will see they are the same. Then, spread out one line so that it is longer. Some five-year-olds (and most four-year-olds) will tell you that there are more buttons in the long line. But most seven-year-olds will tell you the lines are the same. If she gets it wrong, try again, but this time make a "naughty doll" trip over and accidentally disturb one line, so that it is longer than the other. She may well now see that there are the same number of buttons in both lines because her understanding depends upon how she experiences the cause of the change. The doll messed them up; you *changed* them on purpose, and that distracted her from seeing that the number of buttons remained the same.

Virtually everyone who has worked with young children

agrees that there is a big difference in the child's thinking between five and seven. Like moving from babyhood to childhood, the process is a gradual one; yet at the same time it is sudden and complete. One day you realize that some of that innocence and wonder has gone. Her response to the world was in terms of images and actions, now it is in terms of ideas. She may not be an adult, but she is beginning to think like one. She will learn more, and change again, but the age of reason has been reached. Looking back over her pre-school years, it is easy to see why her interests were as they were. Why she needed to explore both objects, and relationships, and why she played as she did. If one could re-run the film of her early years, we might see her progression from the particular to the general: from understanding in certain instances to the development of reasoning and its application to new experiences.

The role of play

Looking back, one can surely see how important it was for her to play with water, sand and building blocks, for these were the elements by which she learned to transform one thing to another and to reverse that process. Her examples were concrete: she learned how to pour water from a jug to a cup and back again. She learned to build, to take down and to rebuild. She did not think everything out in advance: she worked it out with the blocks and sand before her. Now she can abstract those skills: she has learned the rules, and she can move ideas about in the same way.

One can also see more clearly just why making believe was so important, and why she spent so much time playing her games of fantasy. The roles she played were her earliest ideas: her first abstractions. As she played "mommy", and answered back for her doll, she not only saw the world from a parent's point of view, she also switched between the role of parent and child. As the buttons from the sewing box fought a war on the bedroom carpet, she was on one side then the other, advancing one army and causing the other to retreat. This flexibility is, of course, what characterizes the ability to reason.

Now, in middle childhood, practice has not yet made perfect and there is still much to learn, but she has made a start. She needs now to practice her new spectrum of skills, to play the more formal games that will test reasoning ability: games with rules. You will probably notice, at the same time, that her pretend play starts to decline.

Little worlds

As he becomes more social, he also becomes more self-conscious.

ZOHN AHL
Six years on

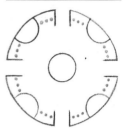

Procedure Zohn Ahl is based on a Kiowa Indian game. The board (above) can be drawn or sewn. The counters are a silver coin (the "Sahe") and three bronze coins. Any number can play, divided into two teams. Each team has a "runner" and four counters. The idea is to get your runner round the course first, each team running in opposite directions. Runners take turns moving according to the way the four coins fall when dropped on the central "ahl stone". Each bronze "head" moves forward a step; "heads" on the silver moves the runner two steps. But four "heads" scores six and four "tails" ten. Landing in a gully means missing a turn; landing in a river means starting again. If two runners land on the same square, the last to arrive wins the round. Otherwise, the first runner to get all the way around wins the lap and a counter from the opposing team. The winner is the team to win all eight counters, or to have most counters when time runs out.

Value
COUNTING
LEARNING TO WIN AND LOSE

TANGRAMS/*Seven years on*

Tangrams are mathematical puzzles that came originally from China. There are few better ways of developing a child's awareness of the conservation of area – that is, the fact that two completely different flat shapes can have the same area. The puzzle is a square of wood or cardboard cut into seven pieces, which are re-arranged to form an enormous variety of shapes – all with the same area as the original square – though they seem much larger.

PLAN

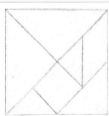

The cardboard should be about 10 in (25 cm) square and, preferably, dark in color. To draw the pattern on the card: draw a diagonal from top left to bottom right; find the halfway marks on the top and right-hand sides and draw a line between them; draw the other diagonal as far as this second line; draw a vertical line from the point where the lines meet to the first diagonal; and draw a line from the halfway mark at the top parallel to the second, diagonal to meet the first. When all these lines are drawn, cut out the shapes using a sharp scalpel or craft knife. When she has had enough of playing freely with the shapes, she can try the patterns, right.

Value
QUIET PLAY; CONCEPT OF AREA

● Dog – a simple first tangram.

● Bird – a more challenging shape.

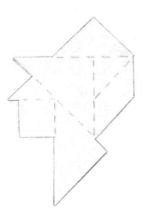

● Face – a difficult tangram for the experienced.

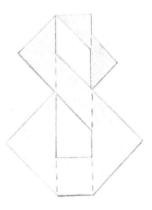

● Figure eight – for tangram wizards only.

At four, he was quite happy to go to the shops in an Indian head-dress, now he is less sure. He will put on Indian clothes to go out to play, but is likely to collapse into fits of giggles if he sees you watching him. His embarrassment may lead to a bout of showing off, or he may retreat into play without fantasy. However, there is safety in numbers, and if he has his friends to support him, cops and robbers, witches and fairies, or teachers and pupils can all continue with an adult audience.

Even at six, though, it may be hard to eavesdrop on his daydreams, and by eight you may see him sitting quietly in thought. When he plays alone, he may need a different sort of prop for his fantasy. He is less likely to be a policeman patrolling the streets in search of a burglar; instead, he tends to create a little world which he controls from the outside; a world he can manipulate and change, where he can try things out, and work things through. He decides upon the dramas, the sorrows and the intentions of his small people. If cars crash, it is because that is his wish, and if people die, or are sad, it may be because he feels this sadness. But he is also outside this world; he decides upon the sorrows, but is not affected by them: they belong to the house, or the station master, and can be turned off by walking away.

A mirror on his problems?

This aspect of play at this age – the playing out of dramas that are both created by the child and at a distance from him – has greatly interested psychologists. It is thought that through this sort of play the child expresses his innermost fears and feelings; that one can gain an insight into his problems by watching him play in his little world.

In some cases this undoubtedly happens: children do work out their problems in this way, but it would be unwise to read too much into your child's fantasy world. As an adult, you do not look at his actions with a child's eye, but with the eye of your own fears, prejudices and hang-ups. If he runs over one of his toy soldiers with a car, it does not have to mean he fears death, or that he is jealous of a younger brother and wishes him dead. He may just have taken your lecture on road safety extremely seriously, and be demonstrating to his little people what can happen if they are not careful.

Don't look for problems: you will certainly see them if you do, and the problems you detect are as likely to be yours as his. He may act out his fears in a natural and healthy way; he may work through deep-seated problems; or he may simply be retelling a favorite story. It is all therapy – coming to terms with his chang-

MESSAGE IN A BOTTLE
Seven years

Procedure Putting a message in a bottle is the kind of simple pastime that fascinates many children of this age. It only needs a brief message, such as "My name . . .; my address . . .; the date . . .; I threw this bottle in the sea at . . . Please write." The chances are no-one will reply, but wondering where it will go and who might find it, as well as looking on a map, are all great fun.

Value
IMAGINATION All kinds of people might find it, almost anywhere in the world.
SUSTAINED INTEREST

Variations Try tying a message wrapped in a plastic bag to a helium-filled balloon.

TOWN PLANNING
Eight years on

Procedure Many children have not the patience or the manual skill to build an elaborate model railway landscape – and they may prefer cars anyway. But a simple and fascinating alternative is to draw the roads for the cars on large, tough sheets of paper – good quality brown wrapping paper will do. Your own street provides an ideal starting point, but he can soon draw another set of streets, complete with road marking and traffic islands, whenever he gets bored with one layout.

Value
IMAGINATION
OBSERVATION Most children will get pleasure from making their roads and road signs correspond closely to the real thing.
DRAWING SKILL

ing world, learning to organize his thoughts, or simple pleasure – all a game worth playing.

Making worlds

These little worlds take many forms. At first he may be content to push his cars along roads he has drawn with chalk on the garden path; later he will demand more realistic roads, and cars to scale. Houses, airports and garages with their little cars and peg people delight his younger brother; he will now demand more realistic people, with suitcases and planes made to the correct scale. The people will need shops to drive to, lamp posts in their streets and baskets to hold.

At six, he will probably be at the intermediate stage in this progression, moving perhaps from peg people to the more realistic "play people" – small plastic models with mobile limbs, whose realism is increased by their ability to hold many different objects. He will have begun to build cars and houses with Lego, and to build garages and houses with boxes.

By the time he is seven or eight he will be dissatisfied with the worlds that others have created for him, and will want something more personal: something that he has made for himself. The classic toys of this era are indeed the train set and the dolls' house, and for the right child they are hard to beat. But not all children enjoy playing in this sort of way: like construction sets, they are toys which give great pleasure, or languish on a shelf gathering dust.

Train sets

Fortunately, it is possible to try out these expensive toys before you buy. If you suspect that he would enjoy a train set, it would be wise to start by building a model layout for toy cars. It is possible to buy or make roadways made of strong cardboard, and likewise houses and trees to line the roads. At first he can build this world in his bedroom, but eventually he will need a permanent corner in which to set up the little world.

For four- to eight-year-olds, a wooden railway system, such as made by Brio, with its bridges, viaducts and little push-along trains, is excellent, if expensive. The somewhat cheaper plastic push-along railways are also excellent, but in the long term, a child who enjoys railways will probably want an electric train set.

Although a road layout or wooden railway can be taken up at the end of play, taking up electric rails and laying them out each time is unsatisfactory. Children soon tire of checking points and making sure that all the connections are good. They want the trains to move: for although much of the pleasure is in designing and building the layout (and planning changes), the trains still need to run. If there is no floor space, you might consider a system that hauls the board up from the floor to the ceiling by ropes and pulleys.

A train set should always be fixed to a board that is large enough to accommodate countryside and stations in addition to the rails. Do not be tempted to put together the whole layout for him: let him decide where the lines and stations should be, and let him add trees, houses and roads of his own making. As he grows older he will be able to make tunnels and bridges, and to re-model his system so that the trains can move in intricate patterns. But even at ten, he will need some help.

The old story about buying a train set for father has more than a grain of truth, so leave the child, rather than the parent, in charge. He will learn little from watching either of you. Train sets have lost much of their popularity, possibly because children stop playing with toys at an earlier age these days. Car racing tracks have taken some of the custom, and although these are more limited in scope and cannot be used to create nearly such an interesting little world, they are often preferred by seven- and eight-year-olds.

Dolls' houses

A first dolls' house can be made quite simply with two cartons placed side by side. A little wallpaper on the inner walls, thick polyethylene for windows, and a brick or wood pattern on the outer walls and the house will be ready for occupation. Snippets of carpet, or cork tiles, can serve as floor covering. Most children will be happiest with a combination of manufactured and home-made furniture. But you may be surprised how important it is to your child that the house contains a bathroom, lavatory and kitchen; and, if the house is on two stories, stairs are likely to be another necessity. Certainly, dolls' house play is largely pretend play, but you should not underestimate the potent charm of simulation.

If she enjoys her cardboard-box house, it may be worth buying a ready-made one. Houses are available with one or two stories, with opening fronts and lift-off roofs, and they range in price from a few dollars to a small fortune. For a young child, furniture should be quite sturdy. A house needs a family to live in it, plus some of the little details of family life: a tiny cake on the table, books in the bookcase, and a diminutive letter ready for mailing on the hall table. Once set up, houses, like train sets, don't take kindly to being moved and deserve a permanent resting place. If that is to be your hall or living room, everyone benefits if the house is pleasing to look at.

STAPLE SEWING
Eight years on

Procedure Making clothes for dolls can be great fun, but many children find it difficult to sew. This need not be a problem if they use alternative ways of putting clothes together. Glue is one good method. But even quicker and least messy are staples. Encourage children to create their own designs, but show them simple but attractive "designer" clothes in magazines to give them ideas – the more flamboyant the better.

Value
CREATIVE Designing clothes can be as creative as any artwork.
USEFUL SKILL
IMAGINATION

COIN SOCCER
Eight years on

Procedure Coin soccer is a simple game which most children of eight can master. It involves two players taking turns shoving a large coin with the edge of a card (such as an old credit card) so that it cannons a smaller coin towards the opposing goal. But the game provides extra food for the imagination if the table top is large enough to accommodate two full soccer teams – plywood is an ideal surface. The teams are ten large coins painted in a favorite team's colors, with players individually identified; the goalkeeper is a cork which can be moved along the goal-line while the other player is "shooting". Ideally, matches should be timed – five minutes each way and scores, with real team names, entered properly in a record book.

Value
MOTOR SKILL
FUN
IMAGINATION The full teams satisfy a child's demand for realism and foster imagination.

Building

While dolls' houses are traditionally for girls and forts and soldiers are for boys, the latter encounter severe competition nowadays from the space station. I am unsure how successful these are as a basis for miniature worlds. In my limited experience, the space station is rarely built more than once, but Lego is not wasted because it can, of course, be used to build all sorts of different worlds. The technical version of Lego, with motors and lights, is even more successful at creating a range of worlds; and the fact that a model works is pleasing to children, especially if they have made it themselves.

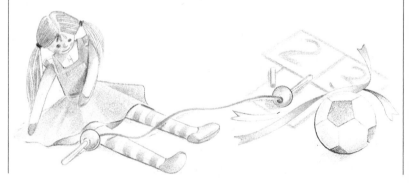

BAN THE WORD
Seven years on

Procedure Children of this age love being in on secrets and silly games. *Ban the Word* involves both parents and children – though you will probably get bored with it long before an eight-year-old. The idea is simply to ban a common word, such as "hand" or "eat" or "outside" for a whole week. Every time anyone uses the word during that week they must put a cross on the scoreboard. The fun is to catch people off guard and get them to say the word.

Value
STRATEGY Tricking people into saying the banned word requires considerable ingenuity. OBSERVATION To spot others using the banned word and avoid using it herself, she must constantly be on the alert.
VERBAL SKILL Searching for ways round using the word stretches her verbal skill.

Variation Instead of banning a word, you could try substituting it with something really silly like "pink bananas" instead of "shoes". A further alternative is to use the game to extend her vocabulary – though you must play too if it is not to become a dull exercise.

CHILDREN'S CULTURE

"Where have you been?"
"Out."
 "Who with?"
 "Oh, you know."
  "What have you been doing?"
  "Nothing much."
A typical conversation between a nine-year-old and her parents. These are the secretive years: the years in which you rarely know where your children are; and hardly ever see them playing unless their secret clubhouse is in your backyard. So elusive are they at this age that adults often think that today's children do not play the games of their youth, or live by the rules of childhood as they knew it; that the culture of childhood is dying.

They forget that as children they believed that they alone knew the games and the rhymes; that they chose to play in the woods and back streets, on the vacant lot and behind the church hall. On wet days it would be the cellar, attic or even the bus shelter. Even in this age of computer games and television, children play a great deal on the streets just as they always have. Of course, they often sit at home watching TV or sneak down to the arcade to play video games; but most of the time, eight-year-olds play many of the games their parents did before them, and have the same notions of honor and fairness that their grandparents had before that. Essentially, they still speak the language their parents spoke and live by the rules of their parents' childhoods, perhaps with the obvious exception of swearing.

When your child starts choosing between the cakes for tea:
"Eeny meeny miney mo,"
or shouts "Not it!" at the start of a game, or chants:
"A my name is Alice,
My husband's name is Al,
We come from Alabama,
And we sell apples,"
you can honestly begin to assume that things have not really changed very much; and when she starts to avoid the cracks in the pavement, you can be certain they have not.

In spite of the cars that clutter the streets, and television, which lures them indoors, children's culture has survived. Girls still skip to the same rhymes, cross their fingers and call "time out" (or "king's X") to demand a truce in which to fasten a shoe during a chasing game.

Children (and some parents) still believe in omens and good-luck charms. They chant to bring luck as they shake a die or take their turn at marbles. They may still avoid stepping on beetles, or cracks in the pavement, and believe that black cats bring bad luck. For some children, ambulances and funerals are unlucky unless you hold your collar until you see a dog. Similarly, when you drive past a cemetery, you hold your breath, and when you drive under a bridge, you duck. Ladders should not be walked under, and blowing on a dandelion, or wishing on a star can make your wish come true.

A child's word is still binding, and she will probably seal it as her mother did with ritual words and deeds.

"My finger's wet," (licking finger)

"My finger's dry," (wiping it)

"Cut my throat," (head back)

"If I tell a lie" (drawing finger across her throat);

or, more often: "Honest injun," "Scout's honor," or "cross my heart and hope to die." She may cross her arms across her chest, hold two fingers in the air, spit on the ground, or lick her fingers and form a cross on her throat. The exact words and actions that children use vary from generation to generation, but not the underlying rule: whatever the words, they are always binding.

If you don't believe her (she might, after all, be crossing her fingers behind her back – quite fair, as far as children are concerned), you can ask her to take some further oath or test: "Look up to heaven without laughing," and tickle her under the chin; or ask her to draw a line in the dust without getting her finger dirty.

At one time, such rituals were not confined to children: in Scotland the pressing together of licked thumbs was a way of sealing a bargain, as it is still in many a Scottish playground. In England, and New York, it is the little fingers that are licked or linked. In the past, if a woman claimed she was not a witch, her word was tested in the same arbitrary fashion.

The code

Children's culture, like children's play, is based on trust. A cry of "king's X" in the middle of a fight can stop the fight while the participants take off their coats. A shout of "dibs" can claim the only sandwich worth eating, or the biggest slice of cake. Although it is possible to complain "you are dibsing everything", it would be a gross breach of the rules for anyone to take something that had been verbally bagged.

Dibs can become a game in itself: "Dibs on the sidewalk," "Dibs on the grass," "Dibs on the fence," can make it

JACOB'S TAIL
Seven years on

Procedure This is a useful game for a group of mixed ages and sexes and has a strong element of ritual that seems to appeal to children around this age. One player is Jacob; all the rest but one line up behind her, arms about each others' waists. The remaining player is the tagger. To start the game she says *"Jacob, what do you want?"* and Jacob replies *"Catch the last one if you can."* The player at the end of Jacob's tail tries to run round to the head, aided by the swinging and squirming of the tail – the tail must not break, though. If he is tagged, he drops out of the game. If he succeeds in arriving at the head without being tagged, he becomes Jacob. The game goes on until all players have been tagged or have been Jacob once.

Value
WORKING TOGETHER The members of the tail must co-operate fully with each other to swing the tail and save the runner.
SOCIAL; EXUBERANT FUN

JAN-KEN-PON
Seven years on

Procedure This is an old Japanese game, well known in the West as *Scissors, Paper, Stone,* and a marvelous way for two children to pass an odd ten minutes together in a confined space. There are many versions, but the best known is for each player to bring her hand swiftly out from behind her back on the cry *Ick-ack-ock* or *Jan-ken-pon.* As she does so, she commits her hand into the shape of scissors, paper or stone. The two players then compare shapes. Scissors snip (and so beat) paper; paper wraps (and beats) stone; and stone blunts (and beats) scissors. The game should be played quickly.

Value
ANTICIPATION, CO-ORDINATION

pretty difficult to walk home. *Dibs* can also get you first go with the ball, or first turn on a new bike; it can even secure you last place if that is an advantage (though often being last can involve being a "rotten egg"). And if you do not want to wash-up, or hold the end of the skipping rope, there is usually a formula.

It is perhaps surprising that among children, who vary so much in size, strength and status, it should be words that decide so many things. Verbal agreement according to an established code seems a remarkably fair – even adult – way of settling potential disputes. But it would be wrong to assume children are always fair. The rules that govern childhood are as rigid as the rules that govern any other society, and to an adult such rules will often seem patently unfair. However, there is little point in saying so, for to do so is to fail to understand (as she will certainly tell you) that to a child the laws are binding. Children trust each other; but that does not mean that they never take advantage of a smaller or weaker child, or accept a child who is "different" with open arms. If she has swapped a bracelet for a couple of old comics, you may feel aggrieved, but she knows that

"touch teeth, touch leather,
No backsies for ever and ever"

is totally binding. Swapping is often not fair, and a child desperate to join the gang may pay dearly for entry. The very existence of rhymes and rituals to seal the bargain suggests it was always like this.

If swapping is "unfair" on some children, "giving" is even more so: for the same rules apply. If something is given it must not be taken back, or the child will be labelled an "Indian giver" or a bad sport. Possession is all, and this applies to things that are found as well as given:

"Finders keepers,
Losers weepers."

It is recognized among children that the uttering of this formula gives a child an absolute right to the article (unless another child shouts for "halves"); however, valuable property is excluded from the code, and to this extent the child's code recognizes adult concepts of ownership. The ethos (if not the practice) of Western society may be very much at odds with the idea of "finders keepers", yet something of the spirit of the child's law remains in the way we deal with buried treasure, or in the rules which govern squatting. And many law-abiding adults may feel that when it comes to wild mushrooms and fruit, it is "finders keepers", even if they grow on private land.

Many people have written with nostalgia about their childhood, about the games, the pranks, and the friendships, and of the tight secret community they inhabited – rather as the middle-aged or elderly look back with nostalgia on the hard but happy times of their youth. For many of us it was perhaps like that: there was freedom and romance in those years. But just as nostalgia for a tight, supportive community can blur the awfulness of poverty and disease, so nostalgia for the good things of childhood can blur the inescapable fact that it is often savage and cruel. The hair-pulling, tortures and fighting; the falling out and the name-calling and taunting of unpopular (or different) children, were always as much a part of childhood as the loyalty and trust. Of course, one could always say:

"Sticks and stones will break my bones –
  but names will never hurt me.
And when I'm dead and in my grave,
  You'll be sorry for what you called me."

But it was not true then, nor is it now. Childhood should be a magic time, but even for those with happy childhoods, it is sometimes quite savage, perhaps necessarily so. Standing on her own feet is, we all know, part of growing up; and learning to adjust to society's written and unwritten codes is an essential "life skill". During these secretive years, she will learn these lessons through her quarrels, in falling out and making friends again, and in the slavish following of the rules of her group. Conformity at any cost is not what many of us want for our children, and certainly not conformity to values other than our own; but it is what most children demand of each other, and as parents we are as helpless as our children to oppose this *status quo*. We cannot fight their battles for them; we can only offer loving support if they choose to rebel against their group, and make sure that it is their battles – not ours – that they are fighting. Being the only girl who never wears a dress, or the only boy with long hair and earrings, can be pretty tough at seven years old.

TWO-LEGGED HORSE
Eight years on

Procedure This noisy and exuberant game should be played on soft grass under adult supervision. The game is played in pairs, and each child clasps her partner's right hand with her own, and her partner's left ankle with her left hand, lifting the leg off the ground. The pairs then lean back and hop round and round. But they must react quickly when the adult gives the following sharp cries: "Gee!" which means hop the other way round; "Gee! Gee!" which means hop and push together; and "Gee! Gee! Gee!" which means hop and pull apart.

Value
FUN This game often goes on until the children are exhausted.
BALANCE
CO-OPERATION

MARBLES
Seven years on

Procedure The lasting attraction of marbles lies as much in collecting the marbles as playing the game. Building up a collection of rare or especially attractive marbles can be very satisfying for a child of this age. There are many ways to play marbles, but one of the simplest and most popular is to use the marbles as shooters. One distinctively colored marble is used as a target. Players then take turns rolling their marbles (six each) as near to the target as possible, from about six feet (2 m). Players can use a marble to knock one of their opponent's marbles away if they wish, but excessive use of this tactic will be regarded as unsporting. The winner is the player with the marble nearest the target at the end of each round.

Value
COLLECTION; RITUAL; MANUAL SKILL; STRATEGY

Variations Other popular ways of playing marbles are described in the text (*page 200*).

COLLECTING AND GATHERING

As September comes around, British school children in their thousands flock to horse chestnut trees in search of conkers, or chestnuts. Where I grew up there was one glorious parade of "conker trees": "the 49 conkers". Everyone called it that, though I do not recall that anyone actually counted the trees. Like most children, we felt we had an unassailable right to the conkers, even though the trees were in the middle of private farmland. Throughout September children trooped across the fields, and although some of us knew our country code, gates were often left open, and cattle would be left to stray from field to field.

We were clearly not popular with the farmer, and at intervals he would ride over the fields in his Land-Rover brandishing a shotgun: or so we believed as we ran for our lives. At the first sound of his engine we would be back across the fields, in fear and trembling. (But what fun, and how often we relived the run.) Many conkers were dropped on the way, but never all of them. At home we would carefully polish them with vinegar, or bake them in the oven. Then we made holes from top to bottom with a hot meat skewer and threaded them with strings or shoe laces in order to "play conkers" – that was why we *said* we collected them. In fact, I think *possession* of the conkers was everything. I do not remember the games of conkers, though we certainly played; yet I do remember the boxes of conkers in my bedroom. I remember arranging them by size, polishing them on my skirt and inviting friends in to see them, but mostly I remember counting and recounting them before bed. Collecting and possessing the conkers was the real job, rather than the game itself, which in truth is rather dull. Admittedly, towards the end of the season, individual conkers became prized for their battle record: in a conker fight, the aim is to split another conker suspended on its string by hitting it with your own. The winner becomes a "oneser", and later a "twoser" if it wins again, and so on. But I think the game remains not an end in itself but merely a focus for the greater pleasure of collecting, and the rituals that go with possession. To understand this is to understand many of the seemingly pointless games of middle childhood, and the sudden crazes that sweep through your neighborhood.

Toffee Wrappers, Barbie and Action Man
A few years ago, 700 seven-year-old children were asked if they had any collections: over 70 per cent of children answered yes.

They collected anything from candy wrappers, bus tickets, leaves, coins, stamps, handkerchiefs, small cars, little dolls, match boxes or bubblegum cards to pictures of pop stars. Every so often manufacturers manage to tap this collecting instinct: suddenly children are all collecting football cards bought in packs of six, or *Star Wars* figures. The manufacturers of breakfast cereals must hope that one of their free gifts will catch on in this way, as sometimes they do, and hamburger chains that give away little gifts (or let you buy them at a reduced rate) are seeking the same route to parents' purses. One can hardly blame them for cashing in: they do not create the collecting bug, merely exploit it.

Many of the traditional toys and games for children of this age group rely on the collecting instinct: marbles, baseball cards, toy soldiers and model cars are obvious examples; in fact it may be true that all the most successful toys for children of six to nine incorporate a strong element of collecting. Part of the success of Lego and Fischer-Technik is almost certainly due to a marketing technique that encourages collecting. *Star Wars* figures were a huge commercial success just because children collected them, and the same is true for *He-Man*, with his many accessories, and the teenage dolls such as *Sindy* or *Barbie*.

Whatever your feelings about these dolls, they are enormously popular: there may be more *Barbie* dolls in the U.S. than there are girls under ten. Unlike the baby dolls that are popular with younger children, *Barbie* is not a friend to be loved or cared for, but an object to possess. If you have ever wondered at the play-value of a miniature wardrobe for toy clothes, or why on earth any girls of eight should covet a plastic bed (even with a matching pillow and quilt), the answer is simple: like bottle caps (which are, after all, rather drab-looking objects), they are there to be collected.

Parents have mixed feelings about collections, particularly those that eat up pocket money. Most of us will readily approve a child's collection of stamps, foreign coins or pressed flowers, but insist that key-rings of dubious taste, or bubble gum cards, are a waste of money. You may disapprove especially if you find, as I did, that my child bought candies he did not like in order to obtain the cards that went with them. So although you may believe that a stamp collection is a valuable enterprise (it *might* teach him the names of some countries he has never encountered) and that pressing flowers or growing cacti have obvious educational spin-offs, we should also be on guard against over-estimating their value.

The purpose of collections, as far as seven- and eight-year-old children are concerned, is generally the same whatever the

SNATCH
Eight years on

Procedure This is a simple and absorbing game that seems to test speed of reaction. One player stands with arms outstretched in front and hands about eight inches apart. The other player dangles a matchbox between the first player's hands and then after waiting a while to build up tension, drops it without warning. The first player must catch it before it reaches the ground. Most people simply clap their hands together to catch the matchbox – and miss. But there are better ways . . .

Value
ANTICIPATION
CUNNING What's the trick?

185

objects. Collections are simply to have and to hold, to look at, to count and to arrange. He may stick his cards in a book, but then he will focus his attention on the spares: the doubles he intends to swap with his friends. Of course he will stick his stamps into books by countries, but this is because stamp albums are arranged in this way: as sellers of used stamps (and governments which print them) well know, children buy stamps by shape, picture or theme as often as by country.

But why should this collecting instinct be so strong? It is not confined to children. Adults collect stamps (and not just as a hedge against inflation); they collect teapots, salt and pepper shakers, clematis plants, roses and larger things, too. I once looked at a house belonging to a man who collected old machinery: garden, house and barn were filled with old plows, winding gear and coal trucks from the local mines; and I once interviewed a student who had about five hundred bags, toys and mugs all featuring mice.

It is often said that language is what distinguishes man from the other animals: but one might also say that while comfort, hunger, thirst, and the production and raising of offspring seem to motivate most animals to action, man can be motivated by far less tangible things. A well-fed child will hock his pocket money for weeks in advance to add another page of stickers to his collection, and a well-fed man may sell his home to buy a stamp.

Children may be influenced by others to form collections before they are six or seven; but the main period of collecting begins with the age of reason – about the same time that they begin to be able to stand outside a problem and to order and arrange things in a logical way. So it may be that this urge to collect, arrange and exchange things is connected with the inclination for abstract thought that characterizes man; but that is pure surmise.

There is no obvious explanation of the collecting instinct, although gathering – the first step towards having a collection – is certainly a very basic human characteristic. It is thought by many anthropologists that originally all men were hunters and gatherers of food, moving from place to place collecting as they went, much as the Bushmen of the Kalahari Desert still do. It is perhaps not surprising that the gathering instinct begins quite early in life. As any parent of a toddler knows, a walk to the shops can be a laborious process as he picks up leaves and stones on the way.

Children continue to be great gatherers throughout childhood, and this tendency can be channelled in a number of ways that are at least as productive and educational as stamp collecting.

MANCALA
Eight years on

Procedure Long known and appreciated all over Africa and the Middle East this is an ideal game for a parent to play with a child, lending itself to infinite variations from mindless fun to real intellectual challenge. The "board" is so simple that a child can make it himself, perhaps from a painted egg carton – it is just two lines of six holes. And the counters could be a collection he has made – of shells or buttons, for instance. The basic principle of the game is to "sow" the counters (*wada*) in the holes (*bute*). The variations are in the way the counters are sown. One of the simplest is to start with four counters in each hole. The first player takes the counters from any hole and sows them, one in each hole, in a clockwise direction. When he runs out of counters, he can go on if the last hole sown has more than one other counter. If so he picks them up and sows round and round in a similar way until his last counter falls in an empty hole. He then captures all the counters in the same hole in the opposite row. But if he lands in a hole with a single counter, the other player takes over. The winner is the first player to get his row of six holes empty.

Value
SIMPLE OR SKILLED; MENTAL ARITHMETIC; PLANNING

STONE TEACHER
Six years on

Procedure This is a traditional game ideal for passing time. The "teacher" holds a small stone which he shifts from fist to fist behind his back. He then brings his fists round to the front and holds them one on top of the other. Saying "Schuster, Schuster! Up, down; up, down!" he rapidly switches the position of each fist. The rest of the players take turns guessing whether the stone is "up" or "down". If a child guesses right, he can move up one step on a flight of stairs, or one paving stone or tile forward; if not, he stays put. The first to reach the top of the stairs or the end of a specified route takes over as teacher.

Value
OBSERVATION Children (and adults) are rarely completely random in the way they present the stones.

Stones can be polished, flowers pressed, and with the help of reference books, insects, plants, and fungi and edible plants can be spotted and gathered. Finding food "in the wild" involves both the ability to predict where the food is to be found, and then observation in order to actually spot it growing. Spotting is a type of hypothesis testing – the confirmation of a prediction – and it is a challenging form of thinking for most children before they are seven. It is interesting that prediction is a common element in the many games children play between seven and ten, so that this difficult and important skill is thoroughly rehearsed, like so many others, in play.

The simplest games of prediction are merely guessing games, the easiest of which is probably *Heads or Tails,* played with a coin. For thousands of years children have played games like *"Button, Button, Who's Got the Button?"* (players guess which hand holds a small object) and *Odds-and-Evens* (players shoot out one or two fingers on the count of three, wagering whether the combination will be an odd or even number). More complex guessing games such as *Paper, Stone and Scissors* (*page 182*) have been played for generations, often as a way of choosing who goes first in a subsequent game. But it is the many varieties of *Hide-and-Seek* which surely sum up the essence of spotting. Whether all seek one (as in *Sardines*) or one seeks all (as in the basic game), or whether there is a race to base (*Drop the Handkerchief, Kick the Can*), the skill is in guessing where the other child might be and testing out that hypothesis.

Most children will play these games from time to time; others will become completely addicted to spotting for its own sake. Go to the roof of any airport and there will be usually more than one child with binoculars watching the planes come in. The child who knows every make of car, or who can identify airplanes as they fly overhead, is displaying the same skill, as is the child who can name every breed of dog. Actually, children often collect without gathering: they tick off cars, or make a note of license plates from as many places as possible. In practice, they collect train numbers, or write down the planes they have spotted, but in principle the pleasure is surely in the spotting; the notes just rekindle that pleasure.

CRAZES

A couple of years ago it was "absolutely essential" for eight- to ten-year-old boys to have a BMX stunt bike. Never mind the cost: everyone had them – or so parents were told. Certainly it seemed that way. On every scrap of waste land children could be seen jumping over boxes, taking off from ramps, twisting bikes around in the air, and bouncing on rear wheels.

Parents could see that it was great fun – and quite understood why their child coveted a bike. Stunt bikes were ideal for middle childhood: competitive, skilled, and at times frightening, they were also a social activity, something for all the gang. The manufacturers pushed this social aspect for all it was worth. Buying a BMX was not just buying another bike. There was a complete package: a group to belong to with its own special words, uniforms, badges and magazines, and for some children there was also an aim in life. Some kids had made fortunes "BMXing" – every child knew that (though few actually knew any kids who had made it).

For the parent it brought some peace of mind. It was a solution to the eight-year-old's desire for a bike. He could ride it – would ride it – on open land, and in the parks, not on the dangerous city streets. If a few bones were broken leaping over boxes, it was better than the nagging worry of a serious traffic accident.

But I realized recently as I watched a solitary boy practicing "wheelies" and "bunny hops" on some open land that this was the first BMX bike I had seen all summer. The craze was over – at least in our part of town.

Perhaps the BMX priced itself out of the market – for it was surely the most mercenary craze of all time. Over a hundred dollars for the first bike seemed a generous enough Christmas present, but when this "had" to be up-graded before Easter to a bike costing twice that amount (and perhaps doubled again after another six months) . . . Few families could keep up, and even if they could, few wanted to. Who, after all, enjoys hearing their child complaining that an expensive bike purchased only a few months ago is not good enough? The basic idea of a stunt bike was an excellent one, among the best new toys for middle childhood, but many feel that the big sell that went with it was exploitative.

It is not the first time that manufacturers have benefited by a craze. Before 1956, how many children wanted a coon skin Davy Crockett cap? The big sales packaging that accompanied the Walt Disney film *Davy Crockett* was enormously successful:

BATTLESHIPS
Eight years on

Procedure This is a simple game that seems to become a craze among each new generation – and it costs nothing to play. In the basic game each of the two players takes a sheet of squared paper and marks off numbers down the side and letters across the top to give a grid reference for each square. Then, in secret, each player marks in pencil different squares to represent the disposition of his navy. Typically, he would have: one battleship (represented by five squares in a row); one cruiser (four squares); two destroyers (two squares) and two submarines (one square). The players then take turns "firing" by calling out grid numbers. As each player fires, he marks a blank grid. The aim of the game is to "hit" all his opponent's ships by calling out the right grid squares.

Value
MATHEMATICS This is a painless introduction to the principle of the graph.
STRATEGY

children were bought furry caps, buckskin outfits, wallpaper, candy bars and charm bracelets by the thousand. And, of course, the crazes will continue to come and go. Five years, which was roughly the interval between skateboards and BMX bikes, seems to be the lull between the big sales campaigns, and one craze per childhood seems to be the pattern to date; but it may change. If parents are willing to buy three bikes in the space of one craze, perhaps they can be persuaded to buy into a whole new craze next year?

"We could be rich if . . ."

Perhaps the most unattractive element of the BMX craze was the notion that a better bike might bring fame and fortune; perhaps it was true that one in a million children made a fortune. Just as one in a million make it in films, become boxing champions or tennis stars. As nine-year-olds, we all tend to believe in miracles. I remember believing that if only I could collect enough bus tickets with numbers adding up to 21, someone would pay me a million pounds. I was not the only one: the story had been around in some form for at least 70 years when I heard it.

Exploiting the cupidity of children seems to me to require an appalling cynicism, even for these days, but one has to accept that today children are big business; in the last 40 years they have become an increasingly important segment of the market. Not only are parents and children more affluent than ever before (and children in poor countries poorer) but children are able to persuade their parents to spend money in a way that would be unheard of 50 years ago. Add to this the fact that so many eight-year-olds do not live with both parents (and thus often have two families to buy for them) and the big sell is inevitable.

Manufactured crazes will certainly continue for all age groups and, like their children, many parents will do the fashionable thing. I must confess that I have a khaki boiler suit (this being 1984), at least one room with Laura Ashley wallpaper, a Victorian bathroom, and a room with a Japanese theme. I sometimes jog around the block, often eat beans and wholewheat pastry, and am trying to reduce my intake of animal fats. In other words, I, too, follow the fashions and crazes which one might expect of a resident of my particular suburb. Of course, I would like to believe that my taste is free from outside influences, but I know otherwise. Manufacturers do not start crazes, they just cash in.

You may feel strongly about a "manufactured" craze, but your best course is probably to try and accept what you can and at least draw the line somewhere. The urge to participate in crazes is not

IF ONLY . . .
Seven years on

Procedure This is a simple, silly game for playing around the house on a rainy day. But be warned; your home may be vandalized by over-enthusiastic children. So lock all valuables away and designate restricted zones. To play the game, one player (or team) says *"If only I were . . . (a king) . . . I would have . . ."* and then list six items that he would have. A king might have: a crown, a cloak of velvet, a retinue of servants and so on. In between the naming of each item, the other players (or team) have just one minute to dash off around the house and find it – or, rather, a good substitute. A metal colander, for instance, might make a good crown, and a richly colored towel a cloak. The wishful thinker can decide whether the substitute is acceptable or not. When the list is complete, another player (or team) take over as wishful thinkers. He might choose to be a racing driver or a sailor or a coal-miner and lists six appropriate items for the rest to find. The game continues in this manner until all players have had a turn – or until you decide the house has taken enough beating. A condition of play must be that all items are put back afterwards.

Value
IMAGINATION;
EXUBERANT FUN

CALL BALL
Eight years on

Procedure This is a simple catching game good for short breaks at school or for picnics. Any number can play, but the best number has about six. To play, all the players stand in a circle, or simply scattered over a small area. Each player is given a number. One throws the ball straight up, calling a number as the ball leaves his hand. The player whose number has been called must catch the ball at first bounce. If he succeeds, he throws the ball up for another to catch; if not, the first player throws again.

Value
ANTICIPATION
EXUBERANT FUN

purely modern. Long before children had money to spend, there were crazes: marbles, hoops, woven lanyards and Rubik's cubes have all had their turn. Some crazes may be more educative and constructive than others, but unless they happen to be in fashion, your child will not readily take to them.

Games over the years

Fashions in children's games – as opposed to heady, short-lived crazes – can stretch over several years, but they, too, come to an end. When I asked a friend if her daughters knew a certain skipping rhyme, she told me they had hardly ever skipped with ropes. Some games – like *Hide-and-Seek* – are now only played in their more elaborate versions by older children, and *Leap Frog* has lost some of its former popularity. Games such as *Johnnie on the Pony*, which were still played in Britain in the late 1950s, are unknown to my 12-year-old son, and to all the children in a recent survey in a major Scottish city. Games like *Blind Man's Buff*, in which one player is the butt of the others' fun, have also declined in the last hundred years, while games where groups play or fight on equal terms have increased in popularity.

Over the years the distribution of games between the sexes has changed, too. Marbles used to be a boys' game, but now girls play as well. Jumping rope, on the other hand, was a game for boys and girls in the last century, but today it is almost exclusively for girls; Hula hoops, once almost universal, became almost extinct in recent years, but are now experiencing a revival.

Children of the same neighborhood will naturally tend to play the same games at the same time, partly because enjoyment is infectious, but mainly because six- to ten-year-olds are great conformists. No need to ask him what he wants to wear when he plays: it is whatever all the other boys are wearing. His gang may wear jeans, tracksuits or go in for "preppy" T-shirts; whatever it is, he will covet it. Ask him his favorite pop group, and it will be the one his best friends favor. At home he can be an individual with his own enthusiasms and private pleasures, quite different from his friends'. But in public the aim is to be invisible.

So he does what they do; if they are busy solving Rubik's cube, he also wants to master it. If they are spending hours playing video games, he will have a similar goal. But before regretting this conformity, remember that joint effort *can* be astonishing – as anyone knows who has ever watched the progress of a school fund-raising drive or a Girl Scout cookie sale.

BALL GAMES

Ball games are among the most ancient of all games, and the most widespread. They can be extremely violent, or very sedate. In some of the earliest recorded games, the ball was simply passed from person to person: Ancient Greeks played *Nausikas* by passing the ball from hand to hand with graceful dance-like movements and song. European ball-dances have long since disappeared, but their influence is retained in our language: we use the word ball for a dance, and ballad for a song. However, it is the rough, even undignified ball games which have been enduringly popular in Europe and the New World. Often enough, they were condemned as a positive evil. As early as 1385 the Bishop of London spoke out against the noisy ball games played in the City of London, and a century later another bishop complained that balls dirtied walls, and broke windows in the cathedral cloisters during divine service.

Some of these games were not so much rough as violent. *Scone* for example, was long ago banned by the authorities in Scotland because of its dangers (but it was played in Brittany until modern times). People lost eyes, even lives, in the brawls it occasioned. Clearly *Scone* and comparable games were not for children; they were violent adult sports, often played between rival villages. Many of our modern sports, including rugby and football, are descended from them.

Increasingly, however, children are becoming involved in scaled-down versions of these essentially adult sports: mini rugby, peewee ice hockey, little league baseball and competitive football are now encouraged in children of eight or nine. I suspect this is a great pity. With the games go adult ideas of the importance of winning and of individual excellence.

There is nothing intrinsically wrong with children taking part in sports, as long as they do so in their own way. Children have always copied the games of their parents, and played their own versions of them in the fields and streets. But in children's games, children's rules apply: the game can stop while laces are tied, or someone gains their breath, and no one bothers too much with the score. But in the mini leagues, the ethos changes: the child cannot say "I wasn't ready" and expect another go, nor can he laugh at his mistakes. Winning is important and will be remembered beyond the game. Of course, the team, not the child, takes most of the credit for winning; but one child may enjoy the credit, or the blame, for the team's result. High scorers

SEVENS
Eight years on

Procedure Ideal for odd moments this game can become rapidly addictive. All it needs is a small ball – a compacted rubber or tennis ball will do – a brick wall and a little space. The game is to bounce the ball against the wall in seven different ways in rapid sequence. Dropping the ball means starting over again. A *Sevens* sequence could be:
1 Straight throw against the wall and catch
2 Catch after one bounce
3 Bounce it from the ground on to the wall
4 Throw it under a leg and catch before it bounces
5 Throw the ball and clap hands before catching
6 Spin once round before catching the ball
7 Repeat first throw. It can be played alone, or in turns with other children; whichever, the object is to better one's previous performance.

Value
SELF-MOTIVATION The strong incentive for a child to better his own previous efforts encourages self-motivation and helps develop a sense of purpose.
CO-ORDINATION, BALANCE, BALL SKILLS

BEACH GAMES/*Eight years on*

Beaches are wonderful, but older children can become bored with building sandcastles and playing the traditional beach ball games. Here are some additional ideas; if you need any further variety, try *Legpull* (*page 183*), *London* (*page 195*), *Rock the worm* (*page 200*) or *Stealing sticks* (*page 202*).

PIGGIE IN THE HOLE

This is a boisterous game involving about six players. The players must all find light sticks, about the same length. They then form a circle about 30 ft (9 m) across and all but one dig small holes. The remaining player digs a larger hole in the center and places a plastic food container (with the lid removed) in the hole. When all the holes are dug, the players move to the center and place their sticks under the container. On the shout of "One, two, three – go!" the players toss the container into the air and run for the small holes. The player who fails to get his stick into a hole is "it", and must drive the container towards the center hole while the others try to stop him by driving it away. But whenever a player's stick is in use, another player can claim an empty hole with his stick – including the player who is "it". Any player left without a hole immediately becomes "it". The round ends when someone finally succeeds in getting the container into the center hole.

For safety, keep sticks always on ground after the starting toss.

Value
EXUBERANT FUN; HAND-EYE CO-ORDINATION; LITTLE EQUIPMENT

MANHATTAN GOLF

This is a quiet game for playing after eating tea off plastic plates. Each player must have his or her own plate. Mark out a "golf" course on the sand, with numbered squares for the holes. The idea is to skim the plates so that they land in the right square. As in golf, you "tee off" in turns for each hole. From there on, the player whose plate is furthest from the hole throws. The winner is the player who finishes in least throws.

BEGGAR, JACK, QUEEN, KING

This is a ball game for four players. The ball should be soft and light. Mark out four three-foot (one-metre) squares on the sand as shown (left). Draw lots to find out who starts out as Beggar, Jack, Queen or King. The players stand in their squares and the game begins when the King pats the ball towards another player. The players then pat the ball to each other with the flat of their hands. Anyone who misses becomes Beggar and the others move up one square to take his place. The King always serves after a miss, and the ball must be hit at least twice before it can be returned to him. The aim of the game is to be King. The winner, if you want one, is the player who is King at close of play.

194

are heroes, and the child who makes a mistake lets down the side.

When I mention my dislike for organized sports, or intensive sports training for children under ten, the reply is usually that a child must start this early if he or she is to excel; that if a country is to do well in international competition, adults must start their children playing competitively and training intensively earlier and earlier. This seems to me to be using children for political ends, and I am not convinced that the price is worth paying. Nor am I convinced it is necessary. Ballet is surely as demanding as most sports, both in skill and stamina, yet Rudolf Nureyev did not start to dance until he was 19, and other exceptional male dancers have started formal training at similar ages.

Of course, children have always been pushed by their parents into excelling, and many children enjoy it. Ask a mother why she pushes her child into modelling at three and she will say "Because she loves to do it". Love it or not, the law sees fit in most countries to insist on protective measures for children who work; but there are no safeguards against parental ambitions. In the 16th century, children were often pushed (even beaten) into excellence in intellectual pursuits, and like the young sportsmen of today, they sometimes succeeded. But one wonders what price the majority of children paid for the success of the few. If it is wrong for a child to work all hours in his parents' shop, is it right for him to further their ambition to have a tennis star in the family? Or, more contentiously, to be the parents of a great musician, or scientist?

Of course, some children choose to spend every minute with a math book, or a violin, but many are pushed along that road. Talented children may enjoy the pressure, and the desire to excel is hardly to be discouraged. But for the majority of children, I feel that competition within the framework of children's own culture, where winning and losing are just passing phases of the game, is sufficient. Children have always played some competitive games (all board and card games are competitive, and so is marbles). They will be under pressure at school and at home to do better than others: it would be nice to leave them some areas in which competition was not of paramount importance. I guess that most parents would like to feel that their children were able not only to compete seriously, but also to enjoy a game for its own sake without having to win; and to make allowances for smaller children, as children naturally do in play, with the result that later they would find it natural to treat people weaker or less able than themselves with a similar consideration.

But perhaps this is old-fashioned. Maybe the traditional

LONDON TOWN
Seven years on

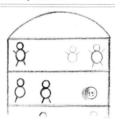

Procedure This is a versatile game of strategy and physical skill that can be played indoors or out, with any number of players. If you play indoors, draw the board shown above on old smooth wallpaper or wrapping paper. Each player kneels on the baseline to shoot a button up the board, either by snapping another button down on the edge or by flicking with thumb and finger. If she misses the board, she loses a turn. Otherwise, she can draw an initialled head (a circle) in the sector the button lands in. The aim is then to build up little stick people on subsequent turns by adding one new feature – first the body, then the legs – every time the button lands in the same sector. Landing on "London" allows a player to add a new feature to her stick people in any sector. Once a player has three complete stick people in any sector, she "owns" that sector, and any player landing there loses a turn. The winner is the player owning most sectors when all are occupied.

Value
STRATEGY; MANUAL SKILL

BRITISH BULLDOG
Eight years on

Procedure British bulldog is a classic street game, ideal for large groups of children needing to let off steam. In its traditional form (see below), it is rough, exuberant fun; even in the gentler version for younger children that follows there is plenty to keep them excited. The game is to run across between two walls or bases without being touched by the "bulldogs" (the catchers). It usually starts with two catchers. At a signal from one of the runners, everyone makes a dash for the other side. Anyone caught becomes a catcher. The game flows back and forth between the walls until the last runner is caught.

Value
FUN The sheer excitement of the sudden dash for the far side after the quiet wait makes this game hard to beat.
TRUE CHILDREN'S GAME with children's ideas of competition and fairness.
AGILITY; FITNESS

Variations Older children can play the rougher street version of the game. In this, catchers must not just touch the runners but lift both of their feet off the ground long enough to say "British bulldog! One, two, three!"

games of childhood molded children for a world where the majority accepted their allotted positions without question or ambition. It is perhaps revealing that the more competitive games like marbles (where the winners get to keep the marbles, and can later gloat over their spoils) are traditionally boys' games, and the less competitive jump rope is a girls' game. Maybe sports are better training for our meritocrats. Directing your child's play is difficult enough – nearly impossible – in these secretive years; you can probably only hope to influence their overall preferences; in which case, you probably cannot go far wrong if you favor an even mixture of true children's games and competitive activity.

True children's games

Perhaps their most obvious hallmark is an imaginative, even quirky approach to the properties of the ball. In the child's world, balls are for throwing on or over roofs to make an exciting catching game; for hurling with great force at the angle of steps, or the curb of a pavement, and for catching without bouncing. They are for throwing at players in a version of *Tag* (which can be played as a team game, or with one person against the rest, just as *Tag* can). They are for bouncing on the floor, with many fancy steps and hand positions, and for throwing against walls in ones, twos or even threes. As in all rhythmic games, there is often a song to sing along with:
"A mimsy, a clapsy,
I roll my hands, touch backsie,
My right hand, my left hand,
High as the sky, low as the sea,
I touch my knee, and my heel, and my toe,
And over we go."
(*Bouncing rhyme, USA.*)

Skipping and jumping games

In America they call it *Jump Rope*, in Britain and Australia they call it skipping, but in all places it is mainly girls who play. Its origins are in the ancient celebrations of springtime and fertility, when the springing-up of the seed was celebrated by hopping, jumping and skipping with a rope made from vine strands. Today, girls in many parts of the world still jump with a single rope, going as fast as they can (even turning the rope twice for each jump), or running and turning the rope at each stride. But the best games are surely those in which gangs of girls jump in and out of a long piece of rope turned by two "enders". "Ever enders" we used to call the women who in principle watched over the children in the school playground, but in practice turned the rope for us. We played games where we all ran in and jumped together:

"All in together girls,
Never mind the weather girls,
When I call your birthday please run out."

We played games where each of us ran into the rope and jumped once before running out, jumping under, or over, but never missing a beat or leaving the rope empty. Best of all were the action games. We would

"Salute to the captain,
Curtsy to the queen,
and turn my back on the dirty margarine."

Or we joined in to rhymes such as:

"Ballerina, Ballerina, turn around!
Ballerina, Ballerina, touch the ground!
Ballerina, Ballerina, do the high kicks!
Ballerina, Ballerina, do the splits!"

And then there are the variations: *Double Dutch*, where two ropes turn in opposite directions, and everyone jumps together; or *Hot Pepper* where the rope turns as fast as possible to:

"Salt, vinegar, mustard, pepper."

For jumping games we had some straightforward, others such as *High Jumps*, where the rope rose higher and higher from the ground; and others that were a sort of combined high and long jump, with an area either side of the rope which had to be cleared. And then of course there is *Chinese Jump Rope* or *Stretchers* (*see margin*).

I have asked many people what they sang as children, and they all agree that the verses made little sense, and this perhaps is another hallmark of the true children's game: you play for the sake of play, not logic. Several of the classic street games, though trials of strength, can often be won by some stroke of luck; in fact winning is often a secondary, if not an irrelevant consideration in many of the true children's games. In *Sentry* (*page 219*) and *Red Light-Green Light* (*page 218*) there is a competitive element, but the rules are arranged so that actually winning involves taking on a new role which is no more entertaining than competing. And in several of the board games described on page 204, a by-product of play is that most of the players receive as much practice at losing as at winning – as if both were important.

Clapping to rhymes

It is not clear whether the two girls who are shown playing hand-clapping games on the 2,000-year-old Ancient Egyptian tomb of Ak-hor would have sung or chanted rhymes as they clapped.

STRETCHERS
Seven years on

Procedure This is a skipping and jumping game with great appeal in some circles today. It needs one very long piece of elastic – rubber bands tied together, perhaps, or a length of trouser elastic. This is looped between two solid chairs or held by two children. Other children then skip over and between the strands in a set sequence:
1 jump legs outside both strands; **2** jump legs inside; **3** cross legs inside; **4** cross legs outside; **5** jump and turn; **6** jump on top of both strands; **7** hop over both; **8** stretch the elastic by jumping sideways; **9** your own variations. Raise the elastic every now and then to make the game more challenging.

Value
PLAY AT ANY TIME with several children, or just one.
CO-ORDINATION; BALANCE; STAMINA

Skelly (see opposite)

JACKS
Seven years on

Procedure This game dates back to the days of ancient Greece and is now played all over the world. It thoroughly deserves this popularity, for few games so simple in concept provide such an unending challenge to the ingenuity of young minds, and children's developing manual skill. Jacks are played with anything from mutton knuckle bones to bean bags (in Japan), but five small stones or the metal "jacks" are fine. The basic idea is to throw a ball up in the air and pick up the jacks in all kinds of ways before catching the ball after it bounces – using the same hand all the while. Most children will invent increasingly difficult moves for themselves, but the simplest game is to pick up the jacks one-by-one or two-by-two.

Value
PLAY AT ANY TIME – alone or in competition with other children – it needs little space. STRATEGY Working out how to perform each move, and working out new moves calls for considerable ingenuity. HAND-EYE CO-ORDINATION; MANUAL SKILL

Children today certainly chant as they clap, and such games are still found in many parts of Asia, Europe and America. My nieces in Scotland sing:
"Come all you brownies,
Come out and play with me,
You can bring your dollies,
You can climb my apple tree,
Slide down my staircase,
Swing on my cellar door,
And we'll be friends then
For ever more."
(*Glasgow*)

To a basic clapping pattern that includes clapping hands together, crossing to slap a partner's opposite hand, and clapping both hands on a partner's unturned palms are added such fancy additions as slapping knees and touching shoulders. Whether or not the Ancient Egyptian girls sang as they clapped, they would certainly not have included advertising jingles in their repertoire as girls do today. But I suspect they may have used the mildly improper jingles you can often still hear:
"Behind the refrigerator, there was a piece of glass,
And if you don't believe me I'll kick you in the . . .''
"Ask me no questions, tell me no lies,
The boys are in the bathroom doing up their . . .''
"Flies are in the garbage, bees are in the park,
Boys and girls are kissing in the dark, dark, dark.''

Hopscotch

Hopscotch is played all over the world, and its origins are in the religions of Europe and Asia. It embodies the leaping and jumping movements of primitive European religion; and the passage of a stone from square to square reflects Asiatic beliefs about the difficult passage of the soul. (Board games such as *Chutes and Ladders* have a similar origin and were probably used initially for religious instruction.) There are many variations both in the worked-out diagram and in the mode of play. Sometimes the child has to hop to each square in turn, sometimes he hops and straddles his feet into two squares alternately, and in others he jumps. There is usually a puck or stone, which must be thrown, or in some games kicked, into each square in turn. In some complex versions, the player must carry the stone on his foot when returning to base, but usually the player simply picks up the stone. *Skelly* (*see opposite*) is an American street game, which combines hopscotch with a form of marbles.

Jacks or *Knuckle Bones* or *Fivestones* was originally played

TRADITIONAL PAVEMENT GAMES/*Eight to ten years*

Hopscotch and *Skelly*, invented by children to make the most of the limitations of pavements, are in fact games to play anywhere offering a surface to chalk on.

Hopscotch is an old but effective way of developing foot-eye co-ordination. It involves hopping in a set order between marked squares, just one foot landing in each square – the idea is to jump the sequence as quickly as possible. Variations in the standard pattern, like those shown, should help sustain interest.

Skelly is traditionally played with soda bottle crown caps filled with wax for weight. But it could be played with Plasticine-weighted buttons. The idea is to flick the cap, with a forefinger, through the squares in a given sequence. Should a player miss a square, the next player has a try; the player who missed must start again, when his turn comes round again, from the square he last reached. If anybody lands in the "no-man's land" around the 13th square, he must go back to the start again.

Value
FUN; HAND-EYE CO-ORDINATION; SOCIAL

199

ROCK THE WORM
Six years on

Procedure An ideal way of letting off steam, this game usually has children collapsing in laughter. It should be played on soft ground or indoors on a carpet with five or more children. All the children line up very close side by side on all fours. Then the child at one end of the row gets up and tries to squirm like a worm across the backs of the others to the far end. Meanwhile, the other children try to shake him off, by heaving their backs while keeping their hands on the floor. When a child reaches the far end – or falls off – he or she joins the end of the row and the next child becomes the worm. This is a safe variation of the traditional *Johnnie on the Pony* or *Hi Jimmy Knacker.*

Value
FUN; BALANCE

with small bones, as we can see in a terracotta figurine (Italy, circa 300 BC and on view in the British Museum) of two girls playing. Today it is still considered to be a girls' game in many areas. In Europe, it is played both with and without a ball, while in America a small ball is often thrown in the air while the jacks are picked up.

When the Europeans arrived in New Zealand they found that the native Maoris had amazingly elaborate versions of *Cats' Cradles.* The pattern, created out of string, could represent houses, canoes, people, even episodes in Maori life. Eskimos too, have developed elaborate *Cat's Cradle* patterns, and some are incorporated in Eskimo mythology. One can play at *Cats' Cradles* alone with a long knotted piece of string, but most of the better patterns require two sets of hands. Most Western children will know one or two patterns, but will not begin to know the richness of the game. The same applies to paper folding. Western children can often fold paper to make planes, fortune tellers and hats: but few can match the art of the average Japanese child. I was amazed at the skill of some five-year-old Japanese children. They made not only the familiar paper bird but also elaborate flowers and animals. It is possible that the early use of chopsticks helps them to develop the fine hand control necessary for paper folding at such an early age.

Marbles
Marbles is a game with a considerable amount of folklore attached. Children have special names for the different types of marbles: aggies, boulders, cats' eyes, glassies and steeleys, and there are elaborate sets of rules. Marble games fall into two categories – surface games and hole games. The surface games include the simple chasing games, in which one player tries to hit the marble of his opponent, and the more elaborate ring games, where he tries to knock marbles out of a central ring or square. There are many variations on this theme, from the small ring which encloses a large group of marbles, to the games which require greater skill. In some of these a small line of marbles is placed within a much larger enclosure and the player must knock the marbles out of the ring, while leaving his own marble inside. Marbles are also shot into holes in the ground, or through gaps made in boxes, and here again there are many variations on basic themes.

Value
In play children practice skills that they need. The six-month-old baby takes an object to his mouth because he needs to explore

and understand the world around him, and he uses his mouth because it is more sensitive than his still-clumsy hands. The three-year-old pretends he is driving a bus because pretending fulfils a need at this time in his mental development. The same holds true for the complex games of middle childhood; and rather as in the law of property, possession is nine-tenths of the law, so in play the value of a game that has been in use for dozens of generations is generally hard to question. They are not automatically always the most creative forms of play, but their key characteristics, especially those that crop up again and again, are the ones to be valued and, if possible, encouraged.

Jacks, *Marbles*, skipping and *Hopscotch*, for example, all make demands upon a child's ability to co-ordinate and on the accuracy of his responses; moreover they are all games in which improving skill can in time be pitted against that of other children; so a young child can join the game and see the heights to which he can aspire with practice. The game's message is not only "play me" but "play me and develop at the same time".

Since a child's muscular co-ordination improves so much during these years, it is of course natural that so many games of this period involve practicing physical skill.

The games have something else in common: rules. The free-wheeling, pretend play that characterizes early childhood has few rules, if any; much of its point is the freedom to improvise. The use of rules certainly reflects the child's new-found ability to think in more abstract terms. Games of middle childhood, with their complex rule structures, elaborate stages, their assigning of roles, picking of sides and running through the order of play, are much more akin to an adult's way of setting about a task. They can, in fact, be seen in terms of plans and operations, and thus to practice the important new crop of mental abilities that developed at about seven – *see pages 170-73*.

But perhaps most characteristic of all is that these are social games. By playing, the child is learning to move within a larger world than in the pre-school years – to interact with others on a more equal footing, and without the allowances that parents usually make for their children. It is interesting that rhyme and song play such an important role, for song often serves to unify a group, especially when its members are not close friends. When people work together they sing; during wartime, demonstrations, religious services, or at times when a group of people feel the need for a unifying influence, they are liable to burst into song. It is interesting, too, that girls' games make most use of singing. Girls seem to look to the unifying influence of song, while boys seem to have an inclination towards initiation ceremonies.

NEW YORK
Seven years on

Procedure There are hundreds of tag games, but most have one great disadvantage – they are not much fun for the child or children who are "on", or "it". *New York* avoids this problem. The players split into two teams and stand on baselines about 20 feet (6 m) apart. One team chooses an activity they are going to act out. They then move towards the other team saying, "Here we come!" and the following exchange takes place:
Waiting team: "Where from?"
Acting team: "New York."
Waiting team: "What's your trade?"
Acting team: "Lemonade."
Waiting team: "Give us some."
Going as close to the waiting team as they dare, the acting team shouts out the initial letters of the activity they have decided upon – say "PB" for playing ball – and act it out silently. The waiting team must guess what the activity is. As soon as they guess correctly, the acting team run back to their base and the waiting team must tag as many as possible before they get back. Those tagged join the other team. It is then the waiting team's turn to choose an activity and act it out. Should the waiting team fail to guess the activity, the acting team try them with a new activity.

Value
VERBAL; CO-ORDINATION

STEALING STICKS
Eight years on

Procedure Here is another classic street game, challenging enough to sustain interest through many sessions, yet not off-puttingly complex. It needs two teams of ten or so players. A line divides the playing area into two territories, one for each team. Some way behind the line is a base where each side has six sticks stored. Teams are not allowed to stand too near their own base. The aim of the game is to steal all the other side's sticks by making forays with one or more players into enemy territory. As soon as a player steps across the line, though, he can be touched and taken as prisoner back to the catching team's base. No more sticks can then be stolen until the prisoner is rescued by a touch from a team-mate.

Value
STRATEGY; AGILITY; FITNESS; TRUE CHILDREN'S GAME; FUN FOR ALL

This can be seen in some of the games they play in childhood, where pain has to be accepted without flinching, and it can be seen in adulthood, when ridicule is the price of acceptance to a group. Of course there are exceptions to these generalities: perhaps the most obvious being the male delight in chanting at football games.

The importance of these traditional games in middle childhood may be beyond doubt; but there is little point in you trying to encourage your children to play them. They will play as they choose. However, you can still introduce them to such games, and they can be invaluable at certain times. When you want entertainment as a family (on vacation perhaps) they are excellent for involving children of different ages. A traditional game may also be the only way to entertain a group of nine- or ten-year-olds at a party. At certain times, typically at social occasions, children like to be organized: if there is no child willing to organize them, they will accept an adult in this role.

The traditional games cannot, of course, teach everything that needs to be learned. Children tend to play games they see others playing; and there are dozens of potentially enjoyable and valuable games that they do not see played. Kites, for example, were unknown to European children before they were introduced from China.

When children do play traditional games, it seems that nowadays they tend to favor only moderately complex ones. The elaborate team games like *Prisoner's Base* seem to be dying out, while very simple tag games also seem to be relatively unpopular. There are a number of reasons why this might be so. Children certainly do not play the traditional games for nearly as long as they did. In many countries, street games are generally given up after the eleventh birthday, when children move into the junior high. Twenty years ago, girls would skip, and boys play marbles, up to 13, or even 14; now they stop much earlier. Thus yesterday's games were led by 12- and 13-year-olds, but today's are organized by eight- and nine-year-olds, and are therefore simpler. This abandoning of play at 11 is not confined to traditional games, but has also adversely affected the sales of the traditional toys of the older child. Another factor may be that competitive sports are taking the place of the traditional, co-operative team games; and another the drift, in the past 40 years, of families away from central city areas into suburban housing developments. Where no one was living before, there are no older children to teach the rules of the more complex games.

When the play of an inner city area of London was recently

compared with that of children of families who had moved out of London to a new town, consisting of vast housing developments blessed with ample play spaces, it was clear that the most complex games had survived far better in the old inner city areas.

WOLF
Seven years on

Procedure This is an ideal game for mixed groups at family gatherings and for parties. One person is chosen as the wolf and goes off to hide. The remaining lambs shut their eyes and count to 500 in fives – the rhythm of counting in fives is much less dull than straight counting. Then everyone looks for the wolf. When the wolf is found, they all go as close as they dare while the leader of the seekers says *"I spy the woolly, woolly sheep, I spy the woolly, woolly rabbit"* and so on until he suddenly decides to point and say *"I spy the woolly, woolly wolf!"* At that, everyone dashes for base (ie a chosen location), pursued by the wolf. Those tagged by the wolf must become wolves too, hide with the original wolf and help chase next time round. The game continues until all the ''lambs'' have been caught.

Value
FUN FOR ALL;
STRATEGY

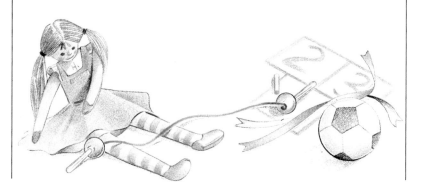

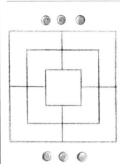

Procedure This is a very simple game with an ancient heritage that can keep two children occupied for hours on rainy days. They need three counters each – two sets of coins will do. The board can be drawn on paper. To play, they take turns placing their counters on the board at intersections. When all the counters are down, they take turns moving one counter per turn to an adjacent intersection, until one player succeeds in placing his or her three counters in a straight line.

Value
PLAY ANYWHERE;
SIMPLE STRATEGY;
QUICK RESULT

BOARD GAMES

Board games originate in every corner of the globe; the Australian Aborigines and the Eskimo are alone in not having developed them. They are universal, just as street games and adult sports are universal.

It is often claimed that societies that invent and play games of chance believe in the essential goodness of a god who cares (or can be asked to care) for the individual; and that societies that do not favor chance games take a more fatalistic view of life. It is a nice idea: certainly the great games of skill (as opposed to chance) – games such as chess, checkers and *Go* – all originate in the East; but as with many reasonable hypotheses, the evidence is not strong.

Many board games need three or four players, which means in practice that the whole family may play together. One might say that they are worthwhile for this reason alone. Since old and young play together, games of chance rather than skill are frequently the choice for family play, but as children grow older they will demand more from board games; for eight-year-olds the blend of skill and chance in backgammon is often appealing, as it is in *Monopoly*. In fact, most modern board games combine luck and judgement in varying degrees. The ones that succeed best for a mixed group of adults and children are those not so dependent on skill that the best player always wins, nor so dependent on chance that the better players become bored. In fact, they combine skill and chance in a similar way to street games.

Perhaps the greatest long-term value of board games is that they teach a child to win *and* to lose. Many find losing excessively difficult, but everyone must learn, and in board games where chance plays a major part everyone gets practice at losing. Some of the games also teach that fighting on in spite of setbacks can pay dividends; but most of all, board games probably exercise everyday social skills.

The most sophisticated board games, such as chess, but also including the best board war games, are tests of strategy. Even in those that require a limited amount of forward thinking, the player must learn to plan two or three moves ahead; to plot his route towards his goal. In effect, he must use his reasoning powers, and in the early years at school, when so much emphasis is put on learning to read and write, these games can play an important complementary role in developing this sometimes neglected skill.

COWS AND LEOPARDS/*Eight to ten years*

Known by a variety of names throughout South-East Asia, *Cows and Leopards* is a simple but fascinating board game for two children of eight or nine. The strategy is challenging enough for the brightest children, yet easy enough for any to learn. You can make the board yourself by drawing or painting on cardboard or, for a longer-lasting board, use a sewing machine to sew the pattern on felt.

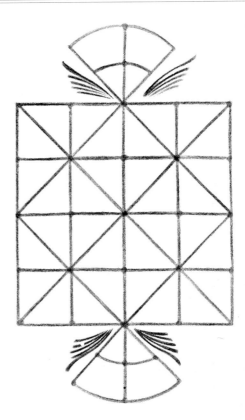

THE RULES

One of the two players controls two leopards; the other controls 24 cows. The cows try to hem in the leopards so that they cannot move. The leopards try to remove the cows before the cows stop them from moving. Taking turns, the players put their pieces one by one on any free intersections on the board, starting with the leopard player. Once both leopards are on the board, the leopard player can use his turn to move one of his two leopards to any adjacent intersection. The cow player cannot move a cow until all the cows are on the board. Leopards can capture cows by leaping over a cow on an adjacent intersection – but only if the intersection on the far side is free (as in checkers). Leopards *must* capture vulnerable cows. To win the game, cows must hem in both leopards so they cannot move.

The pieces *can be just colored buttons, but it is much better to use small plastic cows and leopards if you can – draw the board to match the size of animals being used. Children may be able to make the animals themselves in clay using molds.*

Value
SIMPLE STRATEGY; EASY TO MAKE; PLAY ANY TIME

BARABOO
Six years on

Procedure Most children love hiding games, and this is one of the very best. As with most hiding games, one player shuts her eyes while the rest hide, staying put in their chosen places. The seeker must not only find all the other players; she must actually touch them as well. If everyone hides in awkward-to-reach places, the game is that much more fun, as the seeker has to crawl through small holes or scale walls to make the touch. When a hider is touched, she must help the seeker find the others – though the seeker herself must still make the touch. When no more can be found, the seeker yells *"Baraboo!"* The hiders then softly reply *"Hilow"*. This gives the seekers a clue. The game then continues until all hiders are found.

Value
FUN FOR ALL The seeker is rarely by herself for long.
STRATEGY The best hiders make themselves really hard to touch.
OBSERVATION

CURIOSITY

"Mind your own business,
Chew your own fat,
And don't poke your nose
In my Sunday hat."

"Poking a nose" into something that does not concern you is highly characteristic of childhood, and it will take more than a rhyme to stop a child investigating.

One of the most serious by-products of poverty, malnutrition, and disease is that it can kill a child's natural curiosity: a child who is not nosy lacks the will to learn. Scientists have called this lack of will "functional isolation": the severely deprived child switches herself off from the world about her. When healthy inquisitive children find themselves severely malnourished (as they sometimes do in wartime), there is rarely any lasting problem. But in a child whose natural curiosity has already been stifled, the same degree of hunger can produce permanent damage. In other words, the inquisitive child produces her own stimulation, keeps her own mind active and, despite temporary setbacks, develops into a questioning adult. Remember this when she seems more ready to exercise her mind with jokes than with academic work. Not all jokers end up with good exam results; but they often end up with lively minds.

Small animals, and children, are naturally inquisitive and ready to learn; but as animals grow, they replace curiosity with caution, while man continues to be nosy. How often does one stop to read the scrap of newspaper that was used to pack a parcel? And if someone looks up, how many of us cannot resist looking up too. Even on our death beds, we may enquire about the weather. Of course the number of questions we ask over the years probably decreases, and few of us retain all the inquisitiveness of youth.

Questions can be asked without resort to words; your eight-year-old will probably ask fewer questions than she did when she was three; but she will fiddle and mess about, hover on the edge of conversations, and observe you as you work. When she is about, she is generally nosy, and afraid of missing anything.

To develop this curiosity really is a priceless gift, for although children are born curious, it is the environment around them that feeds this natural inquisitiveness. In the early years you control this environment to a very large degree, either directly, or indirectly in your choice of play school or day care. In the middle school years, you are much less in touch and sometimes a child who has seemed to you to be bright as a toddler will surprise you by failing to impress her teachers.

Why? Sometimes, of course, children are expected to fail, and consequently oblige. About 20 years ago a simple experiment was carried out with a class of children. The teacher was told that certain children were bright, and others dim. By the end of the year the "bright" children were doing well and the "dim" children poorly, even though they were in fact of the same intelligence. Sometimes parents cast their children in these roles. Traditionally it was bright sons and not so bright daughters. Now the roles are less likely to go with the sex of the child; but they may still be there.

Children need to believe in themselves and can often surprise us with their abilities if we allow them to show us. Many a child who cannot remember a single date in history – because nobody expected him to – can tell you every fixture of his favorite football club. His friends are impressed, but his teachers may continue to think his memory is appalling.

A number of years ago I taught a man in his sixties who was taking a degree in his spare time. He was a manager in a large company but had grown up in a poor working-class household and left school just after his fourteenth birthday. Talking to him one evening he told me of one of the most important events in his childhood. A new teacher came to his school and seeing that the children needed stimulation, offered ten shillings to any child who could solve a certain problem by the next morning. Ten shillings was a great deal of money to those children, and some of them worked on the problem well into the night. My pupil found the answer and won the ten shillings – a gift which he described as priceless, for the single reason that it gave him a confidence in himself that he never lost.

Just a little encouragement can go a very long way, provided it is well directed. You may need to closely observe a child to detect her natural aptitudes; single out and encourage a single skill, or group of skills, and you will probably find the response is immediate. And a child who begins to succeed is likely to continue to do so. Equally, a child who begins to fail may continue in the same mold.

Of course, it is easier to stimulate a naturally thoughtful child than one who only seems interested in having a good time. Sometimes it is a matter of finding the right sort of stimulation: a process of trial and error. But above all, remember that whatever a child's school results, and however a child seems to compare

GROWING BANANAS
Eight years on

Procedure Growing a banana plant from seed *is* difficult. It *does* need tremendous care and a little luck. But the impressive results can give a child an enormous sense of achievement if she tends the plant herself. Before planting the seeds, soak them in warm water for 48-72 hours in a Thermos bottle (wash thoroughly afterwards). Then sow $\frac{1}{3}$ inch (1 cm) deep in good potting compost. The seeds need a steady temperature of 70°F (21°C) to germinate, so leave them somewhere warm, such as on a tropical fishtank or on top of a pilot light. Keep the seeds moist and check them frequently. When the seeds germinate, transplant them carefully to three-inch (8 cm) pots. As they grow larger, transfer them to larger pots still – if everything goes well, they may grow to six feet (2 m) in under four months.

Value
CONFIDENCE Seeing the plant grow taller than herself and then you gives a tremendous sense of achievement.
FINDING OUT How much does it grow each month? Is growth even? Why does it need warmth to germinate?
SUSTAINED ACTIVITY
IMPRESSIVE PRESENT

207

KNOCK! KNOCK!
Nine to ten years

Procedure Children of this age seem to love pathetic jokes and terrible puns. Ask two small groups of children to make up jokes to a set formula against the clock and the results should be truly appalling. The old formula of *"Knock! Knock!" "Who's there?" "Walter!" "Walter who?" "Walter wall carpeting":* or *"Knock! Knock!" "Who's there?" "Sam and Janet!" "Sam and Janet who?" "Sam enjanted evening . . ."* provides endless scope for variation, though specifying topics often makes the game easier. Other formulas include the silly books: "Easy Money" by Robin Banks, "Through the Grinder" by Eileen Dinn, "Puddle on the floor" by Rufus Leaky, "Calcium Shortage" by Ben D. Bones (*see page 171*) and so on; or, arrivals at the (animals') ball: "Announcing Mr. and Mrs. Fant and their giant daughter Miss Ellie", "Mr. and Mrs. Lope and their Auntie", "Little Paddy O'Diall and his ancient grandfather Crock O'Diall, and so on *ad nauseam*. Don't expect anything too clever. Award the team who comes up with the worst puns a custard pie.

Value
GOOD PARTY GAME; SILLY FUN; VERBAL

with her peers, a nosy child is an intelligent child. She is nosy because she is intelligent, and intelligent because she is nosy. It matters little what her interests are at this stage: more that she has them. Let her get into the habit of being inquisitive and in a stimulating environment, which you provide by your conversation and by the way that you show her the world, and she will begin to ask stimulating questions. Let her start by learning good habits: she can apply them in sensible and useful tasks in her own good time. Show her that she is capable of learning and finding things out and she will eventually apply these skills in an approved fashion; of course she will need a will to work, but to a child who enjoys learning this comes more easily.

Jokers

Be it never so true that a child's natural enthusiasms need encouraging, whatever form they take, jokers sometimes seriously worry their parents. Indeed, more than a few children in this age group seem to have no interests at all outside pathetic jokes.

"Why is the sand wet?" – "because the sea weed" is the only joke my daughter knows. At least, it is the only joke she gets right. Some parents can find this passion for the trivial quite disconcerting, especially as the enjoyment of the joke seems to consist largely in mindless repetition of the same feeble punch lines.

Like many five- to six-year-olds, my daughter has little idea about what constitutes a joke. If we say "not again" as she begins to say "Why is . . .", she is likely to insist that this time it is different, and change the punch line to "Because the tide came in", or "Because I spilled my juice". Although, like my daughter, many children know one or two jokes at five, or earlier, most children do not really begin to understand the nature of jokes until they are six to seven. People who have tested their understanding of jokes find most five- and six-year-olds pick the literal answer "Because the tide came in", rather than the punch line. Only at seven do the majority of children invariably pick the punch line. This should not be surprising: by their nature jokes are not straightforward, they usually depend on double meaning. Either the child must be aware of both interpretations, or must see that the question was intended to mislead, for example, "Where do you find most fish?" – "Between the head and the tail." Seeing two meanings at once is not easy at this age. Remember, she still has difficulty seeing that water poured from a short fat cup into a tall narrow one is the same amount of water, even if the level looks higher.

Once children can understand jokes, I think they become a

valuable mental stimulus – so never mind that for some time the fascination appears pointless. Jokes are so much part of children's growing up that I am surprised so little is known about their function in child development. There are several questions to be answered: for example, do children use jokes to enter groups and gain acceptance as adults do? Do they only tell and laugh at cruel and embarrassing jokes if they are closely acquainted with the people with whom the jokes are shared? We do not even know that children everywhere laugh at the same jokes, or whether they begin to tell jokes at the same age.

As for the key point – whether joking is a creative form of play – I can only suggest that because it is quite a complex skill, however inane the joke, it is indeed a valuable activity; nothing less than another way of exploring ideas. It probably has the additional virtue of being a social activity. Cracking jokes together produces togetherness.

Television

The only way to stop children watching TV is to move to an isolated spot beyond the reach of even the most powerful transmitter. We tried for some years doing without a TV, but when we found our son was spending all his time in other people's houses watching all the worst programs, we decided that it was better to have the set under our control.

This assumes, of course, that you want to stop him watching it; if your child has not reached this age, you may find it hard to imagine the stultifying effect of constant viewing – and I do mean constant. Children can seem to lose interest in all else – even eating; they watch literally anything that flashes across the screen, and the language of the TV can seem to dominate their speech, thought and behavior to the exclusion of their own personalities.

It is too easy to deride television, and to assume that it always has a bad influence on children. Along with the trashy programs are some excellent shows. *Sesame Street*, and *The Electric Company*, with their high educative content, are watched by very considerable numbers of children in the United States and Israel who might not otherwise receive any pre-school education; indeed many countries produce excellent pre-school programs which, within their objectives, seem to work. One may question how important it is for pre-schoolers to learn the alphabet, but given the premise that it is, then *Sesame Street* succeeds.

What it does not do, and what it cannot do, is stimulate a child's desire to learn outside the context of the program. Children ought not to be passive receivers of information: they

CHARIOTS
Nine years on

Procedure Nothing keeps children away from the television better in summer than a really boisterous, exuberant outdoor game and this is one of the best. The chariots are made with three strong poles roped firmly together to form a triangle. The horses for each chariot are two strong children who lift and pull the front apexes of the chariot with one hand – the rear apex drags on the ground. The driver is a lighter child who lies/stands with two feet resting near the rear apex and both hands on the front bar. The driver can become very skilful at steering the horses. With two or more chariots, you can have a race around a circuit. But race on soft ground (grass or sand) to prevent injury.

Value
SIMPLE FUN; STRENGTH
STAMINA

SPOT THE CLICHÉ
Nine years on

Procedure One of the problems with children who watch a great deal of television is that they believe everything they see. One way to show that television personalities are as fallible and human as anyone is to play this game when watching television together. Write down half a dozen clichéd television phrases, such as "And now over to . . ." or "Just one of the exciting guests we have here for you tonight" or "And we'll be back after the break" – this needs observation on your part. Then, over the course of an evening's viewing, see who can spot these clichés most times – the first to yell out each time scores a point. For subsequent games, the winner decides on the clichés to listen for.

Value
OBSERVATION
DISCOVERY
ATTITUDE TO TV

Variation Television directors use visual as well as verbal clichés, such as zooming in on a person who is being put on the spot. Watch your children's favorite evening show with them and see how many visual clichés you can spot.

have the capacity to learn by doing, which is exactly why *Sesame Street* works: it encourages the child to join in and to shout out the letters and numbers as they appear. But if a child spends most of the day in front of the TV, watching programs in which he cannot join, there is little chance of a general improvement in his knowledge. On the other hand, children can and do absorb some information from television: listen to the rhymes they sing as they clap their hands, skip a rope or throw a ball against the wall, and the influence of TV commercials is obvious.

There is the bonus, too, that from TV they seem to gain an understanding of the techniques of film. It has been shown, for example, that children who watch TV find it easier to judge what a view from the other side of the room might be. In other words, TV helps them to put themselves in someone else's place and helps them to see that two things can happen at the same time, as when the on-screen image cuts back and forth between two events happening simultaneously in different places.

They also gain a broader view of the world and see how others live; from specific programs they can learn about the natural world, about science and technology, literature, and even art, and they may be stimulated to take this knowledge further by reading books, making collections or doing simple experiments. It is also the case that TV can stimulate reading: children who rarely read books can be inspired to do so by watching the story dramatized on TV. On the other hand TV teaches them a great deal about violence, sexual stereotypes, bigotry and greed.

The solution to the TV problem is simple, in principle, if not in practice. The set has an on/off switch. Programs have schedules and there is, in theory, nothing to stop you switching off the undesirable and switching on the good. This sounds like – and is – a Victorian father's approach. And it means, of course, your children will protest: "But everyone in our class watches that," and "I've only watched for half an hour." And inevitably, if she really wants to watch the less desirable programs, she will do so at a friend's house. But the fact remains, if you really feel strongly about the negative influence of television, that there is little alternative but to make this kind of stand. Rational explanations of why you disapprove are unlikely to appeal.

None of this helps parents with the conviction that "must" and "must not" should have no place in dealings with their children. If you also happen to be worried about the influence of bad TV, you have a potentially intractable problem, especially if you are a working mother or father. For the final alternative is to watch TV – good and bad – in company with your children at every opportunity. There is evidence that children learn more from television programs if they watch them with adults, be they parents or teachers. Questioning the violence of a program then and there as it happens, or at least soon after, can influence children's views, and sitting and watching educational programs together does mean that more information is retained.

The best way of cutting down on the sheer volume of TV – as opposed to specific programs – is to provide children with something better to do. This is hardest on dark and cold winter evenings. Hobbies, youth clubs, swimming, or even helping to cook the evening meal, may help to pass an evening without TV; but the best alternative, especially if she is completely addicted to TV, is probably video games. What attracts children to television is often not the content (the fact that they watch all sorts of rubbish is what parents find so worrying) but the action: the dynamic visual activity on a screen. When asked, many children actually prefer video games to TV, and although some video games may seem gratuitously violent, this is not always the case. Some of the most popular games, such as *Breakout, Pinball* and *Pacman* are less violent than the average TV show. Providing a wide range of interesting video games at home means providing a home computer. And although children will start by playing nothing but games on a computer, some go on to become competent programmers.

AD-LIB
Eight years on

Procedure The repetition and simplicity of television commercials and their catchlines are as memorable to today's children as the nursery rhymes of old. You can use this knowledge to play a simple form of charade. The game needs two teams with at least three members. To start the game, one thinks of a well-known commercial. They whisper their choice to one of the opposing team. She must then mime the commercial to the rest of her team. Her team must guess the product in two minutes. If they fail, the person miming has 30 seconds to mime just the product to give her team the chance of retrieving half a point. The game continues with each team taking turns to nominate or guess the commercial. A new player must mime each time, until everyone has had a chance to mime.

Value
COMMUNICATION;
OBSERVATION

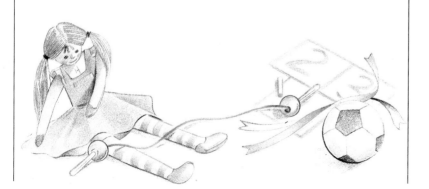

COMPUTERS

Computers impinge on most aspects of our lives nowadays: the tags on the clothing we buy, our bank accounts and bills, even the traffic signals in our cities are all controlled by computers. Like it or not, they are difficult to ignore. Just as many of us grew up in the new era of television, so our own children are growing up in the era of the computer. For parents who have no direct experience of computers, this can be worrying. Behind all those clichés about the benefits of computers, many of us can also see the message: take care your children do not grow up to become the new illiterate – the computer-illiterate.

Those who sing the praises of computers often have a vested interest in making us feel that way: they want us to buy. Faced increasingly with pressures to purchase home computers for their children (as 30 years ago parents were pressured to buy encyclopedias), we need to know whether they really are necessary. Can computers teach him anything which a good book cannot? Are they a better means of teaching? In 20 years' time, will schools really be obsolete and each child sit at home with his or her own computer terminal? And most worrying of all, in these times of growing long-term unemployment, will he be unemployable if he cannot write a computer program?

While many people are happy to put off learning about computers for another year or two, once they have children of seven or eight they begin to feel they ought to do something, if only for their children's sake. They may approach computers with caution, but their children often take to them with greater ease and enthusiasm. Sometimes a child whom years of formal schooling have failed to stimulate can suddenly take off when given a computer. I have a friend who employed a high school drop-out with no qualifications to punch in data on his computer, and found that the boy rapidly became a skilled programmer. The opposite is also true: some highly educated, intelligent people draw a blank when faced with learning to program.

It is sometimes claimed that children who grow up with TV have a special affinity with anything that uses a TV screen. True, children are often better than their parents when it comes to video games or learning from TV programs, but this does not mean that computers are necessarily a better way to teach children. Computer learning has advantages and disadvantages.

The simplest learning programs are those which are rote learning practice, as is needed for foreign language vocabulary,

COMPUTE A STORY
Nine years on

Procedure Current trends in computer design suggest that programming might be a skill that few need in the future (*see main text page 215*). At the moment, though, learning basic programming routines is one of the best ways of coming to grips with just how a computer works and what it can do. Many children will also appreciate the challenge. It can be a taxing, but entertaining mental exercise because it involves pushing buttons and looking at a bright screen – and there is no one to criticize any mistakes.

Eventually, many children will invent their own programs and routines, but this simple adventure plot provides a useful starting point. Individual commands will, of course, vary from computer to computer, so this is only a basic outline.

The idea is that the computer is to be the child's companion in a brief adventure. There are several different ways the story can unfold, depending on the decisions made at each point.

```
LINE
  10 PRINT "WHAT IS
YOUR NAME?"
  20 INPUT NAME$
  30 PRINT
"HELLO";NAME$";
"READY FOR AN
ADVENTURE?"
  40 PRINT "WOULD YOU
LIKE TO GO IN MY
SUBMARINE?" ANSWER
Y OR N
  50 IF REPLY$ = "Y"
THEN GOTO 110
```

Continued on page 214

213

COMPUTE A STORY
Continued from page 213

```
60 IF REPLY$ = "N"
THEN GOTO 2000
70 IF REPLY$ = " "
THEN GOTO 90
90 PRINT "ANSWER Y
OR N OR I'LL ASSUME
YOU MEAN YES"
100 "I'M GOING TO
TAKE YOU ANYWAY"
110 PRINT "SHALL WE
GO UNDER THE ICECAP?"
120 INPUT REPLY$
130 IF REPLY$ = "Y"
THEN GOTO 200
140 IF REPLY$ = "N"
THEN GOTO 1000
150 PRINT "I SAID Y OR
N"
170 GOTO 110
200 PRINT "I THOUGHT
YOU'D SAY THAT"
```

and so on with many
diversions and
alternatives, such as
"it's cold in here; shall
we turn back?" or
"We've sprung a leak,
have we time to fix it?"
or "I see a polar bear"
until line 2000 or, from
line 140:

```
1000 PRINT "SHALL WE
GO TO THE SOUTH
SEAS?"
```

leads off on another
adventure . . . until:

```
2000 PRINT "THAT'S
THE END OF THE GAME,
THANK YOU"
```

Value
COMPUTING SKILLS;
CREATIVE; LOGIC

dates in history, spelling, or arithmetic. The questions are flashed up on the screen, and the machine rings bells or buzzes when the child gets an answer wrong; or puts up stars and flashing lights when he gets it right. If he has to learn by rote (and it is sometimes necessary), then a computer might make it a little less dull: at least at first. I have known children on whom the flashing lights pall after the first week or so. He can use the computer to compete against himself, trying not to make any mistakes: but the motivation to do so must still come from him, and he can test himself in this way just as efficiently with paper and pencil, or get you to test him. If he is a reasonably well-motivated self-starter, he certainly does not need a computer to flash lights when he gets answers right; unless perhaps he is nervous of making mistakes when an adult tests him.

Teaching programs

Teaching programs are much more interesting than rote learning programs. They attempt to get the child thinking logically; perhaps to move an object around the screen, for example to catch a shark in a net or, in the case of Logo, perhaps the best-known of these programs, to move a "turtle" about. They do not tell a child "Do it like this," but let him work it out for himself. Given a background of the school curriculum, which is heavily biased towards learning how to read, write and spell, these programs serve the worthwhile function of exercising his ability to solve problems. Children can learn to reason without a computer: playing certain board games, doing simple experiments, even woodwork or playing marbles or just messing about can teach him to "work out" a properly ordered sequence of actions. Computers are just another way of practicing this skill, not a magic road to becoming a logical genius. He is no brighter because he does it on a computer instead of with a saw and a block of wood; he is merely using a different tool: a tool which is immensely attractive to some but by no means all children.

For children who respond to them, computers can work like magic. This is especially noticeable in children who have difficulties learning in the classroom; some find the terminal a much more sympathetic teacher than a human being. Perhaps this is because it does not judge them before they start to answer, or perhaps because it is lavish in its praise, or even because it looks like a television. No one is sure why, but the fact is that some handicapped, disadvantaged children and not a few perfectly average children, learn much better at the computer terminal than in the classroom. But it would be wrong to imply that it is necessarily so: if your child is slow to progress at school, or simply bored and distracted by his schooling, a computer might help him; but not for sure.

Programming – an essential skill?

Ultimately I suppose we buy computers in the hope that our children will learn to program, to brief the computer in the appropriate electronic language so that it can perform chosen tasks. By contrast, playing video games and using learning packages is to rely simply on ready-made programs. But should we want them to program? It is an excellent training in logical thought and problem solving; but will it, in future, be a qualification for the best jobs?

I would guess not. The reputable computer courses claim that programming is a useful and enjoyable skill, but that it never guarantees jobs. In another generation, programmers (except truly expert ones) may well be a thing of the past. And already electronics firms are thinking in terms of computers that write their own programs. Our children will probably grow up with more and more of their lives controlled by computers; but there is no reason to suppose that programming is an essential skill. Understanding the computer needs to take its place alongside mathematics, science, history, geography, languages and literature; part of a general education, probably no more, certainly no less.

Word processors

When children write essays they often have a general plan, but few write, correct and rewrite as most professional writers do. If the skilled writer rarely gets it right first time, it is not surprising that few children write as well as they could. With a word processor at his disposal, however, the picture changes. Corrections and reorganizing are so simple that children are only too prepared to write, think and then rewrite: making the changes is fun, an opportunity to test the machine's facilities. If he does not like a sentence, he simply writes over it; if he feels that a particular paragraph would read better elsewhere, he can simply move it. Armed with this facility, children's essay writing naturally improves. More interesting still, once he has been taught to look critically at his writing, he will always do so. Most of the research in this area has been carried out with rather older children, but if your child begins to write with a word processor, he will probably develop good habits of composition.

What and when to buy

The market in microcomputers changes rapidly; advice goes out

---

MOVE AND DRAW
Eight years on

Procedure Drawing a house on screen with a computer can be one of the simplest of all computer games – an ideal introduction to computer programing and to computer graphics in particular. It can be developed through various stages to sophisticated programs involving sub-routines for squares and triangles of variable size.
The first stage involves using just MOVE and DRAW commands to place the cursor and rule lines between two specified points. The program could be:

100 MOVE 00

(This positions the cursor at the bottom left-hand corner of the house.)

200 DRAW 00 TO 0.10

(This draws the ground line.)

300 DRAW 0.10 TO 10.10

(This draws one wall.)

400 DRAW 10.10 TO 10.0

and so on. The tricky part is remembering to move the cursor to draw the windows – effectively lifting the pen from the paper.
The second stage is to get the computer to draw a house of any size. This means that the specific statements such as DRAW 0.0 to 0.50 are replaced with general symbols DRAW AB or DRAW BC and so on. The letters A, B, C and so on

Continued on page 216

MOVE AND DRAW
Continued from page 215

represent the apexes and must be defined in the initial statements. Then, to draw the house at different sizes, you simply supply values for AB, BC and so on.
The third and most advanced stage is to program the computer to build the house up from sub-routines for squares and triangles.

Value
COMPUTER SKILLS You introduce programming in three easy stages. The first is not a program, simply instructions. The second uses simple statements that must be thought of in advance. The third requires a flow diagram and uses statements like GOTO. He has to keep track of the sub-routine entries and exits and to make sure the house is larger than the windows.
LOGIC

of date. The best plan is to ask at his school – or look in computer magazines – to see if there are any firms in your area which specialize in computers and the accompanying programs for children. At the same time, visit computer exhibitions, and talk to other parents. If you are buying for a six- or seven-year-old, you will need a machine with large paddles – the name given to the switches that move spots or shapes around the screen. Small children can find it difficult to use the keyboard. Look for bright colors and exciting graphics, and avoid programs that do little more than a moderately good book might achieve. There is nothing to be gained by luring small children from books to computers unless they can add something extra to a child's learning. Although there are programs for pre-schoolers, do not be tempted to buy a computer for this age group. Let your four-year-old have a go by all means, but four is too young to have exclusive use of a computer. Its complexity will make a four-year-old abandon it in the end; and like all toys, an unused computer will be classed as dull, so in your eagerness you may delay his learning.

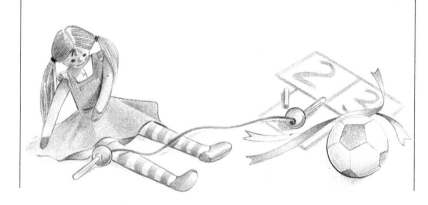

EXPLORING

Driving home from the city in the rush hour I notice little of my surroundings and when I reach home I remember virtually nothing of the journey. Sometimes I find I cannot even remember exactly which route I took. The explanation is simple: I am not in the mood for learning.

But it need not be like that. I remember the excitement of my drive home through the heart of London when I first started working there; and the journey from the airport into Tokyo remains vividly clear, though I was surely tired after 17 hours' travelling with three wakeful children. But novelty is not the only factor. On the first clear sunny day of spring, or the first frosty day of winter, your familiar environment can come to life, and you notice many little things that have passed you by over the months; and as many a corny song proclaims, falling in love (or just being especially happy, or exceptionally fit) can suddenly heighten your awareness of the world around you. And so it is with children. As you drag him around town, he reluctantly follows, and probably learns little because he is unwilling. Let him make the journey by himself, and his excitement and nervousness will arouse all his senses: he will see all there is to see; learn all there is to learn.

As they grow, children venture further afield: the next room, alone in the garden, into the street. We impose boundaries – no futher than the bottom of the hill, not out of calling distance – but eventually they want, and need, to break those boundaries. At what age this occurs, and how far they go, will of course vary. But by 11 most children are travelling some distance to school, and want to go swimming and visit friends in other neighborhoods. Part of growing up is growing away, but letting him go out alone can be worrying at first: however, a short trip on his own to the local shops can provide far more stimulation for a seven-year-old than a family outing into town.

When my middle child of five used to pack a picnic to eat on the patch of grass three houses away, he would come back full of wonder, full of details he had noticed. When much later he took the bus into town to buy coffee for me, he could describe the route, and the shops, quite clearly. At nine he greatly enjoyed a train trip to the next station; but a plane trip undertaken alone to visit his grandparents 200 miles away was not a success. It was all too dramatic. A child who was used to flying might have responded better: while excitement can increase awareness, and

USING A COMPASS
Seven years on

Procedure The intrepid young explorer needs to know how to use a compass if he is to survive in uncharted territory. A few simple finding out games will help him to learn. Show him how a compass works and then set a few questions to answer: **1** Is it true that flowers bloom earlier on south-facing slopes? **2** . . . that snow melts earlier on south-facing slopes? **3** . . . that the pole star points north? **4** . . . that you can tell direction from your watch (not digital!)? **5** . . . that a shadow stick can tell you where north is? **6** . . . that graves in churchyards are aligned east-west? **7** . . . that moss grows on the north side of trees? **8** . . . that snow looks blue on north-facing slopes when the sun shines? . . . and so on. This makes a particularly interesting project for two friends.

Value
INDEPENDENCE: INITIATIVE; FINDING OUT; USEFUL SKILL

Procedure This is a simple stalking game which can be played by younger children particularly well in company with older ones. One player is "the traffic signal" and stands with his back to the others. The rest stand about 15 feet (5 m) away. The idea is to touch the traffic signal without him seeing you moving. He keeps his back turned while saying "one, two, three, four, five" and so on until "ten – RED LIGHT!" As he counts, the other players rush quickly forwards; as soon as he says "Red Light", he turns rapidly round and sends back to the start any players he sees moving, even slightly. He can make the game more interesting by varying the speed at which he counts. The game finishes when all have reached the traffic signal.

Value
CONTROL; FUN

Later progress Older children can try *Sentry*, a really challenging stalking game (*see opposite*).

make a child look outward, real anxiety often turns thoughts and attentions inward to oneself.

Generally it is the city child, with plentiful public transport, who can travel most easily. When we moved to the city from the country a friend who had grown up in the city, but then left it to live in the country, commented that it was marvelous for our eldest child: there was such a large and varied area to explore. From his home there were only two buses a day, and making a solo trip into town was impossible for his children. He recalled traveling on the subway, exploring shops, art galleries and museums with obvious pleasure. Growing up on the edge of the country I had rather the opposite feeling. I felt sad that my children would not be able to follow streams, find badgers' setts, or when older cycle along country roads.

What we both recalled, of course, was the enormous fun of exploring. For him it was the town, for me the country, but for both of us it had been one of the great pleasures of late childhood.

Stalking games

Children cannot go out on trips every day, and if they could their reward would diminish. However, being observant – having a good general level of *awareness* – is a great asset, and it can be developed through play. If, for instance, the situation is not novel, or the company a little stale, a simple competition can heighten his awareness. I suspect it is no coincidence that such a large proportion of traditional middle childhood games are competitive observation ones. *Hide and Seek, Hunt the Thimble,* even *I Spy* are the typical examples, but the classic observation games are surely those based upon stalking.

Stalking games occur in many cultures, and there are many variations, but they all need keen observation, and their competitive element produces the heightened awareness needed to play successfully. The classic stalking game, probably best known as *London* or *Red Light, Green Light,* is a game for almost anywhere, from the beach to the street. Players do not hide, they creep slowly forwards. They can always be seen: but must never be seen to move. If cover is available, *Sentry* is a more exciting game, especially for a large group.

Like many of the traditional children's games, *Sentry* cannot be played without trust. The sentry is faithfully relied upon to keep his eyes forward; there is no referee to enforce the rules, and if someone cheats, the game ceases to be fun. Such an element of trust is present in most children's games (though not in the adult sport we increasingly encourage children to play). Indeed, trust is a characteristic of social play throughout the

SENTRY/*Nine years on*

This is the Rolls-Royce of stalking games, best appreciated after children have tired of simpler ones such as *Red Light, Green Light* (*page 218*). The game needs some cover – say trees in a park – but the sparser it is, the more challenging the game.

1 Agree on two locations (**A** and **B**) 30 to 50 yards (27 to 46 m) apart.
2 Choose a sentry; he stands on **A.**
3 Play begins as the sentry, standing on **A,** faces straight ahead at **B,** *without moving his head,* and counts loudly to 50. The rest of the players – the stalkers – disperse to available cover making certain the sentry does not see them as they go.

4 When the sentry reaches the count of 50, he starts walking towards **B.** He must not move his head – but he may swivel his eyes. When the stalkers judge themselves out of the sentry's range of vision, they are free to move towards **B.** If the sentry sees a stalker, or any part of him, he calls him back to point **A** to start all over again.
5 When the sentry reaches **B,** he turns around through 180°, still not moving his head, pauses to count out loud to ten, then sets off back to **A.** Stalkers out of the sentry's range of vision are again free to move.
6 The procedure is repeated until the first stalker reaches **B** unseen. He then becomes the sentry for the next round.

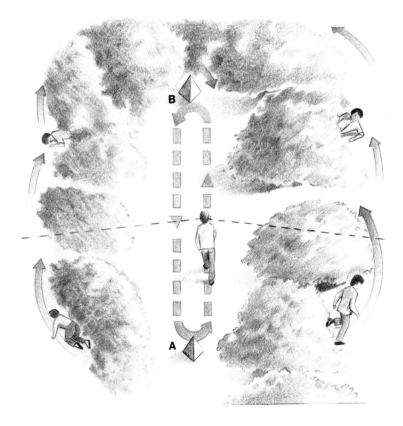

Value
SOCIAL
STRATEGY Stalkers must calculate the sentry's field of vision and plan out a route to the winning post in viable stages.
EXERCISE
NO REAL LOSERS Winning is satisfying, but the reward – being sentry – is not so exciting as being a stalker.

WATERDROP MICROSCOPE
Nine to ten years

Procedure Some children are born observers and will notice for themselves how water can magnify. Others may need encouragement. To make a waterdrop microscope, drill a small hole (about 0.1 in. or 2 mm) in a sheet of aluminium – children should only do this under adult supervision. Then wipe a thin layer of petroleum jelly around, but *not* covering the hole. Drip a little water on to the hole from the end of a finger so that the water sits like a lens over the hole. The specimen could be a plant, a coin or anything that might benefit from a closer look. This should be placed on a sheet of white paper, brightly illuminated by a desk lamp, under the lens. The water lens will magnify the subject to a surprising degree.

Value
OBSERVATION; SIMPLE SCIENCE; EXPERIMENTATION; CONSTRUCTION

animal world: when fox cubs or young lions play-fight they must trust each other not to bite, otherwise the "fight" would cease to be fun, and play would cease to be play. To a child, honor is of great importance, and cheating hardly enters the picture. Perhaps an underlying reason for this is that winning these games is actually not important. They may play each game to win; but they rarely keep track of how often they win or lose. The game is the thing.

There is a further dimension to the better stalking games, one which is particularly important during these middle childhood years. In *Sentry* the players have to plan their route from cover to cover, decide when to run and when to creep and, above all, to work out at which points they are likely to be spotted by the sentry. They need, in other words, to use a strategy, to plan three or even four steps in advance. Obviously this is a skill that everyone needs to develop if they are to think rationally. They will not use precisely the same sort of thinking when they come to solve more complex problems in the classroom, but they will have to think things through. *Sentry* encourages one other important skill: the players must put themselves in the sentry's place and estimate what he or she can see from each position during the passage from base to base. As we have seen, this is a skill that develops at about six and continues to be strengthened through middle childhood.

Some people are born natural scientific observers. My sister is one: she spent much of her childhood searching for small animals and plants, entirely on her own initiative. Country walks with her now are a revelation: I am shown things I would never see myself. While a child is very young the material world seems continually new and exciting, for it is being experienced largely afresh – for the first time. As they grow older, taking more and more for granted because it has already been experienced, they cannot all remain as observant as my sister. They cannot all grow up to be scientists or artists; but even a very basic habit of observation can give so much real pleasure. Encourage her to collect things as you walk; to spot plants, animals, shop signs or cars, and she may carry some of that curiosity and increased awareness into adulthood.

BOOKS FOR MIDDLE CHILDHOOD

A few children start learning to read before they begin school, but most do so in the first two years of full-time schooling. It is not wrong for parents to delegate this responsibility: after all, teachers are trained to teach. But although it is their job, it is not their exclusive right. In the past, teachers sometimes took a high-handed attitude with parents, resenting any interference in the teaching of reading. These days few would take this line; if they do, you can tactfully point out that children learn better if parents and teachers co-operate. Most teachers are delighted when parents show an interest in helping their children read. After all, it is easier for you to spend an hour each week listening to your child – and your child alone – reading than it is for a teacher.

For the child's sake, though, you should make it your business to co-operate with the chosen method of teaching reading. There is no point in adding confusion to an already difficult task. The teacher has 20 to 30 children to teach and cannot work with the idiosyncratic methods of 30 parents. If the school has no formal scheme for getting parents to help, ask if he can bring home his reading book once or twice a week. Most children will be able to tell you whether they are "spelling out" words – that is, using phonics – or learning by "look and say", but check this with the school. "Look and say" gives the child a great deal of initial confidence, and many schools begin with this system. It may not be how you learned to read, but it is how you read now: fluent readers only spell out new or difficult words.

Whatever his efforts at reading, make sure he has plenty of praise. Show him the pleasure you take in his achievement. Do not expect him to be able to "spell out" words unless this is the way he is being taught to read. You must never counteract or undermine the work of the school: think of yourself as a teaching assistant, not his chief instructor, even if in practice you spend more time listening to him than the school does.

On the other hand, don't expect the school to teach him to enjoy books. This is your responsibility. The school will do its best to interest him, but they do not have the time to show each child the pleasures that books can bring. They often read a story at the end of the day: you can read him one, too. They may have a book corner where a child can browse; you can take him to book shops and libraries and make him a library of his own.

The joys of reading need to be sold. Start as you mean to go on, and plug books at every opportunity. You start with the upper

NEWSWORTHY
Eight years on

Procedure This is a challenging game for a small group of children with similar reading ability. Buy two copies of the same morning newspaper and divide the group into two teams. Let both teams read the front page for four minutes. Then retrieve the papers and ask six questions on the news items on the front page. The answers should be written down. Make a note of the scores and do the same with another page of the newspaper, this time with one of the children as question master. Go on playing until everyone has had a turn as question master.

Value
READING They must read quickly and effectively to extract the important points from a story.
DISCOVERY This game may increase their awareness of and interest in the world at large.
MEMORY; OBSERVATION

CABLEGRAM
Eight years on

Procedure A useful diversion for long journeys: the only equipment needed is pencil and paper. The game is based on faulty cablegrams in which only the first letter of each word has come through. Pick a word – such as a personal or place name – of about eight to ten letters. The letters of this word provide the first letter for each of the words in the cablegram. Each player must then guess what the lost message was in two minutes. The message must make some sort of sense, though it can be mysterious. If the keyword was DOROTHY, a possible answer could be: DRIVE ON – REFLECT ON TWO HAPPY YEARS, or better still, DANGEROUS ORANGE RABBITS ON THE HIGHWAY – YIELD. The winner of each round is chosen by general consent. Everyone should have a chance to choose the word.

Value
GAME FOR JOURNEYS;
VERBAL ABILITY

hand, but you can easily lose it. Begin to read to him long before he is lured away by television. Try to sit together with a book every day. Produce books which feed his imagination in a way that most TV cannot, and share his pleasure in them. Talk about the stories you read, not only at the time you read them but whenever the opportunity arises. Could that duck on the village pond be called Jemima Puddle Duck? Could that rabbit be Peter Rabbit? Where did Anne of Green Gables live? Get out the atlas, or, better still, go and see. Most of all, remember that he learns by imitation. He will copy what he sees; if you enjoy books, so will he. He is unlikely to find your message compelling if his books are the only ones that come into your house.

In your fight for his literacy be prepared to be quite creative. Don't treat books as presents for special occasions, but as something one often buys when near a bookshop. Sit next to him as he watches TV, but cuddle him close as you read to him. Most of all, keep the competition firmly in its place: switch off the TV at the end of his program. Make no mistake, television is real competition with the written word. In the average American home, the TV is on for six and a half hours every day, and the average six-year-old has spent 5,000 hours watching it. In Europe children do not watch quite so much TV – probably because it does not run all day as it does in America; but we are catching up fast. It may be some years before we run remedial composition classes in English universities, as they do even in the best North American universities, but can it be far away? How long is it before our children grow up unable to read the instructions on a package of cake mix? A recent survey by the US Department of Education suggests that 20 per cent of adult Americans are functionally illiterate, and another 34 per cent have difficulty in writing the simplest letters, or addressing envelopes. There is no room for complacency: reading must be shown to bring pleasures greater than that of TV if literature is to survive.

Learning to read

Just because he can read a few words, do not be misled into thinking that he has now outgrown pre-reading games (*pages 152-8*). Practice is how children learn. Play *I Spy*, and reinforce his ability to recognize the first letter of a word. Then see if he can tell how words end; spelling out will follow. Read poems to him because they encourage him to listen to the words. Many children like to be told "you're a poet, and didn't know it". But rhyme has an additional function: it helps the child to jump ahead of the sense of the passage with a good guess. At first, the more familiar the rhyme the better: of course he knows "Humpty Dumpty sat on a wall", but he will still feel good if he reads it for himself. The child who pretends to read today will be reading alone tomorrow.

Look for letters on car number plates and advertisements: not because he needs to know his letters, though it is a useful skill, but because it helps him to notice letters and make sense of the different styles of calligraphy and typesetting and sign writing that make up words.

Make sure that he knows his way around a book. Check that he knows he should read from left to right, and from top to bottom on a page and from front to back in a book. Probably the best way to do this is to let him open the book when you start reading, and ask him to turn the pages for you. Best of all, move his finger along the line as you read.

Books for him to read by himself should be simple, repetitive and offer plenty of opportunities to guess when he does not know a word. He needs to gain confidence; never mind the mistakes, or that he "isn't really reading". Trying to read is the first step, however he goes about it. He will need helpful supporting pictures (and possibly rhyme) to assist with this early guesswork, and he needs simple language to go with those pictures: in fact just the qualities you sought in books when he was two. Take another look at some of these early books; don't worry that they seem babyish and remind yourself of the essential qualities. At the same time you can introduce books that stretch his memory and imagination. Teaching him to read and to take pleasure in books ideally proceed in tandem. Many parents forget this and assume that once he can read fluently they should stop reading bedtime stories. Keep on reading out loud until he does not want you to any more; or until you are certain he is addicted. If in doubt about the worth of your labors, remember how much the film or TV performance of a book encourages people to read that same book.

Until he is fluent, the books he can read for himself will be much simpler than the ones you read to him. Remind yourself of his level: "Little Bear ran to Father Bear and hugged him. Father Bear hugged Little Bear." This is from an "I-Can-Read" book – *Father Bear Comes Home* by Else Minarik – and it is just right for an early reader.

LETTERS
Nine years on

Procedure This is another game for journeys or quiet moments at home, needing no equipment. The players sit in a circle, or remember a given order of play. Each player has three lives. One player chooses a letter to start the game off. The idea is then for each player round the circle to add a letter (verbally) to build up a word – but avoid being the person to complete it. Each player must have a word in mind as he adds a letter – though he can bluff – for the player following can challenge him to declare his word. If he has a word, the challenger loses a life; if not, the player loses a life. A player faced with completing a word can try to bluff his way out by adding a likely sounding letter. A game might run as follows. First player says C (thinking of "Christmas"); the second adds A ("car"); the third avoids completing the word by adding L (thinking of "call"); the fourth escapes completing "call" by adding C (as in "calculate") and so on until the last player is faced with *calculatio*. His bluff of *s* fails and he loses a life.

Value
PLAY ANYWHERE; SPELLING; STRATEGY Choosing letters so that your closest rival has to finish the word.

John and Elizabeth Newson's
TOP TWENTY TOYS

These toys have been chosen to cover a wide range of play. Not one of them is the *only* good toy of its kind, but each one illustrates particularly well the design qualities needed in order to fulfill its purpose successfully.

We have not attempted to show examples of big toys here: sit-and-ride toys, dolls' carriages, trucks, tricycles and large block sets, let alone swings, jungle gyms, rocking horses and play houses. Nor have we shown the small-world toys that get added to bit by bit, such as dolls' houses, farmyards and zoos. All these give children enormous pleasure and have long-term play value, but they are beyond the scope of this kind of list.

We have cheated a little by showing a pair or set of toys in a few cases. Sometimes a pair is shown because one is a development of the other but has not superseded it; sometimes a pair is necessary for full use (as in the telephone pair); or a set (such as a tea set) makes all the difference to the toy's attractiveness for play.

Manufacturers' names of the toys illustrated are given in parentheses, but they are not necessarily the only makers of the type of toy discussed. Other manufacturers are sometimes indicated in the text. Although most of these toys are available in good toy stores everywhere, it can be worth your while to seek out stores that sell imported as well as domestic toys.

---

1 Range of crib toys (*Semper/Fischerform*); shown here is **Peek-a-boo** mounted on the **Toy Mount.**

This type of toy is designed either for visual interest or to allow the baby to make something happen. With *Peek-a-boo,* the surprise is under the baby's control – though she will at first make it happen by accident. As she learns that she is responsible for the effect, she will also begin to realize that each hand movement produces a different result. This is one of many toys which use predictable surprise as an essential experience; it also prepares a baby for the idea of an object's permanence. Another stimulating crib toy is Shelcore's *Crib Soft Gym,* an inflatable toy that rotates and squeaks when pulled.

2 Ring Rattle
(*Kiddicraft*)

A first rattle must be neither too heavy nor too noisy: unco-ordinated movements can end in a swipe across the head, while sudden sharp noises are frightening. The *Ring Rattle* is light, bright and easy to hold; it invites passing from one hand to the other, and the colored beads move constantly with a gentle clicking sound. It feels equally good to hands, gums and tongue, so that the early exploratory sequence of look . . . mouth . . . look . . . handle . . . look comes very naturally, while what he hears eventually encourages him to shake the toy for a louder noise.

3 Flip Fingers
(*Kiddicraft*) and **Twin Rattle** (*Ambi*)

Flip Fingers is a modern classic in teether-rattles, which has been much imitated, but never improved upon; *Twin Rattle* is another innovative design which is also likely to defy imitation: each has a deceptive simplicity. The high-quality plastic gives clear, bright colors and a satisfying solidity combined with lightness. *Flip Fingers* can be easily gripped by a poorly co-ordinated child, and the "paddles" are designed with smooth depressions which invite exploring tongue and fingers. *Twin Rattle's* twin cogs revolve endlessly round and round each other in a movement that fascinates grown-ups as well as babies. Both toys actively encourage two-handed play and finger control.

4 Key ring teether
(*Kiddicraft*)

This was one of the first toys to exploit the translucent colors of chunky acrylic plastic; when held to the light, the keys have a glowing quality. Unlike most key ring rattles, these keys have no serrated edges to hurt the baby's gums, but provide biting and licking interest through grooves, depressions and rounded rims. The four linked parts have varied degrees of sameness and difference for the baby to explore, and considerable two-handed manipulation is exercised in turning them through different relationships with each other.

5 Monkey (*Vera Small Toys*)

It is difficult to improve on the traditional teddy bear as a first and favorite friend – especially when it is as huggable as Dakin's *Nature Babies* bear. But other animals can be equally loveable, including a warren of soft pastel bunnies which rattle gently when moved, manufactured by California Stuffed Toys. Vera Small's monkey, pictured here, is the very role-model of a long-lasting companion. Three-month old babies recognize, and are fascinated by the "personhood" of the face, and the long arms, draped protectively over a child, seem to give comfort at bedtime.

6 Baby Trainer
(*Ambi*)

This robust toy is to be strung across the crib, first for gazing play, then for swiping, and finally for manipulation and exercise. Each of the pieces swings independently. The hand-holds at either end are easy to grip, and allow the baby to feel the weight of his body and the strength of his muscles as he pulls up and relaxes; long before that, though, he will enjoy spinning the three-pronged twirler, listening to the rings slipping and clicking up and down, and setting the chunky bell chiming.

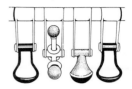

7 Peek-a-boo Bunny
(*Kiddicraft*) and **Dozy Daisy** (*Matchbox*)

Like many other crib toys, *Peek-a-Boo Bunny* is based upon the principle of cause and effect, where the message to the baby is a clear "you made it happen." *Peek-a-Boo Bunny* also has the advantage of capitalizing on a baby's interest in eyes, which are covered and uncovered by the bunny's paws while a lullaby plays. Other toys that reward the baby's efforts include *One Ring Circus* by Fisher-Price and *Pull-a-Byes Bunny* by Tomy. Tomy also produces a line of nice-looking crib toys that includes *Merry-Go-Music Box* and the elaborate *Little Crib Concert.*

8 Funhouse (*Ambi*)

Most activity centers offer the child a variety of visual and auditory happenings as a result of different kinds of manipulations on his part: pressing, twisting, sliding, winding, twiddling and so on. A number, however, are just a collection of unconnected activities, so it is a good idea to look for an activity center with a definite theme, like Kiddicraft's *Seaside* and *Farm*, or this "house": some kind of a story gives parent and child far more opportunity to talk about what is going on.

9 Wobbly fun ball
(*Kiddicraft*)

A toy that rolls a little way, but not too far, will tempt the not-yet-mobile baby to reach, lunge, swivel and finally creep in its pursuit. This substantial yellow floor-ball, in heavy ABS plastic, has a weighted base which makes it roll and wobble eccentrically. The baby will peep through the holes and slots to find two smaller balls inside in contrasting colors, and inside these, shiny jingle-bells. The idea of bells-in-balls-in-a-ball seems to have an intrinsic mystery for most young children; and they find the wobbly action surprisingly surprising. Peeping, poking, fingering and wondering are all stimulated by this toy.

10 Water Mate
(*Kiddicraft*) and
Flutterball (*Playskool*)

These rolling toys, which encourage the almost-mobile child to look and follow, are also fascination toys. The two translucent butterflies, both alighted on the central loose spindle, turn and spin in their bubble. Water has a particular fascination for most babies because of its splash and gleam; and the small duck swimming on forever upright, however the ball is rolled, contrasts by its own stability. It is intriguing that babies, who cannot really understand the paradoxical quality of a stable duck within a rolling globe, still find it extraordinarily compelling to watch. *Water Mate* is of such interest to older children that it seems to act as a focus for interaction between the baby and his brothers and sisters, who take pleasure in demonstrating its delights. Both make good bath floaters, showing their unsinkability in no uncertain terms.

11 Wobble globe
(*Kiddicraft*)

There are many versions of this toy on the market, but this one has a special feature which doubles its play value, particularly as a bath toy: the globe can be unscrewed, half-filled with water and screwed back on. This makes the balls move in a quite different way, and produces a different sound effect – again with the special fascination of trapped water. The globe on its own is an excellent pouring-and-filling toy, with the balls bobbing about inside it.

12 Jack in the Ball
(*Ambi*)

Young children love a surprise that is not too frightening because they were expecting it all along. This version of the old-fashioned Jack-in-the-box gives the child an enjoyable shock over which he exerts his own control. He can also enjoy surprising other people – babies delight in mock-astonishment in adults. Is it a ball? . . . NO! . . . With a squeak, it becomes a roly-poly little man. Surprise toys like this encourage a child's sense of anticipation and climax (which he needs for longer play sequences later on) and also remind him about object permanence. Johnson & Johnson's *Peek-a-Boo* ball, with its pointed rattle that half falls out of the ball, also holds a baby's attention.

13 Soft blocks (Galt)

First blocks are for piling up and knocking down; and although the noisy crash is part of the fun when wooden blocks are piled, the lack of noise is made up for here by the size, which also makes them easier to pile. When babies pile blocks, they can hardly resist the urge to knock them down again; so it's useful to have large ones (so long as they're safe like these) in order to build up some height before the temptation to push is too great. Again, the baby is working on anticipation sequences.

The colors of these fabric-covered cubes are clear and fresh, and because they are washable, they will stay that way. The pictures are also a focus for conversation between you and your baby.

Dick Bruna makes another nice set of washable cloth cubes.

14 Pop-up Men (*Galt*)

This is a toy to be played with at four different levels. The gentle pop-up action holds the child's attention and encourages press-and-let-go finger control even before she can fit the peg-man. As a simple fitting toy, the pegs are easy to grasp, and fitting gives the instant reward of a small bounce. The fact that the pegs are recognizable as "little men" stimulates additional conversation and the beginnings of symbolic or pretend play. Finally, there is a color-matching element. A deceptively simple toy with plenty going on for the child.

15 Cornpopper (*Fisher-Price*) and **Laughalong clown** (*Kiddicraft*)

Push-alongs precede pull-alongs in terms of development because they help the child to feel more stable when he is still walking unsteadily; they also move along in front of the child, encouraging him to look forward and therefore stay upright. Some push-alongs enclose all their moving parts; *Cornpopper,* with its colored balls bouncing around inside a clear plastic bubble, makes a satisfying clatter. The clown shows another function of push-alongs: to give a very small child the feeling of importance: they are a way of announcing "Make way – here I come!" The toy exploits a sight-and-sound effect that children have found funny for generations – the slapping of big floppy feet on the floor – and as a bonus there is head movement and a chuckle.

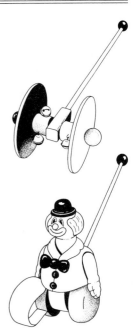

16 Clatterpillar
(*Kiddicraft*)

The pull-along makes a much bigger demand than the push-along on a child's stability and balance skills. Not only does it give no support, pulling her over rather than helping her to stand, but also it encourages her to look round as she pulls it behind her, which at first will cause her to sit down in a hurry. Mastering the skills of pulling a pull-along will give the child very basic mastery over her whole-body movement. Pull-alongs must be stable: those that keep falling over are a constant frustration. *Clatterpillar* is stable even over carpet edges, lawns and uneven pavements and the wave-pattern of its action is visually fascinating. A similar toy is Slinky Brand's *Cater-puller*.

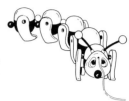

17 Hammer Board
(*Invicta Plastics*) and **All Wood Cobbler's Bench** (*Playskool*)

Peg-pounders such as these are well-tried classics. They help a baby learn to aim, use a tool and manage a controlled force. The board should be sturdy and stable to cope with the wilder blows, and the hammer should be well-balanced – something in which the wooden *Playskool* mallet excels. Unlike plastic pegs, though, wooden pegs may shrink or swell, and a peg that sticks or slips through is more frustrating than challenging. (One solution is to make sure the set is in good working order when you buy it, then keep it away from moisture and heat.) The plastic *Hammer Board* has pegs in a variety of solid shapes, although it is not really a fitting toy, since the pegs are too tight in the hole to be pushed in and out easily by small fingers.

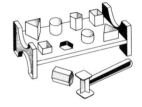

18 Wobbly Colors
(*Kiddicraft*)

Here is an early fitting toy, slightly more difficult overall than Galt's *Pop-up Men*, with a strong focus on color matching. Balls are fitted to their sockets by both color and shape cues, and each socket-block is fitted into the tray – more difficult. The balls themselves are weighted to roll eccentrically, an intrinsically fascinating movement for babies and children, and this also means that they do not roll too far from the less mobile child. There is a "living" quality about these balls, which is very effective in holding the child's attention and which gives a special satisfaction in returning the unstable object into the stable base of its block. The balls are also rattles, making them interesting long before the child understands their fitting and matching possibilities.

19 First Fone (*Ambi*)

The telephone is a powerful stimulus to speech as well as to pretend play, and particularly so if it can be used with an adult or older child: which is why two telephones are much better than one. To serve its purpose, a worthwhile toy phone should be simple, strong and fairly realistic. This is surprisingly difficult to find. Realistic ones often break easily, and the more robust tend to be jazzed up with wheels, faces, rattles and all sorts of other distractions. This model is a basic first telephone, heavy enough not to fall over during dialing, and with all its priorities right.

20 Maypole (*Escor*)

Little children love fitting peg people into small spaces. For younger ones, a toy such as Fisher-Price's Play Family *Little Riders* is perfect. It offers two peg people and five vehicles, including a boat and a tricycle, to fit them into. As the child grows, a toy like Escor's *Maypole* is far more demanding. The maypole's two parts have to be put together, and the little figures have holes underneath them which have to be fitted over pegs on the maypole. This smaller-scale fit needs more precise control from the child, and the aiming skill is a complex one because peg and hole cannot be seen at the moment of fit. In addition, the swaying, spinning maypole is an unstable structure which the child needs to steady as part of the process. This is a nice example of a toy to grow into.

John and Elizabeth Newson's
TOP TWENTY TOYS

In this list we have followed the same guidelines as for the earlier age group, but there is an additional important omission. All the creative play *materials* increasingly come into their own through this age-range. Play dough and clay; different kinds of crayons, paints and felt-tips; sticky stuffs, staples and materials to stick and fasten; every kind of paper, textile and thread: all of these may spell inspiration for one child or another, and variety of opportunity is what counts most. For this reason we have not tried here to choose any particular drawing-and-making equipment.

1 Graded Abacus
(*Escor*)

A toy with which one can almost see the child's thought processes in action. At its simplest, the abacus is a threading toy, and very satisfying as such because of the weight and the "clunk" of the balls as they drop on the posts; the second stage is to fill *all* the posts, resisting the temptation to empty them in between, and thus to understand the pleasure of completion. Color matching comes next; and as soon as matching is combined with the wish to complete, the toy poses a complex mathematical problem. It demands the child's understanding that he must choose *the color he has most of* to place on the longest post, the one he has least of for the shortest, and so on. When he has mastered this toy, he has come quite a long way. This makes the two-graded abacus much more valuable and age-extended than the non-graded version.

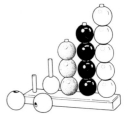

2 Mail boxes: **Lock-a-Block, Prima Forma** and **Shape Box** (*all Ambi*)

Mail boxes help children to develop a concept that adults take for granted – that solid pieces and empty holes can share the same shape. These three illustrate slightly different design advantages and are worth comparing. *Lock-a-Block* discriminates the three basic shapes (circle, triangle, square) in three dimensions; if the child cannot quite match by shape, she has a clue in the color-coded edging of the holes. Having "mailed" two of each, and watched them *almost* disappear as she peeps through the holes, she can unlock the door and find them again. This moment of suspense holds great pleasure.

Prima Forma has no moment of suspense, because the shapes slide straight out again, offering a never-ending mailing game – which is fine while the child is still more interested in the action than in completing a sequence; and this box has six shapes and no clues.

Shape Box is a little more challenging. With eight rather more difficult shapes, they all disappear into the deep box. Like *Graded Abacus,* but unlike *Prima Forma,* this toy stimulates ideas of completion and achievement as well as shape discrimination, and the child proves at the end that she now understands object permanence when she triumphantly removes the lid.

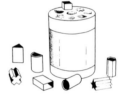

3 Handy Boxes (*Ambi*)

This is a version of the traditional nesting toy, and like similar toys, such as Playskool's *Stacking Barrels* or Chicco's *Building Cubes,* it enables the child to learn about "bigger than" and "smaller than". The repetition of such decisions shows him that this concept is not just about comparing two objects but can be used to put in size-order a whole series of objects. Once he can do that, he can make it all the more complicated with Ambi's *Handy Boxes* by adding the lid each time – perhaps hiding some small toy in one of the boxes and playing guessing games about "which one."

It takes a long time for the hiding-and-finding idea to become boring, which perhaps is why boxes with lids seem to exert so much fascination for young children.

4 Play Buckets
(*Kiddicraft*)

Pouring and sprinkling are favorite activities for all pre-school children, whether with water, sand, dried peas or macaroni. The flat handles make the buckets easy to handle and manipulate. This kind of play is important both in teaching a child about the properties of liquids and other pourable things and in helping her to understand ideas of volume, weight and form: for instance, not everything that can be carried in a bucket takes the bucket's shape. Toy manufacturers do tend to "personalize" their toys unnecessarily; but the cheerful faces on these buckets are more than decoration – they will stimulate the child's pretend play and her sense of humor, too. You only have to fill up the "open-mouth" bucket to see why its eyes have a look of horror! The child may even try giving it a soothing drink from the pointed spout. Both pretend and joking play contribute significantly to language development.

5 Play Shapes
(*Kiddicraft*) and
Popoids (*Tomy*)

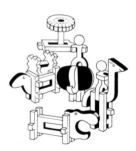

A first construction set with a mix of abstract shapes and representational pieces (animal heads and people). The pieces are easy to fit because of their soft vinyl construction. The representational pieces lead the child to see how he might combine the abstract pieces into an interesting whole. A child may need a warming-up session with an adult, but will soon get the idea of inventing his own constructions. In doing so, he learns to take advantage of accidental combinations and to plan.

Still more important, he works to solve the engineering problems imposed by the fact that the shapes do not necessarily correspond to the objects he had in mind; improvisation and adaptation to circumstances will be skills of lifelong value.

Popoids (Tomy), with their twistable parts and outer space themes, encourage imagination and offer the opportunity to change the shape of individual parts.

6 Inset Puzzles
(*Discovery World*)

Discovery World makes form-fitting wooden knob puzzles with a difference. Each one shows rows of every-day objects such as hamburgers and Christmas trees; beneath each piece is an appropriately scented scratch-n-sniff sticker! Other knob puzzles present zoo animals, pets, crayons: the key quality is that each piece represents a single object. Other useful puzzles, difficult to find but worth looking for, are the *Breakfast* and *Washing* inset puzzles made by John Adams. These pieces are raised above the background, which makes them easy to pick up. Many a child will want to use the pieces for pretend play. She will "eat" the breakfast using the knife and fork, shake salt on the egg, or brush her teeth. Fitting puzzles that support pretend play are rare; this feature immediately enhances the puzzles' value and interest.

7 Kitchen set and
Cups and saucers
(*Galt*); **Cutlery** by
Bambola; bacon and egg
from a joke shop

These high-quality examples of toys for domestic play are all unbreakable; but a less expensive kitchen set can be made up from the genuine articles bought from a discount hardware store. Equipment such as this is enormously valuable in stimulating pretend play, particularly with several children. If we had to choose one part of this group that especially gets this kind of play going, it would be the bacon and egg in a frying pan; so much so, that if we could keep only one item out of all the toys in our playroom, this would be it.

8 Baby doll (*Gadea*)

The first real doll may be the only one you will choose yourself; later on, children develop very clear ideas about what they like in a doll. This doll is for "mothering", nurturing, taking care of, and cuddling; so it is appropriate that it should be as much as possible like a real baby in its general feel. (Don't be tempted, though, to buy a crying doll: it may actually stimulate unkindness in children!) A soft-bodied doll like this one with its cloth torso will settle down much more snugly in its mother's or father's arms, and is easier to dress and undress. Don't choose an all-vinyl first doll unless you are certain it will end up in the bath. You might already have another cheap vinyl doll as bath companion which could be kept permanently naked. Most little boys appreciate a doll to tuck into the stroller (we know one man who has never forgiven his parents for not buying the dolls' carriage he wanted when he was three).

Other nice dolls include *Softina* (Goldberger Doll Manufacturing) and the smaller *Baby Soft Luv,* similar to a real baby in that it smells of baby powder.

9 Music-Box Record-Player (*Fisher-Price*)

This is more than a first musical toy, although its tinkling traditional themes are good for both listening and dancing. The five records offer ten different and pleasant-sounding tunes, giving the child an opportunity for discrimination and choice. He will soon learn the visual cues to play the tune he wants. The actual working of the player demands fitting the record on the turn table plus a series of three actions involving three distinct manual skills: winding up, switching on and placing the arm. This is another toy that gives a big reward for persisting through a sequence of maneuvers; and it is strong enough to withstand handling by a child who is not yet well co-ordinated.

10 Duplo (*by Lego*)

This is an early introduction to Lego, and can be used with Lego as the child grows older. With smaller pieces, and made in harder material than *Play Shapes,* Duplo is a construction set which offers much more than constructional play. The chunky pieces are in fact quite easy to grasp and fit, and the locking mechanism prevents the structure from disintegrating accidentally. For a child with limited attention span and co-ordination, the wheel-bases are a great advantage: she can create a satisfying vehicle by fitting only two pieces together, then gradually improve it with further embellishments, and add a driver. Provision of pieces containing doors and windows, along with convincing animals, people and furniture, immediately extends the toy as a basis for imaginative play and enormously enhances its potential as a focus for language as well as fantasy play.

11 Flootatoota
(*Kiddicraft*)

Drums and tambourines are best for exploring rhythm, but this versatile instrument introduces the child to variations in pitch and tone. The combination of straight and elbow pieces allows assembly into a tightly coiled French horn, a sinuous saxophone or a crazily crooked trumpet. The more the child experiments, the more she discovers: the relationship between the length of the tube and the sound produced; how covering holes or the bell at the end changes the note; the fact that some arrangements produce harmonics, others pure notes. Possibilities range from emitting an Indian war cry to producing six different notes on one fingering by breath control alone.

By taking *Flootatoota* into the bath, a completely different quality of tone can be discovered; in experimenting with "water music" like this, the child learns still more clearly how the length of tube affects the pitch, for she can fill the trumpet with water and pour it slowly away on a sustained note with a glissando effect from high to low. In general, this toy encourages the child both to listen carefully for differences in quality and pitch and to work out for herself scientific principles of sound production.

12 Master Mechanic
(*Kiddicraft*)

This pick-up truck with a working crane is a first tool-using construction toy. A robust and chunky vehicle, it incorporates a carrying handle, foreseeing its role as an inseparable companion, to be lugged around by its devoted owner. Unlike most construction toys, whose parts do tend to get spread around the house, *Master Mechanic* has no detachable parts. The wheels come loose when the nuts and bolts are unscrewed (thus putting the truck satisfactorily out of action and ready to be "fixed"), but nothing rolls away. Nuts and bolts can be manipulated by fingers until the child can manage the screwdriver and wrench, which are anchored by cords to their own toolbox. As well as securing the wheels, turning the bolts will lower the boom and operate the hook, which can be used for lifting cars or buckets. This toy offers excellent manipulative experience at both finger and tool level, and embodies such engineering principles as pulleys, axles and leverage.

A slightly different toy but one that also introduces the use of tools is Brio's *Builder Sets,* which offer a modular system of wooden blocks that can be used with plugs, wheels, and small pliers to make a variety of things that move.

13 Big Builder
sometimes called **Build and Play** (*Jura Castor*)

Another tool-using construction kit, this one can be built up into a variety of structures or vehicles that are actually big enough to climb or ride on. This time the tools really are needed: although the structure will stand with finger-tight screws, actual use demands more leverage than fingers can manage. A comparatively high level of planning and experimentation will be stimulated by this toy, which also begins to give the child experience in working out models from given designs as well as inventing his own. The idea of making something "life-size" is an appealing one, and for that reason *Giant Tinkertoys* (Child Guidance), which are 16 times larger than the regular ones, are also an excellent investment, although the resulting structures will not support a child's weight.

14 Builda Helta Skelta (*Kiddicraft*)

Partly puzzle, partly construction toy, partly sheer fun: *Helta Skelta* is more difficult to build than it looks, as planning is needed to end with the feet all on the same level. Many designs are possible, some rather complicated, and a few are shown on the box for copying – quite a challenge. The builder is rewarded with a complex marble-run, which also taxes the child's logical ability in predicting just where the marbles will pop out. The toy is of interest to a wide age-range, so that older children will enjoy helping younger ones to set it up. A similar toy is *Build and Roll Raceway* (Lakeshore Curriculum Materials).

15 Face paints (*Galt*)

The two quickest ways of becoming someone else are to put on a hat or to paint your face. One of the most successful presents we ever gave was a carrier-bag of hats; and face paints from a toy manufacturer are usually both cheaper and more easily washed off than borrowed or filched adult make-up. With a little practice a child can even become a fierce lion, or a whiskered cat; or there are more metallic-looking colors available for creating robots and space creatures, complete with un-human movements. Much of the fun is in adult reaction to this new person, so you may find yourself entertaining a strange house-guest right up to bath time. Older children like to develop their own artistic skill rather than fantasize, especially if they can find a patient adult on whom to practice.

16 Big Tractor (*Orchard Toys*) and **The Jungle** (*Victory*)

One can't leave out jigsaws from a list of good toys, since the scanning, recognizing and fitting that they encourage are an essential part of a child's learning to organize visual space. Searching for a piece that "looks a bit like this one", recognizing similarities and differences, and realizing what shapes would look like if you turned them round: all useful pre-reading practice, as well as stimulus for a child to talk himself through a problem.

There is a drawback to jigsaws, though: children quickly tire of any one design; so that jigsaws are most useful in play groups and toy libraries, unless you can organize an exchange routine with a neighborhood group. Wooden ones, like *The Jungle,* last best, and are pleasantest to handle: in addition, the animals, which are discreet pieces within the overall design, can be played with separately. *Big Tractor's* 20 pieces are made of strong compressed cardboard, also an acceptable material. It can be given an extra lease of life by letting the child stick it piece by piece (with non-stain plastic putty) on the bedroom wall as a picture.

17 My First Dominoes (*Ladybird*)

Picture dominoes come in many different kinds, each using some variation on the principle of matching. This early version matches numbers, just as standard dominoes match 1–6 spots; but here, pictures are used instead of spots to make the game both more interesting and a little easier, though the counting element is still present. More difficult versions match pictures that are all in the *same class*: for example, vehicle dominoes, in which types of cars are matched, or where front ends are matched to back ends. More difficult still, concepts rather than pictures may be matched – cup to saucer, money to purse, and so on.

18 Cash Register
(*Casdon, Fisher-Price*)

This is one of those toys which children immediately find fascinating in their own right but which have much more lasting value as a prop for role play. Playing store (preferably with a few real cans and other items from the store shelves) is a favorite alternative to playing house for most children. They not only learn to count money and objects but also to negotiate, answer politely (children seem to realize that this is proper for a shopkeeper), and offer alternative solutions to difficult problems ("My little girl doesn't like beans"). The opportunities for language use are endless, especially if an adult is prepared to be an occasional customer; as in a real shop, decision-making, complaining, explaining and just chatting are all part of the shopping experience.

19 Alphabet Teacher
(*Kiddicraft*)

No child should be pressed to read before he is ready, but some children are ready to make friends with letters as early as three. The flip-up keyboard action of *Alphabet Teacher* seems to have a special fascination. Each word-key presents the child with a puzzle: what does it say? When he presses the key, he is either rewarded by the picture that tells him he was right, or corrected if he was wrong. Themes are followed from letters through colors to numbers, so that "c for car" ends up as "six red cars". This toy was carefully researched so that the primary phonic sound of each letter remains true in the word used, and all the words are children's normal names for the pictures shown.

At this stage, we are only trying to help the child to feel at home with the basic understandings of reading, rather than actually teaching him to read. All the same, by the time he has mastered *Alphabet Teacher*, he will have a reading vocabulary of 50 words and ten figures – quite a head start.

20 Tummy Ache and
Jumble Sale
(*MacDonald*)

Group games are a staple for older children. They can begin with simple board games including *Chutes and Ladders, Candy Land,* and various imported games. *Jumbolino* is a Dutch puzzle game in which each player constructs a clown based on the throw of the die. The parts get all mixed up, and it resembles those flip-books where the head of one person is matched with the body of a second and the feet of a third. A similar game is *Jumble Sale,* a British game in which each player draws garments to clothe a character who can end up looking very jumbly indeed. Cunning pays off, yet anyone *might* win. In *Tummy Ache,* another English game, each player has a place setting and has to collect a complete edible meal by drawing cards. The catch is that some are "tummy ache" cards with tadpoles in the lemonade, caterpillars in the lettuce and so on. Games like these open up a vista of increasingly demanding rule-based contests, which the dedicated games player can pursue into adulthood.

CLASSIFIED INDEX OF GAMES

QUIET GAMES TO PLAY ALONE

QUIET SOCIAL GAMES

NOISY GAMES TO PLAY ALONE

NOISY GAMES TO PLAY WITH ADULTS
OR OTHER CHILDREN

INDEX

Main references are in **bold** type; games and brand-name toys are, as a rule, in *italics*.

PICTURE CREDITS

Page 3 John Freeman; 4-5 John Garrett; 6 Nancy Durrell McKenna; 9, 11, 12 John Garrett; 14, 30 Camilla Jessel; 35 Nick Scott; 41, 49 Nancy Durrell McKenna; 61 Nick Scott; 67 Graeme Harris; 74 Nick Scott; 80, 103 Sally and Richard Greenhill; 111 John Freeman; 114 Sally and Richard Greenhill; 123 Nick Scott; 138 John Freeman; 144 Laurie Lewis; 153 Fiona Petersen; 155 John Garrett; 164, 179 John Freeman; 186 Jane Bown; 190 Format Photographers/Maggie Murray; 212 Sally and Richard Greenhill.

EDITORIAL AND DESIGN

Editor John Farndon; editorial assistance Rosemary Dawe, Fred and Kathie Gill; art editor Mel Petersen; designer Arthur Brown; picture research Veneta Bullen; top twenty toys illustrations Paul Saunders.

ACKNOWLEDGEMENTS

Simon & Schuster for permission to reproduce the image from *Family*; Puffin for the image from *Spot's First Walk*; Picture Puffin for the image from *Meg at Sea*, all on page 71. Puffin Books and Harper & Row for the image from *The Very Hungry Caterpillar*; Picture Lions for the image from *Alfie's Feet* and Heinemann for the image from *Helen Oxenbury's ABC of things*, all on page 72. Many thanks also to Tony Sallis; Alan Pearcy; Lucy, Nicholas and Emily George; Lucy Treadway; Siân Petersen and Alexander Duncan; and of course, to Daniel, Anna and Thomas, who taught the author almost all she knows about children.

ABOUT THE AUTHOR

Dorothy Einon was educated at Durham University and at Cambridge, where she earned her Ph.D. Currently a lecturer in psychology (with play as her specialty) at University College, London, she is married and has three children, whose ages span the range covered in *Play with a Purpose*.